"JESUS SAVED AN EX-CON"

RELIGION AND SOCIAL TRANSFORMATION

General Editors: Anthony B. Pinn and Stacey M. Floyd-Thomas

Prophetic Activism: Progressive Religious Justice Movements in Contemporary America
Helene Slessarev-Jamir

All You That Labor: Religion and Ethics in the Living Wage Movement
C. Melissa Snarr

Blacks and Whites in Christian America: How Racial Discrimination Shapes Religious Convictions
James E. Shelton and Michael O. Emerson

Pillars of Cloud and Fire: The Politics of Exodus in African American Biblical Interpretation
Herbert Robinson Marbury

American Secularism: Cultural Contours of Nonreligious Belief Systems
Joseph O. Baker and Buster G. Smith

Religion and Progressive Activism: New Stories about Faith and Politics
Edited by Ruth Braunstein, Todd Nicholas Fuist, and Rhys H. Williams

"Jesus Saved an Ex-Con": Political Activism and Redemption after Incarceration
Edward Orozco Flores

"Jesus Saved an Ex-Con"

Political Activism and Redemption after Incarceration

Edward Orozco Flores

NEW YORK UNIVERSITY PRESS
New York

NEW YORK UNIVERSITY PRESS
New York
www.nyupress.org

References to Internet websites (URLs) were accurate at the time of writing. Neither the author nor New York University Press is responsible for URLs that may have expired or changed since the manuscript was prepared.

ISBN: 978-1-4798-8414-8 (hardback)
ISBN: 978-1-4798-6454-6 (paperback)

For Library of Congress Cataloging-in-Publication data, please contact the Library of Congress.

New York University Press books are printed on acid-free paper, and their binding materials are chosen for strength and durability. We strive to use environmentally responsible suppliers and materials to the greatest extent possible in publishing our books.

Manufactured in the United States of America

10 9 8 7 6 5 4 3 2 1

Also available as an ebook

To Julian and Rodrigo

CONTENTS

List of Figures ix

List of Abbreviations xi

Introduction 1

1. The Incorporation of Faith-Based Organizations into
Criminal Justice Reform 27
With Jennifer Elena Cossyleon

2. Prophetic Redemption 43

3. Making Good through Prophetic Redemption 68

4. "There Is Tension in Democracy": The FORCE Project 92

5. "Imagine a Circle with No One Outside of It":
The Homeboys Local Organizing Committee 115

6. Returning Citizenship 143
With Jennifer Elena Cossyleon

Conclusion 163

Acknowledgments 171

Notes 175

Bibliography 179

Index 193

About the Author 203

LIST OF FIGURES

Figure I.1. A Community Renewal Society faith leader speaking at a worship assembly. 4

Figure I.2. Homeboy Industries members marching to "Ban the Box." 5

Figure 2.1. Community Renewal Society members shaming an elected official. 58

Figure 2.2. Community Renewal Society members staging a "die-in." 58

Figure 2.3. Community Renewal Society members marching. 60

Figure 2.4. Community Renewal Society members staging an action against the Illinois Policy Institute. 60

Figure 2.5. LA Voice members and partners with Los Angeles mayor Eric Garcetti. 63

Figure 2.6. Father Greg washing a formerly incarcerated person's feet. 65

Figure 3.1. A Homeboy giving a testimony at the 2014 Fair Chance rally. 85

Figure 4.1. CRS and FORCE members at a 2014 Illinois House Judiciary and Restorative Justice Committee meeting. 107

Figure 5.1. Jose Osuna shaking hands with Los Angeles Councilman Gil Cedillo. 129

Figure 5.2. Fair Chance hearing at Los Angeles City Hall, 2015. 137

Figure 5.3. Jose Osuna giving public comment at the Los Angeles Fair Chance hearing. 139

Figure 6.1. Jose Osuna holding National Voter Registration Day scrolls, following Los Angeles County's recognition of Homeboy Industries. 145

LIST OF ABBREVIATIONS

ALKQN Almighty Latin King and Queen Nation
AOUON All of Us or None
APPA American Probation and Parole Association
BPI Business and Professional People for the Public Interest
CAP Chicago Area Project
CBO community-based organization
CRS Community Renewal Society
CSG Council of State Governments
EAN Ex-Offender Action Network
FBO faith-based organization
FORCE Fighting to Overcome Records and Create Equality
IAF Industrial Areas Foundation
IBCO institution-based community organizing
ICIRR Illinois Coalition for Immigrant and Refugee Rights
IPI Illinois Policy Institute
LAM Los Angeles Metropolitan Churches
LOC Local Organizing Committee
NIU Northeastern Illinois University
OFBCI Office of Faith-Based and Community Initiatives
OSF Open Society Foundation
PICO People Improving Communities through Organizing
SEIU Service Employees International Union

Introduction

A five-minute film for Fighting to Overcome Records and Create Equality (FORCE), a Chicago-based civic group, opened with still shots of a prison environment—barbed wire, concrete walls, an empty watchtower—and a dismal statistic: "Every year in Illinois, [thirty-five thousand] people are released from prison. Within [three] years, more than half will return" (Community Renewal Society 2012). The next shot cut to Charles, a FORCE member. Charles, well dressed in a brown collared shirt, walked through a verdant park in South Chicago's historic Pullman district as teens played basketball in the background. A program outreach coordinator for the Westside Health Authority—a prominent prisoner reentry organization—Charles sought to redeem himself for his past crimes by "helping [formerly incarcerated] men and women reintegrate back into society."

The film presented several more FORCE members from diverse backgrounds. Marlyse, a Black woman and a mother, spoke proudly of her two young children's education. Ashor, an Assyrian American student, worked in his university's government office and talked about his volunteer work mentoring children. FORCE members such as Marlyse, Ashor, and Charles sought to "make good" (Maruna 2001, 9–10) from their pasts, pursuing careers or volunteer work that allowed them "to give something back to the community." However, records discrimination—institutional practices that impede persons with criminal records from fairly obtaining resources such as employment, housing, and education—stood in the way of FORCE members' efforts to pursue higher education or careers in helping professions. Richard, a Latino violence-prevention worker, lamented as he overlooked a local pond, "You're just discriminated, based on . . . your record, it feels like . . . you don't got . . . no part of the constitution."

The film displayed how FORCE members used collective and political action to resist their exclusion. They took turns boldly stating, "I am not my record," "I am not an inmate anymore," and "I went into the system because of one small mistake." They announced, "I am FORCE," explained what FORCE stood for, and described it as led by formerly incarcerated persons. Marlyse claimed that FORCE was "organizing to create change and justice for other people with records," while footage played of Floyd, another FORCE member, at a CeaseFire rally, chanting and holding signs with a CeaseFire slogan ("Stop. Killing. People.").

FORCE drew from members' faith to enable civic activism. As Marlyse mentioned FORCE's faith allies, footage played of CeaseFire members praying in the street with marchers, followed by Charles imploring viewers to reject records discrimination and believe in forgiveness. The film closed by displaying contact information (address, phone, and email) for the FORCE project at the Community Renewal Society (CRS)—a faith-based social justice organization. Shortly after the FORCE film was produced, FORCE members organized their first successful campaign: the passage of Illinois House Bill 5723/3061 (the Sealing Bill), which expanded the types of offenses sealable for employment application background checks.

CRS and FORCE's Sealing Bill campaign illustrates how faith-based community organizing expands the boundaries of democratic inclusion to facilitate social integration. Like Charles, most FORCE members had gang or drug pasts, but were now going to school, working, reuniting with family, and getting involved with social programming, such as violence-prevention initiatives and halfway houses, in an effort to make good and "reintegrate back into society." In turn, FORCE leaders and members constructed community organizing as a way to make good; they drew from the meanings of recovery to participate in community organizing, reshaping it to include redemption, kin ties, and the construction of the "returning citizen."

Scholarly literature has neglected the issue of religion and empowerment in the lives of former gang members and the formerly incarcerated. Sociological and anthropological research has often focused on religion and rehabilitation, but too often the focus has been on how state-sanctioned social programming fosters victim-blaming discourse and exacerbates precariousness (e.g., Bourgois and Schonberg 2009; O'Neill 2015). Similarly, scholarship in the fields of religion and social work has focused on churches' pastoral role within the state (e.g., Bentz

1970; Cnaan and Boddie 2001; Taylor et al. 2000) as well as how religion may be efficacious in drug rehabilitation (e.g., Jensen and Gibbons 2002; O'Connor and Perreyclear 2002; O'Connor, Ryan, and Parikh 1998). However, major studies on incarceration and suppression policing have often provided only scarce references to how the formerly incarcerated might use religion to mobilize resistance and expand their rights and inclusion (e.g., Alexander 2010; Stuart 2016).

This study is focused on how former gang members and the formerly incarcerated draw from faith-based community organizing in the tradition of "progressive prophetic activism" (Slessarev-Jamir 2011, 4). Helene Slessarev-Jamir (2011, 4), a theologian who has studied American community organizing, has employed the term "prophetic" in reference to "a religious understanding of politics defined by its inclusiveness, its concern for the *other*, for those who are marginalized." Drawing from the work of David Gutterman (2005), Slessarev-Jamir (2010, 676) has argued that "varied ways of framing the prophetic have historically been used in the United States either to enhance or restrict . . . the space necessary for a democratic politics." The Sealing Bill campaign advanced progressive articulations of the prophetic: a concern for those with records living on the margins. It built upon a theological perspective concerned with the marginalized "other," seeking to restore power to those who have little of it (Hart 2001; Slessarev-Jamir 2011, 4).

This book examines how faith-based community organizing fosters empowering social integration among former gang members and the formerly incarcerated. It draws from qualitative fieldwork: participant observation at two field sites and thirty-four interviews with members (all but three of whom were former gang members or formerly incarcerated). The first site was in Chicago, where CRS—a local Protestant-founded community organizing group—fostered the FORCE project (see figure I.1). The second site was in Los Angeles, where LA Voice—a local affiliate of the Catholic-Jesuit-founded PICO National Network—helped foster the Homeboy Industries–associated Homeboys Local Organizing Committee (LOC). CRS and LA Voice waged political and corporate campaigns to regulate the use of criminal record background checks, and to diminish the stigma of a record. They both also helped institutionalize faith-based community organizing among groups of formerly incarcerated persons, through the FORCE project and the Homeboys LOC.

Figure I.1. A Community Renewal Society faith leader speaking at a worship assembly. Credit: Community Renewal Society.

We may conceptualize faith-based community organizing for the formerly incarcerated as a form of *prophetic redemption*, expanding the boundaries of democratic inclusion to facilitate the social integration of those furthest on the margins. Slessarev-Jamir (2011, 1) has claimed that modern prophetic activists draw from a theodicy that seeks to "explain tragic events in the history of Israel as God's punishment for Israel's sins." Modern prophetic activists construct a meta-narrative that draws from the prophetic books' treatment of Israel, including Israel's sins, the prophets unsuccessfully calling for Israel's repentance, Israel's punishment, and the prophets' prediction of God's utopian future. Referencing the work of Gutterman (2005), Slessarev-Jamir (2011) argues that modern prophetic activists draw from the first and the fourth components, which provide a framework useful for holding politicians or corporate leaders accountable for their corruption, greed, and exploitation of others. We use the term prophetic redemption to refer to the application of the theodicy of prophetic activism to efforts to redeem and to socially integrate formerly incarcerated persons living on the margins.

While this book focuses on two case studies of prophetic redemption, other notable examples exist. In the early 2000s, the Rhode Island–based Family Life Center (now Open Doors) lobbied legislators to end a ban on felon access to food stamps; then, in 2004, it successfully campaigned to expand probationers' and parolees' voting rights (Owens 2014). In 2002, the Los Angeles Metropolitan Churches (LAM) protested MCI/WorldCom's high-priced prison phone calls. LAM formed the Ex-Offender Action Network (EAN), and pushed elected officials to reallocate a failing local community bank's federal funds to serve the formerly incarcerated. Their campaign succeeded, and the bank reallocated twenty million dollars for the creation of an employment center for the formerly incarcerated and fifty million in loans and tax credits to employers hiring the formerly incarcerated (Toney 2007).

The Ban-the-Box movement has been the most visible example of prophetic redemption (see figure I.2). The movement, which aims to remove employment application check boxes that inquire about a criminal record, originated in March 2003 when criminal justice activist Dorsey Nunn led a six-person committee and convened a statewide strategy session of forty-two formerly incarcerated people at the Center for Third

Figure I.2. Homeboy Industries members marching to "Ban the Box." Credit: Pocho One Fotography.

World Development's offices in Oakland, California (Toney 2007). Weeks later, at a similar gathering in New Orleans, fifty formerly incarcerated persons from sixteen states created an organization, All of Us or None (AOUON), with several chapters (Toney 2007). Nunn led the San Francisco–based chapter, organizing town hall meetings focused on discrimination against persons with conviction records (Toney 2007). In 2006, AOUON received its first campaign win: their efforts led San Francisco's Department of Human Resources to remove questions about convictions from employment applications, and to implement new job hiring procedures to eliminate discrimination against persons with records (Toney 2007). The Ban-the-Box movement soon swept major US cities, and by 2017 twenty-seven states and over one hundred fifty jurisdictions had passed and implemented Ban-the-Box-style bills, ordinances, and policies (Rodriguez and Avery 2017).

Prophetic redemption has been shaped by two major paradigms in American criminal justice—rehabilitation and punishment. Rehabilitation, dominant during criminal justice reform efforts from 1933 to 1973, has shaped community organizing's pastoral religious displays. Law professor and sociologist John Hagan (2010, 67), who conceptualized this period as the "Age of Roosevelt," claimed that during this time politicians, policy makers, and academics focused on structural factors linked to crime, and articulated solutions through ideas of social reform and individual rehabilitation. Criminal justice activists such as Dorsey Nunn and Susan Burton have borrowed from and built upon this perspective in articulating alternative visions to the current state of mass imprisonment. In turn, we may conceptualize efforts to foster penal reform through the guidance of social service organizations—such as Homeboy Industries—as *pastoral prophetic redemption*. In pastoral prophetic redemption, activists attempt to foster rehabilitation together with facilitating social integration and reducing crime.

Punishment has also shaped community organizing's insurgent religious displays. Hagan (2010), who conceptualized the period of criminal justice reform from 1973 to the present as the "Age of Reagan," claimed that during this time punishment has reigned as the most dominant approach to criminal justice reform—enflaming the popular myth of the career criminal and fear of crime, and shifting the focus away from rehabilitation and social reform (Hagan 2010, 67). It is this perspective that has fueled increasingly long sentences and prison building, which activists like Nunn have committed themselves to combat. We may conceptualize the most polarizing efforts to reject the punishment ideal—such as AOUON's or FORCE's shaming of elected officials—as *insurgent prophetic redemption*. In insurgent prophetic redemption, activists attempt to expand the rights of the formerly incarcerated, but with a less explicit emphasis on personal change. While pastoral prophetic redemption relies on the pastoral role of the church or state, attempting to shepherd the marginalized, insurgent prophetic redemption takes aim at the state and powerful actors, demanding the expansion of citizenship rights.

This book examines how faith-based community organizing draws from the contrasting displays of the pastoral and the insurgent to foster prophetic redemption. While CRS largely drew from the historically Black Protestant church's teachings and practices to mobilize the formerly incarcerated and to polarize public opinion against powerful actors, LA Voice largely drew from Catholic teachings and practices in order to build cooperative support among elected officials—for expanding the rights of the formerly incarcerated—and to enable persons from member organizations to advocate for the continued provision of social services.

This book contends that personal reform is an important dimension of prophetic redemption—one that helps former gang members and the formerly incarcerated distance themselves from past crimes, and to construct meaning from participation in local social movements. As the opening vignette suggested, FORCE members, such as Charles and Richard, extended their efforts to make good and give back to their communities from social programming to faith-based community organizing. So too was Dorsey Nunn's civic activism guided by efforts at personal reform. Nunn had fathered two children prior to being incarcerated, at age nineteen, for his participation in a robbery that had led to murder. As he served a life sentence, he sought personal reform: he desired to be a parent to the two children he had left behind. In prison, Nunn took classes organized by the Black Panthers and the Black Liberation Army. Susan Burton, co-founder of AOUON and founder of A New Way of Life—a prominent Los Angeles–area nonprofit serving formerly incarcerated women—claimed that during her time working with Nunn, "All we wanted was to have a job, be skilled, be trained and be ethical" (Romney 2015).

The book further contends that as they draw from their personal experiences with recovery, formerly incarcerated persons reshape the meaning of community organizing. FORCE and Homeboys LOC members participated in community organizing under CRS and LA Voice, and adapted some of their parent organization's formal community organizing strategies—infusing practices from recovery, such as check-ins, redemption scripts, and testimonies. As they infused recovery practices into community organizing spaces, they constructed kin ties and reconstructed the meaning of being a "returning citizen." The formerly incarcerated constructed returning citizenship as a form of "cultural citizenship" (Rosaldo 1994, 57)—not erasing their pasts but drawing from them to participate in civic engagement and collective and political action.[1]

Faith-based community organizing is not without its critics. Most poignantly, critical race scholars have suggested that faith-based community organizing and prison reform fall short of radical change (e.g., Berger 2014; Davis 2004; Rodriguez 2004). For example, historian and former Black Panther Angela Davis has claimed that faith-based community organizing—particularly some of Nunn's work—often fails to place racial subordination at the center, and is limited in its ambitions to reform the carceral system. Instead, Davis has advocated an abolitionist position: that prisons are fundamentally about racist dehumanization and that we should completely abolish them. Scholars working from this intellectual tradition have examined how civil society organizations, such as philanthropic foundations or nonprofit organizations, function in tandem with the state to reproduce marginality and incarceration (e.g., Gilmore 2007b; Rodriguez 2007; Smith 2007). Some scholars have drawn even sharper distinctions between prison reform and abolition, suggesting that contemporary prison reform amounts to sustained prison building (e.g., E. Stanley 2014). However, such scholarship has largely overlooked the central role that faith-based community organizing has played in abolition-related struggles—as well as the role of personal reform within those struggles.

The two cases in this book, CRS/FORCE and LA Voice/Homeboys LOC, are examples of how faith-based community organizing fosters prophetic redemption—as well as how personal reform and political reform are mutually constitutive. In turn, these cases fill gaps in scholarly literature, conspicuously silent about the symbiotic nature of the personal and the political in criminal justice reform. To understand prophetic redemption we now turn to an "agonistic perspective" (Goodman, Page, and Phelps 2017, 5), examining twentieth-century American crime control contests. Prophetic redemption, rooted in the Black Social Gospel and in W. E. B. Du Bois's work, was initially met with resistance from American sociology (and the top-down criminal justice reform efforts that gave rise to the punitive state), and is now constructed through faith-based community organizing.

Prophetic Redemption and Criminal Justice Reform

Modern prophetic redemption is rooted in the Reconstruction-era Black Protestant church and the work of sociologist W. E. B. Du Bois. Du Bois's *Philadelphia Negro* (1899), the first major social scientific study in the United States, examined social life in a Black neighborhood and was the first text to articulate a relationship between social structures and crime. Du Bois argued that institutional factors, such as racial segregation, were responsible for poverty and urban social disorder, which in turn led to social problems such as homelessness, alcoholism, and crime. In his later writings, such as *Souls of Black Folk*, Du Bois ([1903] 2007) took on a much more scholar-activist tone and advocated for Blacks' access to liberal arts education, enfranchisement, and political struggle. These writings were shaped by Du Bois's position as an active churchgoer, as well as his view of the Black church as the most prominent social institution in poor Black neighborhoods.

Du Bois's scholar-activism was located within the diverse theological, political, and cultural ideas that had shaped Reconstruction-era Black church activism. While early abolitionists such as Harriet Tubman and Frederick Douglass had drawn from their faith to inform their struggles for freedom, emancipation had reconfigured oppression in a way that Black churches struggled to deal with (Dorrien 2015). Historian Gary Dorrien (2015) has argued that a Black Social Gospel emerged from the Reconstruction-era Black church, characterized by four major strands: one strand associating itself with Booker T. Washington's diplomacy, another supporting Black nationalist separatism, a third opposing Washington and identifying with W. E. B. Du Bois's Niagara Movement—which advocated for equal treatment of all American citizens—and a fourth blending Washington's diplomacy with Du Bois's militancy. This "new abolitionism" (Dorrien 2015, 2) reconfigured Black activism from the Reconstruction era to the civil rights movement, and lives on through those who trained under 1960s-era activists—such as Ban-the-Box pioneer Dorsey Nunn.

Du Bois's research on urban social disorder, however, influenced the formation of the Chicago School of sociology—and subsequently the long arc of American sociology and criminology—in ways that initially undermined Black empowerment and prophetic redemption. Compelling evidence suggests that Chicago School sociologists W. I. Thomas and Florian Znaniecki—authors of the landmark *Polish Peasant* (1918)—had plagiarized Du Bois's ideas as they conceptualized social disorganization and crime (Morris 2016). Chicago School founders Robert Park and Ernest Burgess (1921, 724) built upon Thomas and Znaniecki's research, coining the term "human ecology" and suggesting that urban development had consequences for social organization and interactions. The Chicago School's first major study of street gangs built on these ideas of urban development, social ecology, and crime, suggesting that second-generation immigrants were culturally isolated, and that local, urban "interstitial spaces" provided juveniles with spaces to play unsupervised and to graduate into serious forms of illicit street activity (e.g., Thrasher 1927). However, while Du Bois's ([1903] 2007) research had advocated for Blacks' liberal arts education, enfranchisement, and political struggle, Robert Parks—an ally of Booker T. Washington—worked to marginalize Du Bois and to discredit him as an advocate for the Black community (Morris 2016).

The Chicago School's appropriation of Du Bois's insurgent ideas paved the way for Age of Roosevelt crime control efforts—but in ways that shifted power to elites, without regard for power building among the marginalized. For example, Chicago School sociologist Clifford Shaw, a protégé of Burgess's, established the Chicago Area Project (CAP) in 1931, in an effort to analyze a high-crime neighborhoods' unmet needs, inform local social work, and reduce crime. Shaw and his colleagues consequently disseminated their findings through the National Probation Association as well as through the 1934 US Attorney General's Conference on Crime (e.g., Burgess, Lohman, and Shaw 1937; Landesco 1934).

The conference, in turn, informed various state-level attorney general conferences that followed (Thrasher [1927] 1936). In turn, Thrasher ([1927] 1936) revised his second edition of *The Gang* to contain a final chapter on crime prevention that shared findings from research on social policy and programming, as well as a statement from the Attorney General's conference.

Age of Roosevelt crime control efforts advanced antidemocratic institutional arrangements that would later give rise to the punitive state. The Council of State Governments (CSG), an elitist civic organization founded in 1933 at the University of Chicago, presents such an example. CSG founder Henry Wolcott Toll decried the way in which masses could use the vote to influence social policy, as well as the New Deal–era expansion of social citizenship rights (e.g., CSG 1935b, 453; Toll 1928); this occurred at a time when Southern and Eastern European immigrants had *expanded* their citizenship rights by building political machines in large urban areas, such as Chicago (e.g., Fox 2012). Two-fifths of the board members of the CSG's precursor, the American Legislator's Association, were leading eugenicists, and the CSG's membership was open only to members of the three branches of a state government (state senators, legislators, and judges).[2] The CSG disseminated academic information to its members, and had a presence at national conferences, such as the Attorney General's conference mentioned above (e.g., Toll 1934). The University of Chicago played a central role in the CSG; the Laura Spelman Rockefeller Memorial funded the construction of CSG's building at the University of Chicago, and in 1935 fourteen prominent University of Chicago faculty members and administrators served as consultants (CSG 1935a, 147).

The CSG guided the evolution of late twentieth-century American crime control away from rehabilitation and toward surveillance and mass prison building. The CSG advocated for racist and exclusionary laws in the postwar period (e.g., CSG 1972; Kane 1942; Lewis 1963; Oberst 1964). It supported the Omnibus Crime Control and Safe Streets Act of 1968 (e.g., CSG 1968, 385). It published a commissioned report favorably evaluating the passage of the 1968 Safe Streets Act (e.g., Advisory Commission on Intergovernmental Relations 1970). It authored Suggested State Legislation for the US Department of Justice, Law Enforcement Assistance Administration (CSG 1976, vii). In 1987, the CSG even published a Department of Justice, National Institute of Justice–funded study highlighting best practices for prison privatization—when only one private prison existed for a general inmate population.

The Chicago School's advancement of top-down Age of Roosevelt crime control efforts, however, paradoxically provoked resistance that also aided in the development of prophetic redemption. Saul Alinsky, the father of modern American community organizing, had studied at the University of Chicago in the 1930s but challenged its social ecological approach by emphasizing the central role of grassroots political mobilization. Alinsky, who had been born to Russian-Jewish immigrants, had taken Ernest Burgess's undergraduate course in social pathologies, where he became exposed to the concept of social disorganization (e.g., Immergluck 2004). After graduation, Alinsky enrolled under a prestigious fellowship to study graduate-level criminology under Clifford Shaw (Alinsky 1972; Billson 1984). As a research assistant on CAP, Alinsky canvassed local priests in Chicago's Back of the Yards neighborhood and asked them to send their parishioners to the Back of the Yards Neighborhood Council inaugural meeting. The setting—thick with the Congress of Industrial Organization's insurgent labor activity—radicalized Alinsky's perspective.

In an *American Journal of Sociology* article, Alinsky built upon but also challenged the Chicago School perspective, arguing that community organizing must engage "those larger socioeconomic issues which converge upon that scene to create the plight of the area" (Alinsky 1941, 798). His ideas departed from the Chicago School's approach, however, in emphasizing grassroots political mobilization as an answer to social disorganization. Alinsky (1941, 807) asserted the importance of building political power, arguing that to combat social disorganization, a community organizer had to build locally owned organizations and foster members' awareness that "many of their problems stem from sources far removed from their own community." Alinsky advocated for militant labor organizing tools, such as polarization and dramatization (i.e., "agitation") in community organizing (e.g., Alinsky 1957, 3–4). In the end, Alinsky left his graduate studies, voicing resentment at what he perceived to be sociologists' and criminologists' lack of efficacy in combating crime (e.g., Alinsky 1972)—although his ideas on social ecology, social problems, and political empowerment profoundly shaped late twentieth-century American civic activism.

Alinsky's legacy, together with diverse insurgent traditions in American civil religion, extended prophetic redemption through the late twentieth century and into the early twenty-first. Most leaders of the four national faith-based community organizing networks today—the Industrial Areas Foundation (IAF), People Improving Communities through Organizing (PICO), the Gamaliel Foundation, and the Direct Action Resource Network—can trace their involvement directly to Saul Alinsky, through an "apostolic" tradition in which organizers closely train and work with their successors (Hart 2001, 56).

PICO founder Father John Baumann, S.J. is a case in point. Father Baumann studied in the seminary during the beginning of the Vatican II era but became involved in community organizing through participation in the Chicago-based Urban Training Center.[3] There Father Baumann met Alinsky, gained field placement at the Organization for a Better Austin, and had life-changing experiences that convinced him community organizing was "what the Gospels were about" because they focused so heavily on "responding to the needs of people." Baumann's Jesuit superiors later placed him at St. Elizabeth's Church in Oakland, with a Franciscan priest, Father Oliver Lynch, who had been involved with members of the Community Services Organization and farmworker organizers—groups with members who, again, had been trained directly by Alinsky (Ganz 2009).[4] It was from Baumann's work at St. Elizabeth's that PICO (née Pacific Institute for Community Organizing) was then founded.

Diverse strands of religion—from American Protestantism to Latin American Catholicism—further reshaped late twentieth-century faith-based community organizing (Slessarev-Jamir 2011). In the 1960s, IAF community organizer Ernie Cortes—who organized under Edward Chambers, Saul Alinsky's successor as IAF executive director—left Chicago to export IAF practices to his hometown of San Antonio, Texas. There Cortes worked with Catholic priest Father Edmundo Rodriguez and developed a model of congregation-based community organizing that departed from Alinsky's issue-based model. Cortes presented the congregational model at a 1984 IAF retreat attended by Father Bauman, who then subsequently adopted the model as PICO's "relationship-based" community organizing model. LA Voice and the Homeboys LOC, one of the sites in this book, operated within this model.

Institution-based community organizing (IBCO) coalitions—the organizational coalitions among various faith-based and secular groups engaged in community organizing—are facilitating the growth of modern prophetic redemption. Interfaith Funders, a nonprofit network of funders "working to advance the field of congregation-based community organizing," commissioned a study of IBCO growth through a census in 1999 and one in 2011. A report based on this study found not only that the number of IBCO coalitions grown but also that the number of member organizations within IBCO coalitions had grown. Between 1999 and 2011, IBCO coalitions grew 42 percent, from 133 to 189 (Wood, Fulton, and Partridge 2012, 5). During that same time period, the number of member organizations within IBCO coalitions had increased by 12.5 percent, from approximately 4,000 member organizations to 4,500 organizations in forty states (Wood, Fulton, and Partridge 2012, 6). However, whereas the number of congregations involved in IBCO (3,500) remained constant between the two censuses, the number of secular member organizations—such as public schools, labor unions, and neighborhood associations—increased from 500 to 1,000 (Wood, Fulton, and Partridge 2012, 6).

Demographic changes at the turn of the twenty-first century have further diversified prophetic redemption. The Interfaith Funders reports have suggested that the core churches of IBCO—urban Catholic, mainline Protestant, and historically Black Protestant—have faced declining memberships since 1999. In turn, faith-based community organizing institutions have made concerted efforts to diversify the racial and religious background of their member congregations. IBCO coalitions have increasingly waged campaigns on issues facing people of color, partnered with secular institutions, and successfully advocated for the passage of legislation expanding the social rights of the marginalized, on topics ranging from health care to immigration (e.g., Slessarev-Jamir 2011; Wood 2002). Of particular relevance to this study, in recent years PICO has successfully advocated for passage of "Ban-the-Box" legislation through its Lifelines to Healing campaign, which takes aim at anti-immigrant deportations and mass incarceration (e.g., Wood and Fulton 2015).

The Chicago School, however, has given insufficient attention to the above mentioned dynamic changes; this owes to the longer running issue of its narrow scope on top-down criminal justice reform as opposed to grassroots reform. Chicago School–influenced research has generally emphasized functionalist life course and role exit perspectives in the study of social ecology, but not civil religion or grassroots, political mobilization. For example, scholars have typically suggested that marriage, employment, or entrance into military service may lead to exit from gangs, the street, and crime (e.g., Gans 1962; Laub and Sampson 2003; Moore 1978; Vigil 1988; Whyte 1943). Most recently, Chicago School–influenced research has continued to place a large emphasis on studying elites (e.g., Vargas 2016) or on making research accessible for top-down criminal justice reform efforts (e.g., Moser 2013; Papachristos 2009; E. Stanley 2014).

Late twentieth-century Chicago School–influenced research has continued to emphasize marginality in the study of crime and desistance—at the expense of examining insurgent and transformative possibilities. It has noted that neoliberalism and deindustrialization have reshaped the contours of urban marginality, eroding mobility ladders that once helped young men "mature out" of street gangs (e.g., Horowitz 1983; Moore 1991). William Julius Wilson's (1987) research on South Chicago poverty blamed deindustrialization for social disorder and crime, while Robert Sampson, Stephen Raudenbush, and Felton Earls's (1997, 918) Chicago-based research on disorder and crime highlighted the importance of neighborhood-level cohesion, or "collective efficacy," in reducing crime. In turn, research on desistance has focused inward—emphasizing functionalist life course and role exit perspectives—not outward, toward issues of conflict and power (e.g., Decker, Pyrooz, and Moule 2014; Laub and Sampson 2003; Pyrooz and Decker 2011).

In contrast, the sociology of religion has long acknowledged the role of "civil religion" (Bellah 1967)—the intersection between religion and civil society—in fostering belonging. Religious civic groups "engage participants in ways vigorous enough to elicit their communal commitment . . . offer resources for interpreting an ambiguous political world," and contest political power through conflict and compromise (Wood 1999, 329). In addition, social movements literature has suggested that personal reform and political reform are mutually constitutive. Sociologist Francesca Polletta (1998) found that civil-rights-era narratives of participation centered on personal and political reform, and that the telling of such stories deepened social movement activity. In turn, social movement activity shapes participants' lives in meaningful ways, from future political involvement and affiliations to child-bearing decisions and occupational choices (e.g., Fendrich 1993; Gravante and Poma 2016; McAdam 1990; Nagel 1995; Swarts 2008; Warren, Mapp, and Kuttner 2015; Whittier 2013).

Social movements literature has further suggested that community-based organizations (CBOs) play a central role in fostering personal and political reform. CBOs offer residents a place to interact face-to-face (Marwell 2007) and help members to make demands of local and national governments (McCarthy and Walker 2004; Wood 2002). CBOs are "framing institutions," providing language, skills, and resources to combat and cope with social marginality (Watkins-Hayes, Pittman-Gay, and Beaman 2012). CBOs facilitate political reform by building members' personal skills, relationships, and leadership capabilities (Briggs, Mueller, and Sullivan 1997). In a study of six CBOs working for systemic change within schools, Warren and Mapp (2011, 235) found that personal "transformation lay at the heart of organizing efforts," as parents began to see themselves as leaders in schools and communities. Research even indicates that CBOs may reduce crime and increase civic activity (e.g., Owens and Walker 2017; Sharkey, Torrats-Espinosa, and Takyar 2017).

This book advances ideas of prophetic redemption through perspectives rooted in the sociology of religion and the study of social movements. Where most Chicago School–influenced research has focused on marginality, life course, and role exit perspectives, this book emphasizes civil religion as a form of empowering social integration, examining how faith-based organizations (FBOs), such as CRS and LA Voice, may mobilize members for collective and political action—and how such activities may be rooted in members' efforts to experience personal reform. In addition, where most social movement scholarship has focused on relatively privileged groups, this book examines FORCE and the Homeboys LOC, organizations composed of former gang members and the formerly incarcerated. In this book we consider the following research questions: How do faith-based organizations foster community organizing to expand the rights of the formerly incarcerated? How do former gang members and formerly incarcerated persons participate in faith-based community organizing? How do they construct meaning from it?

Getting to Know Activists Fostering Prophetic Redemption

This book is founded on fieldwork conducted between December 2012 and November 2015. I conducted participant observation at FORCE from December 2012 to April 2014, and with the Homeboys LOC from June 2014 to November 2015. I participated in regular meetings, some leadership trainings, worship assemblies, coalition meetings, and lobby day visits to the state capitol. I also sent letters to elected officials, and set up a few meetings with elected officials—though this was the extent of my behind-the-scenes participation. I was not in the room for prep sessions with leaders before major events, or the debriefs that subsequently followed.[5]

As mentioned previously, the CRS was locally based and Protestant-founded and had "incubated" the FORCE project. The Homeboys LOC, in contrast, had been formed through Homeboy Industries and LA Voice-PICO. Catholic-Jesuit priests had founded both PICO and Homeboy Industries, and while PICO had grown to one hundred fifty chapters nationwide, Homeboy Industries was the largest gang intervention program of its kind—employing roughly five hundred current and former gang members.

This book also draws from semistructured interviews with thirty-four respondents: twenty-four from FORCE and ten from the Homeboys LOC.[6] Respondents ranged from casual members I saw only two or three times to organization founders; most respondents had criminal records, a few had a gang past but no record. (Three respondents were in FORCE but had neither a criminal record nor a gang past.) FORCE respondents were mostly Black, while a few were Latina/o and three were white. Homeboys LOC respondents were mostly Latina/o, while a few were Black and none were white.

CRS, which labeled itself as Chicago's oldest social justice organization, was a large activist organization originally founded by the Congregational Church (a predecessor to the United Church of Christ) as the Chicago City Missionary Society in 1882. CRS's mission statement declared that it was a "faith-based organization that works with people and communities to address racism and poverty. Community Renewal Society transforms society towards greater justice and compassion." CRS proudly proclaimed its radical, racial history—providing legal counsel for slaves after an infamous slave ship mutiny—on its website. CRS's religious organizational culture emphasized structural dimensions of justice and compassion, articulated through its "theory of change": public engagement, public will/opinion, civic demand, and public policy/ practice change. CRS had a very professional website, listing its twenty-two-member board of directors and twenty-six-member staff—which included three organizers. CRS worked with dozens of affiliated congregations. Most CRS clergy and members were from large Black Protestant congregations on the South Side, but other congregations were also represented: largely white, suburban churches on the West and North sides, and a largely Latina/o and Black Catholic Church.

Eduardo (Eddie) Bocanegra—who had a high level of visibility in Chicago-based violence prevention starting about 2011—had been approached by Chicago-area community organizers who wanted him to lead efforts to organize the formerly incarcerated. Eddie became a CRS organizer-in-training in return for CRS's support of his organizing activities with FORCE. CRS's lead organizer, Alex Wiesendanger, assisted Eddie, who was FORCE's lead organizer, by providing training and support.

I met Eddie while serving on a panel at the Loyola University Chicago School of Law. I exchanged numbers and had lunch with him, and was later invited to FORCE's "launch meeting" in December 2011. At its inception, FORCE was a small community organizing group with a core membership no larger than a dozen persons. FORCE was composed exclusively of adults, many with gang pasts, mostly men, all Black and Latino except for one person who was Middle Eastern. Most were from the Chicago area, though a few had been led to Chicago through the postincarceration experience (serving time away from home, entering halfway houses, etc.). Eddie proudly stated at every meeting that this group was "ex-offender-led"—one of the first of its kind—and that efforts should be focused on recruiting persons with records. My presence as a person who was not formerly incarcerated made me an anomaly to FORCE. As I raised the prospect of doing participant observation with FORCE, Eddie put the discussion before the group and publicly supported me, telling members that what I wrote could help others to learn about their group and be good for the growth of such activities.

LA Voice had been founded much more recently, in 2004, from two Los Angeles–based organizations: the Hollywood Interfaith Sponsoring Committee and Community Voice. LA Voice drew from Catholic teachings on human dignity; its mission statement declared that the organization "teaches people to speak, act, and engage in the public arena" and that it sought to "transform Los Angeles into a city that reflects the human dignity of all communities, especially those in greatest need." Its mission statement also drew from Catholic ecumenism, stating, "We are an interfaith, multi-racial community organization that unites people from diverse backgrounds." LA Voice's website was very modest, decorated with a collage of many dated photos featuring Black, Latino, and white people of all ages; they stood together and smiled, marched holding banners, or simply sat at a table wearing T-shirts and LA Voice stickers. LA Voice had a small board of directors—three drawn from Catholic-affiliated organizations, and one from a Muslim-affiliated foundation. It listed ten staff members, including five organizers, and worked with forty congregations across Los Angeles. Many (but not most) leaders were drawn from Catholic-affiliated organizations, while members were drawn from a diversity of religiously affiliated organizations— Catholic, Jewish, Episcopalian, Muslim, and Mormon.

Homeboy Industries and LA Voice put forth the support for the Homeboys LOC. Jose Osuna—a Homeboy Industries employee—had been asked by Homeboy's founder, Father Gregory Boyle, to become involved with LA Voice. Jose was the second Homeboy to become involved, after Homeboy Industries' associate director Hector Verdugo. Jose became involved with LA Voice in 2014, at a time when LA Voice's campaigns began to move quickly in the direction of violence-prevention and reentry-related issues. After learning about community organizing, Jose felt that Homeboy Industries should play a more significant role in community organizing.

I met Jose upon one of my visits back to Los Angeles from Chicago (where I held a position as an assistant professor in sociology at the Loyola University of Chicago). I was visiting Homeboy Industries to reserve the lobby for a reading of my book *God's Gangs*, about how FBOs help young men to exit gangs, when I inquired about the possibility of teaching a "civic engagement" course at Homeboy Industries. I asked because, after I had gotten involved with community organizing through FORCE, I felt that community organizing might be well received by Homeboy Industries' members. The staff person helping me told me, in a somewhat dismissive tone, "that won't really be useful." Instead, she told me that most Homeboys were "trying to learn how to hold a job" and become better parents. Then she paused for a moment, thought, and told me that—if I was really interested—I should "go through" Jose Osuna, because he was already representing Homeboy Industries to LA Voice.

I initiated contact with Jose via LinkedIn, requesting to have a one-on-one with him and arranging to have lunch at Homeboy Industries during one of my visits to Los Angeles. I had never met Jose, and I had not overlapped with him at Homeboy Industries when I conducted research for my earlier book. As I sat with him, however, I found Jose exceptionally approachable. He spoke highly of LA Voice and PICO, and his participation with them—even leading a workshop at a regional conference. I shared with him my experiences with FORCE in Chicago. At the end of lunch, I asked if I could become involved with the Homeboys LOC as a participant observer. He told me he would be willing to put it before the group. Soon after, at one of the Homeboys LOC's first meetings in June 2014, I brought a copy of my book to share with others and Jose presented me. I told the group that I felt it was my responsibility to "give back" to Homeboy Industries; I also told them that I thought members' voices were important, and that a project on civic engagement could be one way to give back. I was received warmly; when I asked for comments, one member, a Black woman in her thirties, told me, "Thank you for saying what you said."

Both CRS/FORCE and LA Voice/Homeboys LOC engaged in the traditional activities of faith-based community organizing: one-on-ones, meetings, organizer trainings, leadership assemblies, worship assemblies, and lobby day trips. Both also conducted policy analysis, but this was outside the purview of my fieldwork. It was always unclear to me at which stage policy research became involved, how CRS or LA Voice leaders had conversations with coalition partners, or how much pre-planning went into regular meetings. Leaders nonetheless emphasized the importance of these organizations and settings as facilitating civic engagement. Campaigns typically focused on those issues most relevant to members or their communities; CRS campaigns had traditionally focused on housing, education, and taxes, while LA Voice campaigns had traditionally revolved around housing, education, health care, immigration, and voting.

Several concerns related to law enforcement and mass incarceration became increasingly important to these groups' civic activity. First, CRS or LA Voice–affiliated leaders and members voiced the concern that persons with substance abuse problems were often incarcerated without receiving adequate treatment. Second, members also asserted that those convicted of drug crimes or nonserious felonies received sentences that were much too severe. Third, members declared concerns with formal discrimination against those with criminal records; "records discrimination" prevented the formerly incarcerated from being able to find employment in the formal labor market. Fourth, members also outlined concerns over informal discrimination against the formerly incarcerated. Some likened the postincarceration experience to a "life sentence," due to obstacles that prevented the formerly incarcerated from securing employment or housing.

This book utilizes the "extended case method" (Burawoy et al. 1991). The purpose of the extended case method is not to engage in theory refutation, but to reconstruct theory through anomalous cases. Whereas literature in the fields of sociology, criminology, and social work has overlooked civil religion among former gang members or the formerly incarcerated, the cases of CRS/FORCE and LA Voice/the Homeboys LOC provide such examples of civil religion. In this book we consider how former gang members, and formerly incarcerated persons, experience and participate in faith-based community organizing. We find that faith-based community organizing, for and among the formerly incarcerated, expands the boundaries of democratic inclusion and facilitates social integration. Pastoral and insurgent religious displays enable collective and political action, provide members the opportunity to experience personal reform, and construct cultural citizenship around the experience of being formerly incarcerated.

Goals and Aims of This Book

The aim of this book is to examine how faith-based community organizing fosters prophetic redemption. I contend that faith-based community organizing has emerged as an inadvertent response to broader shifts in the penal field, such as the rise of public-private partnerships, giving a platform for faith-based groups to advocate for change. CRS and LA Voice are two such examples, rooted in longer histories of civic activism; recently they have extended their efforts from housing, education, or tax reform to issues facing the formerly incarcerated, such as records discrimination. In addition, I contend that faith-based community organizing's religious displays afford members opportunities to experience social integration, through belonging, empowerment, and redemption. While CRS and LA Voice drew from deeper traditions in American civil religion to enable collective and political action, FORCE and Homeboys LOC members drew from their experiences with recovery to participate in such spaces—and to reshape the meaning of such action.

Chapter 1 draws from a social movements perspective to examine how 1990s-era probation privatization contests reshaped the penal field in ways that led CBOs and FBOs to become more deeply incorporated in criminal justice reform efforts. As neoliberal think tanks aggressively promoted transferring probation activities to for-profit firms, the American Probation and Parole Association (APPA)—a CSG-related organization representing probation officers—fended off such threats by building public-private partnerships with CBOs and FBOs. The CSG and APPA still sought to preserve the influence of elite civic organizations in criminal justice reform; in fact, APPA leaders authored a text that offered strategies for preventing CBOs and FBOs from becoming empowered actors in local criminal justice reform efforts. However, FBOs did not react to the new and quickly changing penal landscape in entirely predictable ways. Once seated at the table of criminal justice reform, faith leaders participated in both pastoral and insurgent displays of prophetic redemption. The efforts of CRS/FORCE and LA Voice/the Homeboys LOC trace their origins to these evolving contests over criminal justice reform.

Chapter 2 builds upon a gap in the field of criminology by investigating how CRS and LA Voice, as umbrella faith-based community organizing groups, shaped the social integration of former gang members and the formerly incarcerated. CRS and LA Voice's contrasting religious traditions shaped how they facilitated members' participation in community organizing. LA Voice leaders drew from Catholic theologies and practices, and a relationship-based model of community organizing, to foster members' civic participation; in turn, the relationship-based model allowed Homeboys LOC members to form individual and organizational partnerships in ways that carried out Homeboy Industries' broader institutional mission of providing social services. I term this approach pastoral prophetic redemption. By contrast, CRS leaders drew from the historical Black Protestant church's theologies and practices, and an issue-based model of community organizing, to foster members' civic participation; in turn, the issue-based model allowed FORCE members to emphasize power discrepancies and the need for social justice, and to publicly condemn state and elected officials. I term this insurgent prophetic redemption.

Chapter 3 examines how former gang members and the formerly incarcerated narrated becoming involved with faith-based community organizing. Respondents' narratives contrasted their backgrounds in gangs and drugs with their efforts to experience personal reform; they had been in rehabilitation, and made efforts to "give back" to their community, through highly personal interactions—such as mentoring—in order to "make good" and distance themselves from their past. As they attempted to make good, they became involved in a range of civic participation culminating in community organizing. By virtue of their lived experiences, they sought to play key roles in reforming their neighborhoods. Their personal efforts to make good, in turn, resonated with faith-based community organizing's prophetic mission, and provided a bridge to become involved in collective and political action.

Chapter 4 considers how FORCE members engaged in CRS's style of insurgent prophetic redemption. FORCE leaders translated Alinsky-influenced community organizing principles, such as "power" and "self-interest," and practices, such as "elevator speeches" and "one-on-ones," in ways that resonated with members' experiences on the street and in recovery. FORCE members, in turn, drew from recovery to reconstruct the meaning of community organizing; they drew from recovery's ritual verbal displays, such as "check-ins" and "testimonies," to turn monthly meetings and one-on-ones into settings that allowed them to give back and perform being reformed. Last, CRS organizers deprivatized members' efforts at personal reform, such as personal testimonies, for collective and political action.

Chapter 5 explores how Homeboys LOC members engaged in LA Voice's style of pastoral prophetic redemption. Homeboys LOC leaders drew from relationship-based community organizing principles, such as fostering racial and religious "diversity" or giving a "voice" to those on the margins, in ways that built relationships with elected officials, and partnerships with nonprofit organizations, and advanced Homeboy Industries' mission of providing services and employment to at-risk and formerly incarcerated people. Homeboys LOC members, in turn, drew from the discourse of recovery to construct the meaning of community organizing, such as by making good through testimonies—though leaders deprivatized such testimonies in ways that advanced Homeboy Industries' public profile more than it publicly held elected officials accountable.

Chapter 6 examines how members constructed being "returning citizens" through their experiences with community organizing. It argues that "returning citizenship" is a form of "cultural citizenship" (Rosaldo 1994, 57), and that narratives of participation in community organizing shape the construction of such citizenship. Most respondents drew from two main narratives, cultural deficit narratives and structural barrier narratives, to articulate community organizing participation. Cultural deficit narratives described households and neighborhoods as lacking collective efficacy—characterized by absentee parents, gangs, violence, drugs—while structural barrier narratives framed social problems as structural: due to unjust laws, poverty, inadequate housing and education, or mass incarceration. Most respondents drew from these narratives to describe how community organizing built relationships that provided social support—even kinship—to foster collective efficacy and overcome structural barriers. Returning citizenship rearticulated dominant, individualistic notions of citizenship (i.e., being "positive" and "productive") into collective notions, and provided a collective subjectivity upon which political resistance to exclusion could be mounted.

In closing, this volume brings the concept of prophetic redemption to bear on discussions of religion and criminal justice reform. Criminal justice reform need not be concerned simply with inward-looking displays of faith-based personal reform, such as alcohol and drug recovery, but can also encompass civil religion: meetings, assemblies, organizer trainings, public testimonies, and lobby day visits to the state capitol. Civil religion, in turn, may facilitate empowering social integration, through pastoral and insurgent religious displays that expand the boundaries of democratic inclusion and facilitate the social integration of those furthest on the margins. A close look at the prophetic nature of faith-based community organizing reveals that formerly incarcerated people participate in campaigns not only to expand their rights but also to make good from their pasts and to reclaim the honor and dignity lacking in the stigma of a criminal record.

1

The Incorporation of Faith-Based Organizations into Criminal Justice Reform

WITH JENNIFER ELENA COSSYLEON

On February 27, 2014, US President Barack Obama announced a new initiative to target Black and Latino incarceration: "My Brother's Keeper" (White House 2014). President Obama made his announcement at the White House, flanked by young, mostly Black, men of color. The setting was formal—all the men were dressed in suits or ties—but the mood was casual and lighthearted. It opened with a personal testimony from a high school graduating senior from Hyde Park, located on Chicago's South Side, who loved baseball and dreamed of going to New York University. The audience, all much older adults, responded with generous applause and laughter. Faith leaders—including the PICO National Network's Reverend Michael McBride—had met Vice President Joseph Biden the previous year and demonstrated support for reducing gun violence through executive and legislative action.

My Brother's Keeper was a public-private initiative that drew upon pastoral religious displays. The name of the initiative was biblical, drawn from Judeo-Christian notions of love and the role of a good shepherd. My Brother's Keeper sought to reduce incarceration—especially among Black and Latino men—through top-down notions of social reform: encouraging localities and community leaders to address the school-to-prison pipeline. The initiative encouraged an ambitious focus on six strategies, including improving the health of preschool-aged children, advancing third-grade reading scores, increasing high school graduation rates, completing postsecondary education or training, and entering the workforce. It sought to reform the school-to-prison pipeline by building coalitions of elected officials, corporate businesses, large philanthropic foundations, and religious groups.

My Brother's Keeper fell into a line of recent top-down "prisoner reentry" initiatives—such as the Serious and Violent Offender Reentry Initiative and the Prisoner Reentry Initiative—that attempt to stem incarceration through public-private partnerships, but ultimately absolve the elite actors, agencies, and organizations most responsible for mass incarceration. Obama declared that "nothing keeps a young man out of trouble like a father who takes an active role in his son's life," but stated that "government cannot play . . . the primary role" and ignored how existing legislation ensures a large prison population. Obama announced the "good news" that the private sector "already" knew the importance of his initiative, but admonished communities of color by saying "no excuses" and "it will take courage." Obama blamed cultural pathologies and evoked government only to guide research into "what works" to create "better husbands and fathers, and well-educated hard-working, good citizens."

Sociologist James Beckford (2012, 16) has conceptualized state government funding of faith-based groups and activities as a process of "interpellation," one in which the "policies, mechanisms, and practices . . . recognize and summon religious identities." In contrast to scholarship on "post-secularism," which celebrates public-private faith-based partnerships as religious reenchantment, Beckford (2012, 16) argues that such institutional arrangements signal nothing new—they simply "extended the reach of long-standing arrangements between the . . . state and religions." Obama, in his announcement, showcased the work of the South Chicago program Becoming a Man, touted the "evidence" behind it, and claimed he would not increase but make federal funding "smarter." The evidence, however, a University of Chicago study, was very weak: statistical differences in arrest rates washed out a year after the study's implementation (e.g., University of Chicago Crime Lab 2012). President Obama's announcement functioned as a pastoral religious display advocating for existing public-private institutional arrangements.

Faith leaders, however, demonstrated grassroots resistance by challenging Obama's claims about responsibility. While Obama claimed that government was not responsible for the crisis of missing Black and Latino fathers—and that the private sector represented the greatest promise for reform—faith leaders asserted that the government was responsible and called on the president to support incarceration and immigrant reform. The PICO National Network (2014a) published a press release quoting pastor Michael McBride as saying, "It is a moral contradiction that we as a nation expect the active presence of our sons and fathers, and at the same time deport fathers of citizen children, and incarcerate boys and men of color for nonviolent drug offenses." PICO leaders not only participated in the My Brother's Keeper announcement and initiative, but also used such civic engagement to articulate resistance and to foster grassroots activity—such as with LA Voice and the Homeboys LOC.

Recent scholarship has varied widely in its depiction of the broad, bipartisan support for anti-incarceration initiatives, such as My Brother's Keeper. Some scholars have emphasized prisoner reentry as a key feature of criminal justice reform, labeling it as a "movement" (e.g., Toney 2007; Travis 2007). Others have suggested that "conservatives" should be credited for "leading" the prison reform movement, and that elite civic organizations—such as the Urban Institute, the Open Society Foundation (OSF), and the CSG—have played only supporting roles (Dagan and Teles 2016). Yet others have questioned the usage of the term "movement" to describe prison reform, pointing out that the CSG only facilitates top-down policy reform (e.g., Gottschalk 2015).

A social movements perspective examining 1990s-era probation privatization contests, however, provides a more complete framework for understanding the interpellation of religion in criminal justice reform. First, political opportunity theory (e.g., McAdam, Tarrow, and Tilly 2001; Tilly 1978) suggests that the openness of a political system shapes social movements—that the direction and effects of social movements are heavily influenced by "state structures, policies, balance of power, competing interests, and preexisting agendas of elected officials and various state agencies" (Whittier 2009, 15). The 1994 Crime Act and the 1996 Welfare Reform Act provided political opportunity—expanded institutional latitude—for the CSG and the APPA (one of its related organizations) to facilitate probation-community partnerships that deepened CBOs' and FBOs' position within the penal field.

Second, research on political "threat" (e.g., Almeida 2003; Prieto 2016; Reese, Giedraitis, and Vega 2005; Tilly 1978; Van Dyke and Soule 2002) has further suggested that perceived threats play a prominent role in explaining why some groups mobilize when others do not. For-profit privatization represented a threat against the stability of the probation occupation (often protected by state employment laws and high rates of union representation), and influenced APPA leaders to seek and embrace public-private partnerships with FBOs and CBOs. In turn, community-probation partnerships allowed probation administrators to outsource some of their activities, while also building support with locally influential organizations.

A social movements perspective applied to elite civic organizations in the penal field provides a fuller portrait of how FBOs and CBOs became more deeply incorporated into criminal justice reform. Political opportunity theory suggests that instability among elite alignments may create political opportunities for mobilization and that elite allies may offer resources for mobilization (e.g., McAdam 1996). Similarly, political contests between elite civic organizations on the right created the conditions for FBOs and CBOs to deepen their position within the field. While nationally elite civic organizations drew from the tropes of "broken windows" (Kelling and Wilson 1982) and "prisoner reentry" to design criminal justice reform partnerships as top-down—and based on elite-sanctioned, evidence-based practices—regional and local elite civic organizations adapted "prisoner reentry" in ways that allowed faith leaders and the formerly incarcerated to carry out prisoner reentry as a form of prophetic redemption. As they were invited to the table of criminal justice reform, faith leaders and formerly incarcerated persons reacted in unexpected ways: they rearticulated the meaning of prisoner reentry as grassroots and political.

While religious interpellation has given FBOs a platform for prophetic redemption, what is less clear is the nature of these recent reconfigurations. We now examine how 1990s-era probation privatization contests deepened the role of CBOs and FBOs in criminal justice reform, and how this inadvertently provided an opening for faith-based community organizing groups to resist top-down criminal justice reform and mobilize grassroots action.

Probation Privatization and the Incorporation of CBOs and FBOs

Neoliberal Age of Reagan criminal justice reforms underlie many changes in the penal field that have more deeply incorporated CBOs and FBOs. In the early 1980s, President Ronald Reagan's administration heralded aggressive encouragement of public service privatization by releasing a list of eleven thousand government functions that could be privatized. In the spirit of Reagan's advocacy for privatization, in 1986 the state of Kentucky provided the US Corrections Corporation a contract to run Kentucky's Marion Adjustment Center—the first privately run adult state prison in the nation. Months after, the CSG released a federally funded study on prison privatization, drawing from the Marion example (e.g., Hacket et al. 1986). In response, conservative think tanks aggressively pursued prison privatization. The Heritage Foundation voiced support for wholesale prison privatization—from special needs populations to general offenders—arguing that privatization was inherently cost-effective (e.g., Joel 1988). As studies critiqued the idea that prison privatization was necessarily cost-effective, prison privatization tactics became increasingly aggressive, attacking the collective bargaining laws that protected employment in the public sector (e.g., Thomas et al. 1999, 24).

The APPA, a CSG-related organization, occupied a political position threatened by the aggressive promotion of for-profit privatization of probation. The APPA's membership base was largely composed of well-paid civil servants protected by collective bargaining who felt that privatization endangered their job security (e.g., Bosco 1998). In turn, the APPA defended its members by taking a public stance against aggressive for-profit privatization of probation. In 1987, the APPA released a position statement that resonated with CSG's nuanced stance—some privatization, in some circumstances, could be appropriate. The APPA's statement created backlash as pressure mounted through other groups in the penal field. At the American Correctional Association's annual meeting, president Perry M. Johnson (1993) delivered a keynote address in which he urged a rethinking of corrections—an "exchange rate for punishment"—in which alternative sentencing and offender fines could substitute for prison. In addition, the neoliberal National Center for Policy Analysis issued a report attacking the APPA, supporting legislation (the Conditional Post Conviction Release Act) to extend bail into probation and parole (e.g., Reynolds 2000); it argued that probation was broken, and that probationers were committing murders every day. The National Center for Policy Analysis framed probation leaders' resistance to privatization as a "turf war" (e.g., Reynolds 2000, 9).

Two landmark legislative bills created a political opportunity for the APPA to reshape the penal field in ways that defended probation from for-profit privatization. First, the 1994 Crime Act opened a space for nonprofits and FBOs to participate in probation-related activities. The act provided a six-year, $8.8 billion grant for "community policing," created the Office of Community Oriented Policing Services to administer such grants, and built probation-police partnerships by relocating some probation work to the neighborhood—alongside private, nonprofit organizations, such as FBOs. Second, the Charitable Choice clause of the 1996 Welfare Reform Act clarified religious organizations' eligibility for federal social service contracts. These federal changes allowed FBOs—many of which were the last standing institutions in deindustrialized, low-income neighborhoods—deeper engagement in the probation and social service fields. In turn, the deepening engagement of FBOs in the fields of probation and social services placed the APPA in a political position to deflect for-profit privatization pressures by developing community-probation partnerships with FBOs.

The Boston Strategy to Prevent Youth Violence was illustrative of the new public-private, community-probation partnerships that incorporated FBOs. The Boston Strategy consisted of three significant components—Operation Ceasefire, the Boston Gun Project, and Operation Night Lights—and was carried out through collaborations with police, probation, and community groups (Reinventing Probation Council 2000). Operation Night Lights began before the 1994 Crime Act, and involved the sharing of information between probation and law enforcement, and probation officers' evening visits to high-risk youth probationers' homes. Operation Ceasefire utilized community groups, especially local clergy and community leaders—such as Boston's Ten Point Coalition—in mitigating gang disputes. Collectively, the Boston Strategy produced the steepest US decline in homicides. From 1995 to 1996, homicides dropped from ninety-six to sixty-one, and eventually dropped to seventeen between January and August 1999 (Reinventing Probation Council 2000, 28).

APPA-affiliated leaders took a significant step in reconfiguring probation, top-down, by exporting Boston Strategy–influenced FBO partnerships. In 1997, John DiIulio facilitated a gathering at the Manhattan Institute's Center for Civic Innovation, which led to the founding of the

Reinventing Probation Council. The council aimed to nationally reconfigure probation and comprised fourteen persons—including five presidents and past-presidents from the two big national probation associations (the APPA and the National Association of Probation Executives). The first Reinventing Probation Council report, "'Broken Windows' Probation" (1999), noted that "widespread political and public dissatisfaction" with probation was justified (1999, 1) and emphasized the need for "active partnerships with community and neighborhood groups" (1999, 5). The report drew attention to a handful of localities' efforts in implementing innovative probation models—in particular the Boston Strategy—while elaborating key strategies to reorganize probation.

The report—far from advocating for grassroots reform—warned of violent probationers and advocated for extending broken windows policing to probation. It encouraged community betterment activities with agencies, businesses, nonprofits, and FBOs—not for residents but to shore up probation's legitimacy. A follow-up Reinventing Probation Council (2000) report plainly advocated for probation-community partnerships rooted in deception and the displacement of community leaders. Shortly thereafter, Rhine et al. (2001) published an article in *Perspectives*, the APPA's flagship publication, explaining that seven cities had been selected to receive technical assistance for "broken windows probation" implementation; in turn, the APPA's related organization, the CSG, continued the effort to expand broken windows probation through the implementation of initiatives much larger in scope.

Prisoner Reentry, CBOs, and FBOs

While the APPA led efforts at broken windows probation implementation, a few powerful civic organizations—such as the CSG—soon began top-down efforts to deepen CBO and FBO involvement in the penal field; the two efforts would dovetail to form what is now recognized as "prisoner reentry." Starting in 2000, billionaire George Soros's Open Society Foundation (née Open Society Institute) funded the Urban Institute and the CSG to produce research and develop public-private partnerships. These and other OSF recipients reframed the effort to deepen the role of FBOs, in the penal field, through the development of the concept of "prisoner reentry."

Jeremy Travis (2005), who claimed credit for the popularization of the concept of "reentry," recalled that usage of the term originated in 1999, when US Attorney General Janet Reno asked Travis (then director of the National Institute of Justice) and Laurie Robinson (assistant attorney general for justice programs) how to address the issue of the large number of people exiting and returning to prison. Following their discussion, in October 1999, Reno issued a call for proposals for partnerships to develop "reentry courts." Travis claimed to have intentionally chosen the term "reentry" because he viewed it as politically neutral—in contrast to progressive efforts to abolish prisons or concerns with "superpredators" (Bennett, DiIulio, and Walters 1996) that had fueled dramatic prison growth in the late 1990s. Following its introduction, several presidential administrations, national organizations representing elected officials, federal and local agencies, policy think tanks, associations representing practitioners, and advocacy groups used the term "reentry" to mobilize prison reform advocacy around the issue of containing mass incarceration's mounting economic and social costs. The term enjoyed broad bipartisan support for reducing incarceration, with scholars later referring to it as a social "movement" (e.g., Toney 2007; Travis 2007).

Collaborations between OSF, the Urban Institute, and CSG reframed criminal justice reform from broken windows to prisoner reentry, and expanded political opportunities to deepen CBO and FBO involvement in the penal field starting in 2000. That year, Travis left the National Institute of Justice to take a position as a senior fellow at the Urban Institute, where he and criminologist Joan Petersilia co-chaired a series of eight roundtables on prisoner reentry, convening academics, practitioners, civil servants, advocacy groups, funding agencies, and foundations. Susan Tucker, an OSF program officer, attended the Urban Institute's inaugural Reentry Roundtable in 2000, and that year the OSF made a series of commitments to the field of prisoner reentry (Open Society Institute 2001). The OSF funded eleven nonprofits, some of which expanded broken windows probation—such as the Urban Institute and CSG—but also CBOs that expanded the definition of prisoner reentry to include collective and political action, such as Family Life Center, Critical Resistance, and the Ella Baker Center for Human Rights (Open Society Institute 2001).

OSF funding for many prison reform programs continued to 2002. In 2001, the OSF funded the CSG's newly created Reentry Policy Council, which counted, in its initial meeting, several members of OSF-backed programs that played formative roles in early development of prisoner reentry, including Travis, Paparozzi, and Tucker (Open Society Institute 2002). Then, in 2002, OSF lured Eric Cadora away from the Center for Alternative Sentencing and Employment Services to work for Tucker, developed Justice Reinvestment, funded a Justice Reinvestment initiative out of George Washington University, and funded the CSG to provide states "technical assistance" implementing Justice Reinvestment (Open Society Institute 2003).

In 2001, President George W. Bush established the White House Office of Faith-Based and Community Initiatives (OFBCI). John DiIulio, who had earlier facilitated the founding of the Reinventing Probation Council, served as the OFBCI founding director. The OFBCI sought to increase the capacity of FBOs by acting as a liaison and connected CBOs and FBOs—then dubbed "armies of compassion"—to trainings and information, helping thousands of FBOs apply for federal funds and deliver federally funded services (White House 2008).

The OFBCI further secured the CSG and APPA's position in deepening the role of FBOs in social services and the penal field. A slew of federally based funding followed the OSF, Urban Institute, and CSG's reform efforts, much of it based on the public-private partnerships first articulated in the Reinventing Probation Council's "'Broken Windows' Probation" report. Although DiIulio had denounced his disparaging remarks, in which he had called juvenile delinquents "superpredators," the OFBCI was simply a veiled attempt to advance the suppression-style policing he had earlier advocated for; the OFBCI institutionalized a series of large federal initiatives to popularize what was initially conceptualized as broken windows probation.[1]

- In 2003, the Serious and Violent Offender Reentry Initiative provided $100 million of reentry-related funding for state programs through five US departments: Justice, Labor, Education, Housing and Urban Development, and Health and Human Services (Lattimore et al. 2008).

- In 2005, President Bush initiated his Prisoner Reentry Initiative, providing reentry-related funding through a Department of Labor and Department of Justice joint venture: in 2006, the Department of Justice provided prerelease awards between $450,000 and $1.8 million, for thirty grantees in twenty state prisons systems, while the Department of Labor awarded the same grantees with $660,000 per year for postrelease services for up to three years (US Department of Justice 2008).
- In 2007, also as part of the Prisoner Reentry Initiative, the Department of Justice awarded twenty-three state prison systems between $225,000 and $450,000, and in 2008 the Department of Labor awarded those same grantees $130,000 (US Department of Justice 2008).
- In 2008, President Bush signed the Second Chance Act (House Resolution 1593) into law; it has since been renewed several times, authorizing more than $475 million in total (Bureau of Justice Assistance 2018).
- In 2010, the Bureau of Justice Assistance launched a public-private partnership, the Justice Reinvestment Initiative, with the Pew Charitable Trusts; the stated aims were to improve states' efficiency with reducing crime and prison spending. By 2013, seventeen states had participated (Urban Institute 2013).

The CSG played a prominent national role in the evolution of federal prisoner reentry initiatives. Between 2000 and 2015, the CSG received over $100 million of Department of Justice funds—in part to provide technical assistance to CBOs and FBOs providing prisoner reentry—and produced suggested state legislation for Justice Reinvestment.[2]

Regional and Local Reconfigurations of Prisoner Reentry

Regionally prominent philanthropic foundations played a role in the development of prisoner reentry, and the interpellation of FBOs, in the two cities of this study: Chicago and Los Angeles. Such prisoner reentry initiatives popularized not only public-private reentry initiatives but also civic action. In 2001, the California Endowment provided $900,000 in funding for OFBCI-related efforts to the LAM.[3] Subsequently, in February 2002, the LAM formed the EAN and staged a protest against MCI/WorldCom's high prison call rates (Toney 2007). In turn, the California Endowment provided $50,000 of funding for the EAN in September 2002.[4]

Public-private reentry partnerships had helped to align CBOs' and FBOs' efforts with elite civic organizations' articulations of criminal justice reform. In December 2002, a few months after funding EAN, the California Endowment spent $147,000 to host the Urban Institute's fourth Reentry Roundtable, themed on mental health.[5] By early 2003, the California Endowment had helped to converge EAN interests with those of the OSF, CSG, and Urban Institute. In January 2003, EAN founder and leader Ernest Austin (2003) spoke before California's Little Hoover Commission—the state's independent oversight agency that investigates government operations. Austin spoke not about the high cost of prison phone calls, but rather about the need for reentry, and public-private partnerships that included CBOs and churches. Weeks later, the Urban Institute's Jeremy Travis (2003) gave testimony to the Little Hoover Commission. Travis mentioned Cadora's work on "million-dollar blocks" (neighborhoods in which incarceration of residents cost over one million dollars annually), and publicly advocated for reentry and Justice Reinvestment—taking money out of corrections and putting it back into local nonprofits—for one of the first times.

Regionally elite civic organizations' efforts to deepen FBOs' involvement in local penal fields did more than just converge interests around prisoner reentry initiatives and public-private partnerships—they also fostered local and regional civic action. The California Endowment's first consistent set of grants to an FBO doing explicitly reentry-themed work went to the Regional Congregations and Neighborhood Organizations Training Center, from 2002 to 2008; Slessarev-Jamir (2011, 82) cited this group as an example of prophetic activism, "organiz[ing] congregations on the issues of substantive citizenship rights that are particularly relevant within African American communities." In addition, in 2011, Lenore Anderson, director of the OSF-funded Ella Baker Center's Books Not Bars campaign, founded Californians for Safety and Justice with funding from OSF, the California Endowment, and six other foundations. In 2014, Californians for Safety and Justice led a successful state referendum, California Proposition 47, on CSG-influenced Justice Reinvestment–styled reform. Both LA Voice and the Homeboys LOC participated in the Prop 47 campaign.

PICO California's local and regional civic efforts built upon the CSG and APPA's top-down "broken windows probation" strategy. In the 2000s, the California Endowment provided PICO California with millions of dollars of funding, and in 2007, PICO's Oakland chapter, Oakland Community Organizations, led efforts to advocate for a full Ceasefire program with public-private faith-based partnerships.[6] Members organizing these efforts visited Boston to meet with Jeff Brown, one of the founders of the Boston Strategy, and were eventually successful, in bringing a Ceasefire program to Oakland in 2012. This was the first Lifelines to Healing campaign, and PICO's national community organizing efforts—advocating for violence prevention, Ban-the-Box ordinances, and immigration reform—were soon named after this campaign. Then, in 2014, PICO National Network leaders met with Vice President Joseph Biden, as mentioned earlier, and the California Endowment's work with PICO was highlighted as My Brother's Keeper initiated research into inventorying successful social programs (Kapor Center 2014).

At the same time, PICO California leaders took part in insurgent religious displays related to immigration reform and criminal justice reform. After President Obama's announcement for My Brother's Keeper, PICO leaders published a press release voicing concern with the US government's excessively punitive prison sentences and immigration deportations (e.g., PICO National Network 2014a). Subsequent press releases chided President Obama for an "unacceptable delay" (e.g., PICO National Network 2014c) of administrative action on immigration reform, telling the president, "We need more than words. We need action" (e.g., PICO National Network 2014b). In October 2014, Oakland Community Organizations clergy leader pastor Ben McBride and two other members of PICO California joined over forty clergy leaders and activists in an act of civil disobedience and arrest, in Ferguson, Missouri, over the death of Michael Brown. These efforts informed PICO California's organizing efforts in subsequent years. In 2016, as PICO California statewide director, Pastor Ben McBride invited a panel of speakers from Missouri—leading activists with Hands Up United—for a symposium on police accountability in Oakland. The following year, PICO brought activists from Oakland to California's Central Valley for a symposium in which they shared their success in organizing for police accountability.

Regionally elite civic organizations also deepened FBOs' involvement with criminal justice reform in Chicago. The chief executive officer of

Chicago's Safer Foundation, Diane Williams, had attended the Urban Institute's inaugural reentry roundtable, and Chicago had been one of the sites included in the Urban Institute's first major study on reentry. In turn, the city became the first locality with an official reentry initiative in the United States: the Chicago Mayor's Reentry Initiative of 2006. This initiative fostered public-private partnerships that included CBOs and FBOs, and the implementation of a Ban-the-Box policy in the public sector. The Safer Foundation and Chicago Metropolis 2020, a group of venture capitalists that led the city's reentry initiative, sponsored a conference in April 2007, "Overcoming Legal Barriers to Reentry," which included Exodus Renewal Society member Chris Moore as a panelist. Moore would later co-chair the FORCE campaign launch meeting with FORCE member Eduardo Bocanegra in 2011. In 2013, CRS circulated a fact sheet with a list of organizations supporting the Sealing Bill. Among them were several of the organizations funded by the Mayor's Reentry Initiative, such as Heartland Alliance, St. Leonard's Ministry, and North Lawndale Employment Network.

CRS and FORCE also drew from Urban Institute, OSF, and CSG-related research in their campaign work. CRS's Sealing Bill fact sheet cited employment recidivism figures from psychologist Arthur Lurigio's (2005) American Correctional Association presentation of findings from the Safer Foundation's Recidivism Study; Lurigio, in addition to Williams, had attended the Urban Institute's inaugural reentry roundtable. The Safer Foundation study figures were also cited in the FORCE informational video mentioned in this volume's introduction, as well as in fact sheets for several more campaigns, such as CRS and FORCE's Absolute Bars campaign (for abolishing lifetime bans against people with records from employment in Illinois schools, parks, and health care) in 2014. In addition, CRS's sister organization, the *Chicago Reporter*, published an investigative journalistic story that drew from Cadora's work on million-dollar blocks, shortly before FORCE's 2014 lobby day visit to the state capitol (e.g., Caputo 2013).

CRS and FORCE leaders, however, were not limited to pastoral displays of reentry as criminal justice reform; as with some PICO members, they participated in insurgent displays against elected officials and corporate bodies. In 2013, CRS lead organizer Alex Wiesendanger staged a protest on the front lawn of Mayor Emanuel's house. In addition, as we will see later in this book, in 2013 FORCE members shamed Walgreens at an action in an officer's church. Last, in 2015, inspired by nationwide Black Lives Matter protests, a few CRS and FORCE members organized a protest at City Hall; Alex wore a mask bearing the word "Mayor," and members dramatized a scene of police brutality while Alex exhibited apathy. In the latter two actions, activists were successful in getting modest demands met.

Apart from their deepening role in local penal fields, the two cases in this book (CRS/FORCE and LA Voice/Homeboys LOC) also participated in local politics alongside other progressive, labor, nonprofit, and faith-based groups. This, too, was not entirely predictable. LA Voice's campaigns, for example, supported the highly progressive—and somewhat militant—labor-community coalitions backed by the Service Employees International Union (SEIU) (e.g., Milkman 2010; Soja 2014). These coalitions involved highly prominent faith-based groups, such as the Interfaith Movement for Human Integrity (formerly Clergy and Laity United for Economic Justice) and its respective anti-incarceration campaign, Justice Not Jails. Homeboy Industries members, however, did not stand with LA Voice in all campaigns. Homeboy Industries members stood apart from LA Voice—and even organized to carve out an exemption for themselves—in a Fight for 15 campaign to raise the city minimum wage to fifteen dollars an hour. On the other hand, CRS circulated fliers for Fight for 15–themed events and FORCE sometimes met at the SEIU's offices. FORCE members, however, were not involved in the Fight for 15 campaign.

Conclusion

CBOs and FBOs now have a greater opportunity to take a seat at the table of criminal justice reform. Privatization contests in the 1990s fundamentally reconfigured corrections, facilitating public-private partnerships that deepened the role of CBOs and FBOs. However, while it was never elite civic organizations' intention to allow groups invited to the table opportunities for insurgent displays, that is precisely what happened. Instability among elite civic groups reconfigured the penal field in ways that allowed some CBOs and FBOs to stake greater claims for civic and political participation.

The threat of for-profit privatization in probation created opportunities for CBOs and FBOs to build alliances with elite civic organizations, such as the APPA. While the Heritage Foundation and other conservative groups pushed aggressively for the wholesale privatization of the entire corrections field, the APPA drew from the 1994 Crime Act and the 1996 Welfare Reform Act to deflect such pressures; the Crime Act provided funding for community policing, and the Welfare Reform Act allowed CBOs and FBOs to receive funding for social service provision. The APPA's resistance to for-profit privatization took form through the notion of broken windows probation, supporting the popularization of community policing models, such as the Boston Miracle. These Manhattan Institute–led efforts, however, clearly stated opposition to community and faith-based leaders' political empowerment. As broken windows probation began to take hold, federal changes—such as President Bush's 2001 OFBCI executive order—further cemented the CSG and the APPA's position within the penal field, and deepened the incorporation of CBOs and FBOs into criminal justice reform.

The inadvertent consequence of bringing CBOs and FBOs "to the table" was that, once there, they would refashion criminal justice reform. This is most apparent in the post-2000 rise of "prisoner reentry," and regional and local rearticulations of it. While nationally prominent philanthropic foundations and think tanks refashioned broken windows probation as prisoner reentry, regionally and locally prominent organizations reshaped prisoner reentry arrangements through grassroots activism. While the CSG, the OSF, and the Urban Institute provided the technical assistance to institutionalize top-down federal reentry initiatives—starting with the Serious and Violent Offender Reentry Initiative, and continuing with the Prisoner Reentry Initiative, Second Chance Act, and Justice Reinvestment Initiative—the California Endowment and the Safer Foundation provided funding to CBOs and FBOs that would engage in much more grassroots forms of civic and political action. The cases in this book, CRS/FORCE and LA Voice/the Homeboys LOC, present two such examples of how faith leaders and formerly incarcerated persons drew from faith-based community organizing to rearticulate the meaning of prisoner reentry from top-down criminal justice reform to grassroots resistance.

Scholars have varied in their conceptualizations of contemporary criminal justice reform—labeling it a movement or not, or giving credit to post-2000s conservative politics. This book, however, builds upon perspectives rooted in social movements and the sociology of religion, suggesting that contemporary criminal justice reform is grounded in probation-privatization-related political threat and opportunity, and the interpellation of religion. These reconfigurations, however, have reshaped not just oppression but also resistance. While elite civic organizations may have innovated prisoner reentry to reposition themselves in penal field contests, CBOs and FBOs reshaped the meaning of prisoner reentry in ways that enabled grassroots collective and political action. We now examine how faith-based community organizing groups reconstructed the meaning of prisoner reentry, participating in not just state-sanctioned social service provision but also prophetic redemption—religious displays that expanded the boundaries of democratic inclusion and facilitated the social integration of the formerly incarcerated.

Prophetic Redemption

I'm not asking you to do anything. I'm reminding you that it
is your obligation as people of faith.
—Marlon, asking members to support Illinois HB 5723 at
the CRS Fall 2012 Worship Assembly

CRS held its biannual worship assembly on October 13, 2012, at Pullman
Presbyterian, a Black Protestant church on Chicago's South Side. About
two hundred people gathered, representing largely progressive Protestant churches, of different denominations, from across the Chicagoland
area and Cook County. The church, with its modest high ceiling and
glass chandeliers, was decorated with industrial burgundy carpet and
a large wooden cross behind the stage. At the center of the stage, an
image: a sky and flying doves. The words "Jesus," "savior," and "healer"
surrounded two large screens projecting the altar and main speaker.

Pastor Eddie Knox, the extremely charismatic African American
leader of Pullman Presbyterian, walked up to the altar and enthusiastically got congregants to participate in the worship assembly with call-
and-response interactions. He shouted twice into the microphone, "Are
you excited?!" Pastor Knox then opened with a prayer that focused on
the downtrodden. Proclaiming that we were all there to serve God's will,
Pastor Knox finished with three thunderous amens. The drummer and
choir at the back of the stage immediately launched into a melodic rock
performance of "God Is Good All the Time," imploring us to move to
the music as they swayed side to side, smiling and wearing their bright
orange CRS "Faith in Action" T-shirts.

This worship assembly was a community organizing event in the tradition of "progressive prophetic activism" (Slessarev-Jamir 2011, 4). Helene Slessarev-Jamir (2011, 4), a theologian who has studied American
community organizing, has employed the term "prophetic" in reference
to "a religious understanding of politics defined by its inclusiveness, its

concern for the *other*, for those who are marginalized." Drawing from the work of David Gutterman (2005), Slessarev-Jamir (2010, 676) has argued that "varied ways of framing the prophetic have historically been used in the United States either to enhance or restrict . . . the space necessary for a democratic politics." CRS's message of "faith in action" was focused on progressive articulations of the prophetic: a concern with those living in poverty, those subject to racial discrimination in housing and education, and those suffering from excessively strict drug laws.

At one point, the pastor invited FORCE members, led by Marlon Chamberlin, to the stage for a somber moment of reflection. A short video clip on FORCE (mentioned in this book's introduction) played via projector in front of CRS members. The clip featured several FORCE members, all with records—and all with difficulty in overcoming the stigma thereof to find work—publicly advocating for legislation to help expand the sealing of criminal records: the Illinois Sealing Bill (House Bill 5723). Then, Marlon, a FORCE leader in his early thirties, took to the stage. Those of us in FORCE walked up to stand beside him in solidarity, as he stood next to the pulpit.

Wearing a long-sleeve dress shirt of orange (CRS's color), Marlon gave his personal testimony of returning from prison. Marlon had been incarcerated for ten and a half years under mandatory minimum sentencing; he had a son who had been two years old when he went to prison and was now twelve. Although Marlon filled out several applications for employment, he never received callbacks for job interviews. Marlon's son told him he was afraid Marlon would return to the streets and prison if he could not find work. Marlon told the congregation that Illinois HB 5723 would allow the sealing of criminal records for persons who had nonviolent convictions and had remained crime-free for four years. Unapologetically, Marlon commanded the congregation to "rise up and step up." He told them, "I'm not asking you to do anything. I'm reminding you that it is your obligation as people of faith."

Following Marlon's poignant directive, CRS leaders gave instructions for the main activity of the day: breakout sessions that immediately followed. CRS leaders led organizing workshops focused on how to move legislative bills through the Illinois General Assembly, how fair tax works, and how to hold house meetings. CRS then caucused representatives from each congregation to vote on a "platform for renewal."

Delegates voted to place the Illinois Sealing Bill on the platform for renewal. This would be one of CRS's cornerstone bills for the following year. Eventually, after several lobbying trips to the state capitol, CRS and FORCE members successfully gathered enough support from elected officials for the Sealing Bill. It narrowly passed the Illinois House of Representatives—by three votes—as Illinois HB 3061 in May 2013. It became effective as of January 1, 2014.

Structural changes in the field of faith-based community organizing have influenced shifts toward campaigns expanding the rights of the formerly incarcerated. CRS and LA Voice waged local and regional campaigns to reduce incarceration and prison spending, and to limit the use of background checks in employment applications. CRS and LA Voice leaders drew from religious displays to support collective and political action on behalf of the formerly incarcerated, though the nature of such activism contrasted by site. While CRS leaders institutionalized an insurgent prophetic redemption, placing emphasis on polarizing types of civic engagement, LA Voice exhibited a softer type of civic engagement. LA Voice leaders institutionalized pastoral prophetic redemption, articulating the importance of CBOs and relationship building into civic efforts.

Marlon's directive and CRS members' subsequent support for the Sealing Bill highlights an important and understudied dimension of the postincarceration experience: how particular types of social reception may foster social integration. In this case, CRS—which drew from a much deeper tradition of racial and social justice—extended its campaigns from addressing issues on behalf of the poor and the marginalized to issues that the formerly incarcerated more explicitly confronted. As CRS leadership drew from the displays of prophetic activism, the CRS rank-and-file membership responded by expanding inclusion of the formerly incarcerated, such as by voting for their congregation to support the Sealing Bill on CRS's legislative agenda.

As we have seen, we can conceptualize faith-based community organizing, for and among the formerly incarcerated, as *prophetic redemption*. Prophetic redemption provides religious and civic practices that act as "rituals of reacceptance and reabsorption" (Hagan and McCarthy 1997, 181), such as CRS's campaigns, worship assemblies, testimonies, organizing workshops, and lobby day visits to the state capitol. These displays not only enabled collective action but also helped foster social integration. These differing forms of prophetic activism—the insurgent and the pastoral—created a setting in which formerly incarcerated people were not only embraced but actively encouraged to participate. FORCE members such as Marlon made good and redeemed themselves from their past crimes by engaging in civic activism.

Faith-Based Community Organizing for and among the Formerly Incarcerated

CRS and LA Voice waged several corporate and legislative campaigns aiming to expand the rights of the incarcerated and formerly incarcerated. These campaigns were successful, in all cases, though some compromises limited the scope of reform, while other campaigns took years to take effect—but incorporated more robust policy.

From fall 2012 to summer 2013, CRS and FORCE organized in favor of Illinois HB 5723, which failed before successfully passing as Illinois House Bill 3061. Dubbed the Sealing Bill, HB 3061 expanded the list of sealable offenses—those offenses that the formerly incarcerated could petition the courts to seal. Sealable offenses initially consisted of only some class 4 felonies, nonviolent drug felonies, the lowest of all felonies, but the Sealing Bill expanded that the list and allowed petitioning of the courts to seal some nonviolent class 2 felonies as well as all class 3 and class 4 felonies, as long as the individual's criminal record had remained clean for the past four years. Following a CRS-FORCE lobby day visit to Springfield, members enlisted the support of key conservative legislators, though some types of nonviolent class 2 felonies had to be negotiated out of the bill.

CRS/FORCE also initiated a corporate campaign against Walgreens starting in fall 2012. FORCE members, many with criminal records and college degrees, applied for jobs at Walgreens stores. After no one received a callback, FORCE contacted Walgreens to set meetings about the company's diversity policy and the felony conviction question. After a long campaign, FORCE members managed to influence Walgreens officials to remove the felony conviction question from their application. Later, when FORCE saw that none of their members—or anyone they knew—received callbacks for interviews, they pushed Walgreens to work closely with several nonprofit organizations providing rehabilitation and job training for the formerly incarcerated: St. Leonard's Ministry, Grace House, Westside Health Authority, and Heartland Alliance. Finally, in the spring of 2013, Walgreens finally hired its first formerly incarcerated person who had applied through the rehabilitation and job training sites it agreed to partner with.

CRS and FORCE initiated two more legislative campaigns from fall 2013 to summer 2014. First, they sought to remove absolute bars on ex-offender employment in the parks district, health care industry, and schools. Second, CRS launched the Reclaim Campaign in November 2013, aiming to release all persons awaiting trial for nonviolent offenses, shut down a wing (one-third) of Cook County Jail, and redistribute one-third of the County Jail's five-hundred-million-dollar budget toward restorative justice and Chicago public school education. In the end, CRS's leaders negotiated for a legislative bill that would reduce trial wait times—among the highest in the nation—from thirty to ten days. The bill was expected to result in a forty-million-dollar cut from Cook County Jail costs, to be redistributed as originally planned: toward restorative justice and education.

In Los Angeles, in June of 2014, several secular organizations and FBOs organized for a citywide Fair Hiring (later Fair Chance) Ordinance—the most ambitious of its kind in the nation. Building off successes in Northern California, groups based in Northern and Southern California pushed for an ordinance that would remove the felony conviction question from public and private employment applications. In addition, the ordinance would also restrict employers from conducting background searches until after an interview was conducted, and prevent them from inquiring about or making decisions regarding a past crime unless it directly pertained to the job in question. Dozens of groups, including AOUON and A Better Way of Life, as well as two of the groups at the center of this book—LA Voice and Homeboys LOC—held a well-scripted rally in front of newly elected Mayor Eric Garcetti's City Hall office. Garcetti's response involved joining the crowd and speaking in favor of the action to the media.

Later in the summer, as the Los Angeles Fair Hiring Ordinance was under study by the City Council, LA Voice solicited the Homeboys LOC for participation in organizing for California Proposition 47. Known as the Safe Neighborhoods and Safe Schools Act, Proposition 47 aimed to reclassify nonserious, nonviolent "wobbler" felony crimes into misdemeanors; so long as a defendant had no serious convictions, the felony would instead be charged as a misdemeanor. This would reduce sentence length for an estimated forty thousand offenders per year, allowing currently incarcerated inmates to leave jail/prison early. The estimated annual savings of three hundred million dollars would be redirected into a new state fund, of which 25 percent would be allotted to grants to help reduce grade school truancy and drop outs, 10 percent to grants for victim services, and 65 percent to support mental health and drug abuse treatment services.

Rituals and Social Integration

Marlon, whom we met earlier, had experienced many of the structural obstacles facing the formerly incarcerated—such as being socially marginalized, having a criminal record, and being unemployed—but faith-based community organizing provided rituals that helped to socially integrate him. While literature in criminology may help to explain how Marlon experienced marginality, it falls short of explaining *how* he experienced social integration—and the central role of civil religion.

In an interview, Marlon described his youth as unremarkable—growing up in a working-class home and trying to stay out of trouble. He claimed this changed when he found out his girlfriend was expecting a child. Feeling compelled to become a financial provider, Marlon turned to dealing drugs and soon after found himself arrested. In 2002, he was convicted of a major drug crime and sentenced to twenty years in federal prison. Marlon caught a break, however. While incarcerated, President Obama signed into law the Fair Sentencing Act of 2010. Marlon's sentence—a product of hundred-to-one crack-to-cocaine sentencing disparities—was reduced to ten and a half years, and he was soon released.

When he was released to a halfway house in 2012, Marlon vowed to not repeat his mistakes. He enrolled in Harold Washington College for a prerequisite class to get ready for college, and took a three-month construction course at Dawson Technical Institute. However, while Marlon was staying in the halfway house, Eddie Bocanegra visited. Eddie was on a covert mission to organize some house members; he screened *The Interrupters*, a documentary about violence-prevention efforts in Chicago's most disadvantaged neighborhoods, and fielded questions afterward. Marlon said he had already wanted to involve himself in "getting back out and trying to help out the community"; he found a church and a support group to prevent him from returning to the streets, and wanted to mentor young men to prevent them from going to prison. In turn, Marlon interpreted Eddie's visit and invitation to connect as an opportunity to make good. After the film, Eddie distributed his business card, and Marlon followed up with a phone call. Reflecting on this experience, Marlon described it not as a chance encounter but as a spiritual experience—it was "ordained to happen." Soon after, Marlon became involved with FORCE.

Marlon's experiences with prison and recovery are reflected in functionalist-oriented scholarly literature. Criminologists Scott Decker, David Pyrooz, and Richard Moule (2014) adapted sociologist Helen Ebaugh's (1988) research on "role exit" to explain how gang members disengage with the street. Drawing from interviews collected in Los Angeles—including some with members from Homeboy Industries—Decker, Pyrooz, and Moule argued that desistance occurs as gang members entertain "first doubts," become socialized with non-gang activity (i.e., "anticipatory socialization"), and then experience "turning points" that accelerate desistance. In Decker, Pyrooz, and Moule's research, former gang members described leaving the gang through activities located within family and work.

The life course and role exit perspectives help to explain—but fall short in fully accounting for—how Marlon left the street. He experienced "anticipatory socialization" through his halfway house and by being involved with social programming. A significant "turning point," during that stay, was receiving Eddie's business card, giving him a phone call, and becoming involved with FORCE. At the same time, the life course and role exit perspectives do not explain how Marlon desisted from illicit street activity. He did not simply adopt conventional practices, such as living a private religious life or becoming a nurturing breadwinner, but experienced desistance and social integration by actively engaging in and constructing new ways of being in the world. Marlon's effort to live his faith publicly falls into a longer civic and religious tradition in America, such as the work of activists affiliated with the Southern Christian Leadership Coalition or Clergy and Laity United for Economic Justice (e.g., Hondagneu-Sotelo 2008).

In contrast to American sociologists and criminologists' use of the life course model to explain desistance, Australian criminologist John Braithwaite (1989) placed the context of social reception as central to the process of desistance. Braithwaite theorized that contexts that allow "rituals of reacceptance and reabsorption" following disapproval produce reintegration and reduce deviant behavior (Hagan and McCarthy 1997, 181); in contexts where no rituals for reacceptance followed deviant behavior, stigmatization is relentless, reintegration does not occur, and deviant behavior is more likely to continue (Hagan and McCarthy 1997). Recently, American scholars have adopted this perspective to explain how actors from mainstream institutions may engage in and produce permanent stigmatization and alienation of gang members—but also how CBOs may reach out to gang members to allow them to learn, make amends, and become socially reintegrated (e.g., Brenneman 2011; Flores and Hondagneu-Sotelo 2013; Hagan and McCarthy 1997; Rios 2011).

Faith-based community organizing provided formerly incarcerated persons with rituals of reacceptance and reabsorption, through the types of prayers Braunstein, Fulton, and Wood (2014, 713–14) found to serve as cultural bridging activities: interfaith prayers, "prefigurative prayers" that outlined a vision of an inclusive democracy, or prayer forms that "enact[ed] relationships" or allowed members to share practices. First, leaders drew from prophetic teachings to encourage members—some of them privileged and from the suburbs—to accept and advocate for the formerly incarcerated. At a CRS leadership assembly, a poor elderly woman spoke passionately about organizing for housing reform, and quoted Luke 10, beseeching members to be a neighbor to others. She urged us to be the good Samaritan, warning that "it doesn't take a lot to become the man who fell among thieves." Second, CRS and LA Voice provided "platforms" (Braunstein 2012, 120) that enabled ritualized displays, such as testimonies; this allowed members to bear witness and to create solidarity with those on the margins. At an LA Voice leadership assembly, Imam Marcus opened by giving a testimony and a Muslim prayer. With an intense delivery, Marcus told participants that his brother could not find work due to a decades-old felony. He decried the injustice before quoting the Qur'an and telling us that, as believers in God, we were like a body: when one part hurt, the rest of us could feel it.

In prophetic redemption, non–formerly incarcerated persons played the role of "cosmopolitans": persons from relatively privileged locations who had experienced identity shifts away from deep racial or nationalistic attachments and were key constituents enabling democratic inclusion (Slessarev-Jamir 2010, 682). CRS and LA Voice leaders bridged a cultural divide and fostered a sense of belonging, with the intended aim of mobilizing members for collective and political action. CRS and LA Voice leaders framed the formerly incarcerated as the "other," and encouraged members to embrace them as an act of faith, supporting campaigns to expand their rights.

Prophetic Redemption

LA Voice and CRS contrasted in their use of religious displays. We can conceptualize CRS's style of prophetic activism as *insurgent*. This strand has been deeply influenced by Saul Alinsky's "issue-based" community organizing model and is characterized by public, polarizing displays targeting elected officials. Alinsky, in his definitive guide for organizers, *Rules for Radicals* (1971), asserted thirteen rules for community organizing that drew upon zero-sum and collective conceptions of power. First, he stated, "our concern is with the tactic of taking; how the Have-Nots can take power away from the Haves" (1971, 127). Second, his first rule explained that power was collective, as it had "two main sources, money and people" (1971, 126). The rest of Alinsky's rules further asserted zero-sum and collective notions of power by encouraging adversarial relations in the public sphere. Eight of the rules mentioned the words "enemy," "opposition," "your people," or "the target," while another three explained how to gain the advantage in adversarial relations through "ridicule," "threat," or provoking violence from the opponent (Alinsky 1971, 126–30).

Gamaliel national network director Dennis Jacobsen (2001), in a theological guide aimed at clergy, advanced Alinsky's ideas for a new age; Jacobsen argued that empires, from American government to multinational corporations, are predisposed to broaden their power against the interests of the nonelite—and that the cozy relationship between some religious leaders and elected officials makes organized religion complicit with such aims. In contrast, Jacobsen likened challenging power to the biblical act of coming "out of Babylon": to "live in a constant state of resistance to classism, racism, and militarism," "to connect with a community of faith and faithfulness," and "to act in accordance with one's conscience" (Jacobsen 2001, 5). CRS made use of polarizing, Alinsky-style discourse that drew from "coming out of Babylon." As a result, we can conceptualize CRS's use of issue-based community organizing, and the way in which it draws from insurgent religious displays to facilitate prophetic redemption, as *insurgent prophetic redemption.*

Another type of prophetic activism is much more deliberately *pastoral*, emphasizing collaborative partnerships and the provision of social services—rather than public, polarizing displays targeting elected officials. The work of Susan Burton—whom *New Jim Crow* author Michelle Alexander (2017, 3) has called a "21st century Harriet Tubman"—stands as an example of pastoral prophetic activism. In her book, Burton states that she does not perceive the terms "helper," "advocate," "organizer," and "rebel" to be mutually exclusive, but that they simply describe different facets of her work (Burton and Lynn 2017). Burton, who once experienced cyclical drug abuse and incarceration, dedicated her life to liberating others similarly oppressed by the justice system, opening several safe houses for formerly incarcerated women. Burton's safe houses provided housing and other basic necessities for women she recruited by waiting at the bus stop where prisoners were released. In 2006, Burton earned an OSF Soros Justice Fellowship, and implemented an intensive, six-month program called Women Organizing for Justice. At retreats, Burton led women in conversations ranging from slavery to Jim Crow, drug laws, and Black Lives Matter. Burton and the women she worked with had also become politically active, lobbying for California Assembly Bill 109 (i.e., "Realignment"), which devolved state prisoners to county jails, as well as California Proposition 47. Two of Burton's organizations, A New Way of Life and AOUON, worked with LA Voice and were instrumental in the passage of Los Angeles' Ban-the-Box-style law, the Fair Chance Ordinance.

Burton's work as a healer, leader, and activist exposes the limitation of issue-based community organizing—it underestimates the power of meaningful relationships in fostering collective and political action. While Alinsky emphasized issue-based community organizing and viewed community leaders as persons to be manipulated, Edward Chambers—Alinsky's successor as head of the IAF—has since advocated for building relationships with community leaders. In his seminal text to organizers, *Roots for Radicals*, Chambers (2003) centered meaningful relationships in the work of community organizing. Chambers conceptualized several tensions inherent in social movements—such as self-interest and self-sacrifice, power and love, and change and unity—and advocated for a vision of community organizing that prioritized resolving such tensions through pursuit of self-interest by "being among people," multiplicative power ("power with"), and embracing conflict that leads to accepting others' uniqueness and building consensus.

The broad shift in community organizing strategies, beyond Alinsky-style insurgency, was driven not by IAF leaders as much as by community organizers' desires to connect with others in more meaningful ways. PICO founder Father John Baumann, S.J., recalled experiencing discontent with the Alinsky model of community organizing after a decade of organizing.[1] Baumann was drawn to organizing because he felt that it was "the way to be in the world . . . living the Gospel," but that at the same time he felt the Alinsky approach was disrespectful, didn't respect Catholic notions of "human dignity," and led him to distance himself from the Church and his congregation. In turn, Baumann embraced the changes that came with Chambers's reconceptualization of the IAF's organizing model—most notably Ernie Cortes's work formally training others on relationship-based community organizing.

Cortes's relationship-based model shaped the PICO National Network's approach to organizing. Baumann had studied theology just as Vatican II reforms had been issued, and he recalled taking the changes seriously. As mentioned earlier, after tiring of the "disrespectful" nature of the Alinsky model, Baumann drew from the Vatican II call for reforms to guide his shift toward a relationship-based model of community organizing that respected "human dignity." Such reforms within PICO have been associated with discouraging the use of the term "target," for fear of straining relationships with powerful actors or organizations (e.g., Braunstein 2017). Instead, there has been a broader, intentional shift away from the secular militancy of issue-based community organizing (Braunstein, Fulton, and Wood 2014). For example, LA Voice executive director Rev. Zach Hoover emphasized the term "faith-based community organizing" rather than "institution-based community organizing"; he also spoke of the pride he experienced when LA Voice organizers expressed joy at being able to reflect on their faith, in LA Voice, more so than with other faith-based community organizing groups.[2] To be sure, LA Voice engaged in some forms of militancy, such as holding a forum before the LA mayor's race, asking future mayor Eric Garcetti to support a Fair Chance Ordinance, following up with Garcetti after his election, and demanding public support from the mayor. Nonetheless, these insurgent displays were largely away from the purview of the public, enough that LA Voice's emphases on ecumenism and human dignity were much more salient. We can conceptualize LA Voice's use of relationship-based community organizing, and the way in which it draws from pastoral religious displays, as *pastoral prophetic redemption*.

Some scholars and theologians have roundly criticized FBOs' pastoral displays. For example, Jacobsen admonished the "practical, working theology" of most US churches, characterizing "food pantries, homeless shelters, and walk-a-thons" as a mere service-oriented approach toward addressing human suffering and need. Similarly, sociologist Nina Eliasoph (2013) has critiqued the personalistic "volunteerism" that reformer Jane Addams' civic efforts have inadvertently influenced today. This concern with volunteering and civic engagement might be extended to CBOs and FBOs doing prisoner reentry work, such as social service provision or employment services; research suggests that as the formerly incarcerated participate in job placement services, they double-down in ways that fuel the contingent labor market and further erode the stability of work (e.g., Peck and Theodore 2008). However, the work of reformers such as Susan Burton suggests that the pastoral does not necessarily lie outside of or undermine the prophetic. Instead, it is possible for pastoral displays to foster collective and political action for those on the margins.

CRS and LA Voice both allowed a theological concern for the "other" to materialize into campaigns for marginalized persons, including the formerly incarcerated. CRS and LA Voice conducted public policy research, coordinated meetings with partnering CBOs, trained members in community organizing, and held leadership assemblies. Both also led marches, walks, and rallies, held meetings with elected officials, and mobilized members for lobbying elected officials. Nonetheless, they did so through contrasting religious displays: the insurgent and the pastoral. While CRS drew largely from insurgent religious displays, LA Voice drew largely from pastoral religious displays.

Insurgent Prophetic Redemption

CRS's institutional mission emphasized "racial and social justice," celebrated its association with the United Church of Christ and the *Amistad* slave ship mutiny, and drew from historically Black Protestant church practices to facilitate members' "coming out of Babylon." CRS held major worship assemblies twice a year, presenting legislative campaigns through song and prayer, with elected officials in attendance. At biannual worship assemblies, a pastor would lead us in an opening prayer, long and stream of consciousness with a focus on love and justice. After members collectively said "amen," a church choir would punctuate the silence with loud, ecstatic music and singing. Songs included traditional and popular hymns such as "He Has Done Marvelous," "Lord You Are Good," and "Freedom." Drawing from the Black church's strong tradition of call-and-response dialogue, after the opening music a pastor usually led members in a "responsive reading," such as John Corrado's "Hey Ain't That Good News." Throughout the event, music continued to be used generously, interspersed between agenda items or to highlight legislative updates (e.g., the "litany of victories").

Assemblies were large gatherings, often attended by hundreds of members, and rotated between member churches. Church music could be heard outside of the church walls, and as members trickled in late they would find a church crowded with members standing, singing, and clapping to the music—and eagerly greeting each other in awkward spaces such as the crowded pews or narrow walkways. Organizers also handed out an event program, often with a cover adorning a provocative image of Martin Luther King, shouting and with a clenched fist. The program contained an agenda, with times listed next to items, and responsive readings. In the pews, a few members held up signs with progressive messages, such as "Justice Is What Love Looks Like in Public," "Doctors for Rehabilitation Not Incarceration," and "Jobs Not Jails." Just before the assembly got started, a CRS leader would rehearse the litany of the day with members. One such litany, in support of reducing jail wait times and building peace hubs, began with the leader shouting "Repair!," after which the congregation responded with "Justice!" They rehearsed litanies—Repair! Justice! Restore! Lives! Rebuild! Communities!—several times as the event officially began.

CRS members engaged in an insurgent manifestation of prophetic, progressive activism—displaying inclusivity to those on the margins and hostility toward those with tremendous amounts of power. CRS leaders adapted traditional church songs, as well as the responsive reading, to denounce oppressions and demonstrate solidarity with marginalized persons. Once, the CRS choir played the old civil rights hymn "Victory Is Mine" as a projector displayed stanzas that replaced "I told Satan to get thee behind" with various public figures and offices, such as "the Governor," "IHDA" (the Illinois Housing Development Authority), and "Rahm" (Chicago's mayor). On another occasion, the CRS choir played "This Little Light of Mine," with references to Illinois, "families torn apart," and "violence in our streets." At the fall 2012 worship assembly, Pastor Knox led the congregation in singing from the text in our programs, adapting popular Christian songs by replacing lyrics in the text with terms such as "poverty," "racism," and "economic inequality."

CRS leaders communicated notions of community organizing as high-conflict and polarizing through their use of metaphors. During the fall 2012 worship assembly, as the opening song came to a close, Pastor Knox triumphantly announced CRS's recent "victories." He thrusted both fists in the air, and likened CRS to "a world-class athlete" who had been "in training." He asked, "Who was with me in Springfield?!" Against waves of clapping and cheering, several persons took turns walking to the altar and announcing CRS's recent public policy accomplishments—

the most notable of which was the acquisition of fifteen million dollars in affordable housing from the governor. For every accomplishment, the choir and congregation erupted into an adapted version of "Victory Is Mine." As the song came to an end, Knox acknowledged the new CRS-affiliated congregations with representatives in attendance. Proclaiming that CRS's power was growing, the pastor yelled that he wanted CRS to be stronger, unstoppable.

CRS extended its campaign work from the poor, children, and the homeless to issues concerning the formerly incarcerated. At the time FORCE became part of CRS, CRS centered on expanding the social rights of those furthest on the margins through campaigns focused on gun control (e.g., "Stopping Illegal Gun Trafficking"), progressive tax reform (e.g., "Fair Tax for Education Funding"), economic development (e.g., "Employment"), and housing (e.g., "Land Banks"). CRS partnered with FORCE, and campaigns grew to include Illinois HB 5723/3061 (the Sealing Bill), Restorative Justice Peace Hubs, Opposing Mandatory Minimums, the Reclaim Campaign (reducing the maximum time a person can be held before a preliminary hearing from thirty to ten days), and the Absolute Bars campaign to remove lifetime bans against the formerly incarcerated in health care, education, and parks and recreation.

CRS's worship assemblies created a space in which marginalized people could engage in the key discursive practices of community organizing. Formerly incarcerated persons—in addition to other CRS members—rotated leadership positions. This included serving as an assembly "chairperson"—announcing the starting of the assembly, formally presenting the pastor, and presenting the "guideline for the agenda." This also included other activities at assemblies, such as presenting legislative campaigns during the "presentation of the platform," giving testimonies to gain support for their campaigns, and announcing organizing "wins" during the "litany of victories."

CRS's key discursive practices also included confronting a "target," when an elected official or other person with power was at the event. The assembly chair, in a highly choreographed performance, would bring the elected official up to the stage for a member to "make the ask." This involved a member presenting grievances and a policy solution and then publicly asking the target for support (e.g., Wood 2002). CRS leaders

Figure 2.1. Community Renewal Society members shaming an elected official. Credit: Community Renewal Society.

Figure 2.2. Community Renewal Society members staging a "die-in." Credit: Community Renewal Society.

constructed "making the ask" as confrontational. They demanded only a yes or no answer. As the elected official gave his or her response, CRS organizers led members in a collective response. If the official's response was no, the group's retort was to shame the official, such as by reading a litany from the worship assembly program. One such litany, performed at the Martin Luther King 2014 worship assembly, was "we pray that God change your heart and bend your mind towards justice." During the assembly, an elected official refused to support a legislative item, and the emcee led the membership in responding with the litany (see figure 2.1). Lead organizers, before and after worship assemblies, emphasized that "making the ask" "took power" and reversed typical power relations. At the same time, "the ask" was used to create organizational sustainability. Lead organizers gave organizers-in-training the responsibility of "making the ask"—even if they were unwilling—in order to deepen their investment in specific campaigns and broader civic activism.

CRS's lobby day visits to the state capitol were infused with insurgent displays. At the 2013 visit, members protested for the passage of gun trafficking legislation by staging a "die-in." Roughly five hundred members packed the capitol's first-floor rotunda and, upon the leaders' cue, lay down on the tile floor (see figure 2.2). As a CRS leader spoke out against rising homicide rates and the importance of regulating gun control, we lay motionless on the ground—each of us symbolizing each Chicago gun death in 2012.

At the 2014 lobby day visit, hundreds of members poured out of the capitol building for an action. We walked down the sidewalk to the building that housed the Illinois Policy Institute (IPI), a neoliberal think tank, although we had no city permit for the protest (see figures 2.3 and 2.4). As we arrived, a CRS clergy leader spoke through a megaphone, accusing the IPI of spreading lies about progressive tax reform. The pastor chanted, "IPI, stop your lies!" We joined in and collectively chanted, "IPI, stop your lies!" IPI employees came out to witness the protest—one video-recording us, as if trying to gather evidence of any inappropriate activity. In response, we sang the civil rights hymn "Ain't Gonna Let Nobody Turn Me Around" and shouted several more chants ("We are CRS," "What do we want? Fair tax! When do we want it? Now!" and "Get this burden off our back, the people want a fair tax!"). We returned to the capitol to finish lobbying legislators for tax reform.

Figure 2.3. Community Renewal Society members marching. Credit: Community Renewal Society.

Figure 2.4. Community Renewal Society members staging an action against the Illinois Policy Institute. Credit: Community Renewal Society.

Pastoral Prophetic Redemption

LA Voice's institutional mission drew heavily from Catholic social teachings on ecumenism and the importance of "human dignity," claiming to teach those in "greatest need" how to "engage in the public arena." LA Voice was formed in 2004 from two Los Angeles–based organizations: the Hollywood Interfaith Sponsoring Committee and Community Voice. LA Voice worked with twenty congregations across Los Angeles, as part of the PICO National Network, which was founded in 1972 and had chapters working in one hundred fifty cities across the country. In contrast to CRS, LA Voice had a very modest website, decorated with a collage of many dated photos, with Black, Latino, and white people smiling, standing together, and holding banners. The website mentioned LA Voice's emphasis on learning political strategy and addressing health care, neighborhood safety, education, housing, and voter turnout.

LA Voice's organizational culture, influenced by Catholic ideals of ecumenism and human dignity, enabled such a diversity of churches and member organizations that it was difficult to identify a modal group. At a large training, with about seventy-five persons in attendance, members represented several churches—Catholic, Episcopalian, and Mormon—as well as Muslim and Jewish religious and faith-based groups, and students from a local low-income high school. LA Voice's rich religious diversity inhibited the type of hierarchical and authoritative political culture more characteristic of CRS. In contrast to CRS's ecstatic assemblies, LA Voice's meetings were very casual, informal, and diffuse; one large training began with "sharing a meal," a "call to order," and a "welcome."

LA Voice's large trainings, leadership assemblies, and campaign-based workshops reflected its rich member diversity. Events opened with a prayer focused on justice, love, multiculturalism, and inclusion. Whereas CRS leaders used assemblies to agitate members, Hoover spoke in softer tones to encourage inclusiveness and to celebrate diversity. At a leadership assembly, Hoover commented on the "wonderful group of beautiful people" in the room, before introducing a Muslim member, Imam Marcus, for the prayer. Imam Marcus, in contrast, spoke with less restrained passion. He quoted the Qur'an and told us that it urges us to be "just to others—even if unfair to the self." In another instance, at the training, Imam Marcus quoted the Qur'an as well as Maya Angelou's concept of a "diversity tapestry," and used these teachings to reflect on "revolution," religious diversity, and finding the "other."

LA Voice's leadership assemblies were much more contemplative than those at CRS. Rev. Zach Hoover described the purpose of one meeting: "to come together to share thoughts, reflections." With a commanding tone, Hoover quoted scripture—Luke 6:44, the tree of fruit being the harvest of one's work—to describe the organization's one thousand members and seven recent political actions. However, Hoover then turned the podium over to several members who, through a large projector, used Microsoft PowerPoint to talk about current campaigns and progress in achieving goals. The speakers stammered, the presentation was not very polished, but the large group sat attentively.

LA Voice's religious and organizational culture, and its relationship-based model of organizing, fostered political action with little public display of polarization. One example of this was a march and rally in favor of the campaign for the Los Angeles Fair Chance Ordinance. On July 6, 2014, Homeboy Industries members marched from the group's downtown building on Alameda Street to City Hall, along with members from LA Voice, the National Employment Law Project, and other locally based secular and faith-based nonprofit organizations such as A New Way of Life, AOUON, the ACLU of Southern California, Asian American Drug Abuse, Community Coalition, Los Angeles Alliance for a New Economy, the LA Black Workers Center, LA Reentry Partnerships, and LA Voice.

The march drew its inspiration from progressive, prophetic activism, such as the 1960s civil rights movement and Martin Luther King–led peaceful demonstrations—as well as contemporary faith-based community organizing marches. Jose and leaders from LA Voice and the National Employment Law Project walked alongside Homeboys and Homegirls holding signs in support of the social rights of the disadvantaged and formerly incarcerated. Marchers held signs with the "Ban-the-Box" slogan, as well as "Education Not Incarceration" and Homeboy Industries' own slogan, "Jobs Not Jails." The racial and religious diversity of the march was striking: the marchers were Black, white, Latin, and Asian men and women and from multiple faiths.

The march and rally—despite drawing symbolism from progressive, prophetic activism—lacked any political "targets" and instead empha-

Figure 2.5. LA Voice members and partners with Los Angeles mayor Eric Garcetti.
Credit: Pocho One Fotography.

sized cooperative relationships. Before the march, Jose told the group
that he wanted the march to be orderly and positive, with "no anger." The
energy behind the march seemed to be toned down compared to CRS
marches I had participated in. Jose enthusiastically shouted two chants
("ban the box" and "jobs not jails"), but some Homeboys/girls' seemed to
participate halfheartedly, with little enthusiasm in repeating the chants.
In addition, contrary to the norms of faith-based community organizing, as members arrived at City Hall they were not dressed in ways that
asserted their organization's power—such as by wearing boldly colored
matching T-shirts. In contrast, members from a few allied groups, such
as AOUON and the LA Black Workers Center, wore all orange or black
T-shirts representing their organization and demonstrating their power
and presence. Although the rally featured testimonies, Mayor Garcetti
arrived after all persons in attendance had finished speaking and left
without taking any questions. Garcetti had told members of the various
nonprofits in advance that he was favorable to a Fair Chance Ordinance,
and demonstrated this by giving a speech to a friendly and racially and
religiously diverse crowd (see figure 2.5).

LA Voice held a prayer vigil in front of Los Angeles County Jail that also drew heavily from its religious culture of ecumenism and human dignity—and its aversion to conflict. The event was well attended by a racially and religiously diverse group of people, praying in different faiths and languages, representing a range of interests—from immigration and wages to the Fair Chance Ordinance, incarceration, and housing. The event came on the heels of Pope Francis's visit to the United States, and his picture was displayed on a projector as dozens of people trickled in to the event and sat on a lawn. The event started with a Muslim call to prayer, and increased in intensity as a woman from a Catholic church admonished the "brokenness" of the justice system for the exclusion it created. Rather than identify a target or issue, however, the woman ended her reflection by praying, "We hope you experience the holy one."

The LA County prayer vigil provided a platform for members to give testimony and bear witness to inequality. A white woman from LA Voice spoke in English and Spanish about "transforming the city" and "human dignity," and used the projector to show the large number of organizations represented by people in attendance. Lively speeches, music, and testimonies followed. An elderly white clergy member played his guitar and sang, "Woke Up This Morning." A dean from a local evangelical seminary referenced the pope's visit, and spoke a few words about love in Spanish. A woman from an LA Voice–affiliated Catholic church reported about her recent trip to Philadelphia to see the pope, and drew from that experience for a reflective prayer; she cited scripture from the book of Genesis, and asked us to say aloud "We see you" ("Te vemos" in Spanish) after every testimony.

The persons who gave testimony at the prayer vigil drew from scripture—or referenced the pope's visit—to advocate for greater social rights for the marginalized. The second testimony was from an older Latino man, who had already served twenty-nine years in Folsom Prison. He spoke about being forgiven by the mother of the boy he had killed. He explained that the boy's mother saw God in Mary—because Mary had forgiven Jesus's murderers—and in turn he was able to see God through the boy's mother. Sensing our forgiveness toward him, he encouraged us to support the Fair Chance Ordinance. He told us, "This is what Fair Chance looks like." In unison, we responded with the reflection refrain,

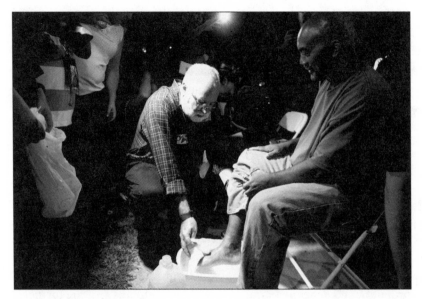

Figure 2.6. Father Greg washing a formerly incarcerated person's feet. Credit: Pocho One Fotography.

"We see you." One woman, a Latina SEIU-affiliated janitor, advocated for others because she had once been further on the margins, fleeing the El Salvadoran civil war and fighting for a fifteen-dollar minimum wage. She too spoke about "lifting others," dignity, and Pope Francis. Again, we said "We see you." Several speakers displayed prophetic activism, advocating for others, and lamenting immigration deportations, ICE raids, low wages, and the lack of affordable housing. We said "We see you" after every testimony.

The prayer vigil finished with a foot-washing—a symbolic gesture in the Catholic faith meant to demonstrate paying forward good deeds (see figure 2.6). Father Gregory Boyle from Homeboy Industries described the prophetic message—that it symbolized receiving someone into a community. Father Greg invited participants toward the front of the gathering to wash others' feet. As soft Spanish Catholic music played on a guitar, participants lined up to wash the feet of those sitting in chairs. It was very quiet and relaxing, with people silently shuffling to make space or participate. Father Greg was center-stage, washing the feet of the man who had been to Folsom. Just before we left, event organizers made an announcement over the speaker, asking and reminding us to sign cards with two Los Angeles County Board of Supervisors measures, one to restrict ICE in the Los Angeles County jail, another to redirect a hundred-million-dollar surplus in the county budget toward affordable housing. This was the extent of LA Voice leaders' public displays targeting elected officials—much less polarizing than those of CRS leaders.

Conclusion

Faith-based community organizing, for and among the formerly incarcerated, builds upon broader contemporary efforts to expand the boundaries of democratic inclusion. Where faith-based community organizing had previously largely focused on housing, education, or health care, it is increasingly focused on criminal justice reform. In turn, the settings of faith-based community organizing facilitate prophetic redemption among former gang members and the formerly incarcerated. CRS and LA Voice are examples of such shifts in the field.

Faith-based community organizing's shift toward campaigns to expand the rights of the formerly incarcerated is significant because sociological literature—from Du Bois's research to the Chicago School—has long posited that social disorganization is a cause of crime, and that policies to socially integrate marginalized people may reduce street crime. As a result, some campaigns have aimed to expand the rights of the formerly incarcerated to ameliorate marginality, foster social integration, and reduce crime. However, a further consequence has been understudied: how civic and political action itself may ameliorate marginality and foster social integration.

CRS and LA Voice drew from deep traditions in American civil religion to expand the boundaries of democratic inclusion and to facilitate the social integration of former gang members and the formerly incarcerated. While CRS drew from insurgent religious displays rooted in the historically Black Protestant church, LA Voice drew from pastoral displays rooted in Catholic teachings. CRS leaders shamed elected officials who opposed legislative bills to reduce the stigma of a criminal record, while LA Voice leaders fostered cooperative relationships between a diversity of congregations and social-service-providing CBOs and FBOs.

Both urged relatively privileged persons from their member congregations to support expanding the rights of the formerly incarcerated, but both also urged former gang members and formerly incarcerated persons to become more deeply engaged with civil religion.

The settings of faith-based community organizing, as well as the discursive practices within, provided former gang members and the formerly incarcerated with ways of experiencing social integration. CRS and LA Voice coordinated meetings with partnering CBOs, trained members in community organizing, and held leadership assemblies. They also held marches, walks, or rallies, arranged meetings with elected officials, and mobilized members for lobbying elected officials. In turn, CRS and LA Voice provided contexts that allowed "rituals of reacceptance and reabsorption" (Hagan and McCarthy 1997, 181). Whereas scholars of desistance have emphasized functionalist-oriented life course and role exit perspectives in explaining desistance, collective and political action may also allow marginalized persons to develop social ties and maintain desistance from crime.

Chapters 4 and 5 provide a richer examination of how CRS and LA Voice's religious theologies and faith-based community organizing approaches shaped prophetic redemption among two key member organizations—FORCE and the Homeboys LOC—as well as how members within these organizations drew from street gang and recovery culture to deepen participation with and reshape the meanings of faith-based community organizing. We now turn our attention to how FORCE and Homeboys LOC leaders' and rank-and-file members' experiences led them to become involved with collective and political action.

3

Making Good through Prophetic Redemption

Eddie Bocanegra, a thirty-seven-year-old second-generation Mexican American and FORCE's founder, was held in very high esteem as a Chicago-based violence-prevention worker. Eddie had been a "violence interrupter" for CeaseFire, one of several former gang members who were tasked with responding to acts of gang violence, intervening, and cooling heads to prevent outbreaks of bloodshed. Eddie could relate to gang members because he had grown up in Little Village, a heavily immigrant, low-income neighborhood in Chicago. Eddie's father, a mechanic, had been an alcoholic. Eddie had experienced poverty, gangs, and violence, and had even witnessed dead bodies as he rode his bicycle as a child. Only later did he come to understand these experiences as having caused posttraumatic stress disorder—just as a deployment to Iraq had caused the disorder in his brother. In prison, Eddie took college classes—including in sociology—that helped him develop an understanding of how his childhood had shaped his behavior as a teen.

Eddie was eventually featured in *The Interrupters*, which examined how street workers sought to prevent gang violence by healing the wounds of violence. It offered an unflinching view of the pain of living in Chicago's poorest neighborhoods, as well as the resilience and compassion of people living on the margins. It explored how former gang members, such as Eddie, sought to make good and to redeem themselves. As a seventeen-year-old, Eddie had taken the life of another gang member and been sentenced to prison. He had served fourteen years. But Eddie was determined to dedicate the rest of his life to preventing others from engaging in violence.

Eddie channeled some of his efforts outside of CeaseFire, which he felt was a platform for great violence-prevention work but lacked "accountability" in its current form. In his free time, Eddie created a weekend arts program for children who had experienced the loss of a loved one to violence. Eddie's boss "hit the roof" when he found out about the arts program—thinking the scope of Eddie's work should be limited to working with the most hardcore gang members. The arts program, however, engaged many of the partners and children of the population CeaseFire targeted. The program became very successful and, ironically, much later graced CeaseFire's website as an example of its best work. As he became a rising star in Chicago-area violence prevention, Eddie was recruited as an organizer for CRS. He then folded his interests in violence prevention into community organizing, and worked on campaigns to help formerly incarcerated persons get jobs and avoid the streets and violence.

Eddie's experiences demonstrate how former gang members' efforts at rehabilitation and violence prevention may lead them to participate in collective and political action. While the Chicago School pathologized gangs, drugs, and crime as symptoms of social disorganization, literature in critical criminology has found gangs to be sites of sociability, generativity, and resistance against modernity (e.g., Brotherton 2007, 2008; Garot 2010; Hagedorn 1994, 2007b; McDonald 2003). David Brotherton and Luis Barrios's (2004) study on members of a New York chapter of the Almighty Latin King and Queen Nation (ALKQN) suggested that gang members' lives were characterized by generativity, and that such generativity fostered collective resistance against exclusion and inequality; for example, the ALKQN had adapted twelve-step programs to provide recovery and political empowerment to members with substance abuse issues (Brotherton 2008; Brotherton and Barrios 2004). Similarly, although he was no longer a member of the Latin Kings, Eddie drew from their literature—which included a social justice mission—to recruit streetwise youth into political work.

Eddie's personal reform efforts were rooted in "redemption scripts" (Maruna 2001, 85). A redemption script's first major component is "generativity"—helping others (Maruna 2001, 99–100). As the above vignette suggests, Eddie did violence-prevention work and community organizing as a way to help others and to give back to his community; Eddie became a violence interrupter with CeaseFire, started an arts program outside of CeaseFire, and became a CRS community organizer. In addition, the way in which Eddie credited sociology classes for his personal changes reflected the second major component of a redemption script (2001, 88): the articulation of a "real me" in opposition to past crimes. Sociology had helped Eddie understand his childhood experiences, and to develop a deeper understanding of his own behavior and his relationships with others. Last, Eddie expressed the third component of a redemption script—communicating a strong sense of control over one's destiny—through his violence-prevention and community organizing work. In line with the "compensatory model" (Maruna 2001, 148), Eddie did not blame himself for his past crimes but felt responsible for helping others to avoid his fate. Thus, Eddie's efforts to prevent violence were rooted in "tragic optimism" (Maruna 2001, 97).

Some critics have charged that prisoner reentry programming emphasizes the need for former prisoners to transform and responsibilize *themselves* into law-abiding citizens (Biebricher 2011; Clark 2005). State-sanctioned social programming, rather than empower, manages the marginalized, and inscribes them as risk-bearing subjects (Fairbanks 2009; Gowan and Whetstone 2012; Haney 2010; Kaye 2013; Miller 2014). Halfway houses, reentry institutions, and recovery programs regulate access to shelter, food, and one's children through performances of rehabilitation (Carr 2010; Haney 2010). As a result, state-funded programming may emphasize soft skills at the expense of efforts—such as political mobilization—to expand the rights of the formerly incarcerated (Biebricher 2011).

FORCE and Homeboys LOC members' civic activism was waged not in spite of but because of personal reform efforts. FORCE and Homeboys LOC members sought to responsibilize themselves and achieve the American dream: to gain a career, a home, and a family. While they had experienced racism, poverty, marginality, and gangs or illicit economic activity, as adults had faced obstacles due to their criminal records. In turn, they sought to improve family ties, overcome poverty, and provide better opportunities to their children.

Therapeutic discourse may enable new forms of collective resistance (e.g., Whittier 2009). Redemption scripts, as a form of therapeutic discourse among former gang members and the formerly incarcerated, had enabled collective and political action. FORCE and Homeboys LOC members sought to make good by "giving back" to their communities, through mentoring or violence prevention—but also through faith-based community organizing.

Making Good: From Personal Recovery to Community Organizing

FORCE and Homeboys LOC leaders and members served as street intellectuals who helped to mobilize formerly incarcerated persons and gang members. Similar to Brotherton's (2007, 258) analysis of the ALKQN, leaders discerned "politically fertile social conditions" for mobilizing resistance to oppression.[1] Leaders recognized that members lacked "activist human capital" (Van Dyke and Dixon 2013, 198), but also recognized that they sought to make good through redemption scripts that emphasized volunteering, mentoring, twelve-step recovery groups, parenting classes, social work, and violence prevention. In turn, FORCE and Homeboys LOC community organizers elicited members' participation—attending meetings, giving testimonies, and canvassing neighborhoods—through "vocabularies of motive" (Mills 1940, 904) that framed collective and political action as a way of giving back and making good. Leaders bridged faith-based community organizing practices with members' efforts to make good through "cultural brokerage" (Giorgi, Bartunek, and King 2017, 125).

The first three case studies, Eddie, Marlon, and Jose, trace how Eddie started FORCE and recruited Marlon, as well as how Jose started the Homeboys LOC. These experiences with gangs and crime—but also recovery and local social movement activity—resembled the experiences of more prominent activists, such as former gang member-turned-novelist Luis Rodriguez or A New Way of Life founder Susan Burton.[2]

Eddie

I met Eddie while serving on a discussion panel at a screening of *The Interrupters* at Loyola University Chicago Law School, shortly after I had arrived to take a faculty appointment at the Loyola Sociology Department. The screening was in a packed house: 250 seats filled, along with 70 persons in the balcony overflow seating. On the panel was the film's producer, novelist Alex Kotlowitz (of the Chicago-based novel *There Are No Children Here*), as well as Eddie and another interrupter, Cobe Williams. Also serving on the panel was Kathryn Saclarides, executive director of ENLACE, a violence-prevention organization located in Little Village. Kathryn had collaborated with Eddie to start the arts program featured in *The Interrupters*. Everyone in the packed room sat quietly during the film's screening.

In one of the film's most memorable scenes, Eddie shared that he had served a fourteen-year sentence for taking the life of another gang member. We watched as Eddie retraced his steps, in the film, of the fateful interaction years earlier, and recalled that he had meant to only hurt the boy he killed. With some emotional restraint and taking a deep breath, Eddie described his involvement with outreach as a "coping mechanism." But with tears streaming down his face, he confessed to having to "stay busy" and to "keep moving" to avoid dwelling on the past. During the question-and-answer session following the screening, it was clear from several tear-filled responses that some audience members had a degree of familiarity with the film's content, and that the images and scenes evoked intense—almost uncontrollable—emotion.

I had a one-on-one with Eddie following the screening at a restaurant in Pilsen owned by friends of Eddie's family. Eddie was dressed professionally: khakis, a button-down shirt, a sweater, and a tie. I was wearing similar clothes, though not nearly as pressed, and my glasses not nearly as clean. Eddie carried a polite, thoughtful conversation. We discussed education, career goals, and a desire to "give back to the community." I spoke about having earned a PhD, and how I was working on a book about faith-based recovery from gang life. Eddie shared that he was about to graduate with a bachelor's degree and was planning on enrolling in a master of arts program in social work at the University of Chicago. It was his ambition to break the stereotype of formerly incarcerated persons as deficits to their communities. Eddie shared with me that he had been approached by Chicago-based community organizers and that they had told him they wanted him to lead efforts to start an "ex-offender-led" community organizing group.

Over a period of three years, I would get to know Eddie much better. Eddie and I talked about not only organizing but also the politics of academe, family, and work-life balance. Eddie's most influential mentor was Dr. Francisco Gaytan, an assistant professor at Northeastern Illinois University, where Eddie had received his bachelor's degree. Gaytan had introduced the notion of "social capital" to Eddie, and lacking any sophisticated training in sociological theory, Eddie simply took it to mean that he understood the lives of gang members, prisoners, and the formerly incarcerated in ways that others—such as myself—never could. Eddie became convinced that decisions at the table of criminal justice reform should be made not by experts without a background in gangs and prison but rather by people with lived experience such as himself. He believed he had a type of social capital that could inform policy, and that groups like FORCE could help make his voice—and those of others with similar experience—relevant in the spaces where they needed to be heard.

Just after Eddie and Kathryn married, I visited Eddie's house. It was generously decorated with portraits of Eastern Orthodox saints. Eddie mentioned that he attended church regularly. Later, when I asked if he had converted because of Kathryn, Eddie paused and kindly told me he had done his "research" and really believed that the Eastern Orthodox Church was the "one true" church. Then, just after Eddie and Kathryn had a daughter, Eddie stepped down as a CRS/FORCE organizer. He told me that having children "changes everything," and that he was turning his focus to school, work, and home. Eddie then left his CRS job for a higher paying, full-time job as executive director of violence prevention for YMCA Chicago. Eddie's goal within five years was to remain with the YMCA, grow his family, and graduate with a master's degree in social work from the University of Chicago.

Just after starting his position with YMCA Chicago, Eddie was interviewed by WBEZ, a Chicago public radio station, in a piece titled "After Committing Murder as a Teen, a Chicago Man Dedicates His Life's Work to His Victim." In the interview, correspondent Shirley Alfaro asked Eddie about his experiences in prison and exiting prison. The theme of redemption remained central in Eddie's narrative of his life trajectory, though he confessed being unsure of whether he had forgiven himself. At the end of the segment, Alfaro asked Eddie, "Have you ever met the family of William, the life that you took?" Eddie responded, "I don't feel like I deserve the opportunity to talk to them yet . . . all the work that I'm doing is so that one day I can meet [his] mom and say, 'I don't expect you to forgive me for what I've done. . . . But I just want you to know that everything I'm doing with the rest of my life is for him.'" Eddie's response elicited feelings of shame and undeservingness, but also his determination to make good. Eddie was working to prevent such tragic violence through social-service-based violence prevention and civic and political engagement.

Marlon

Marlon, a thirty-five-year-old African American with a major drug conviction, succeeded Eddie as FORCE's lead organizer. As we have seen, Marlon met Eddie during a visit Eddie made to Marlon's halfway house. Eddie had visited in an unassuming manner, simply screening *The Interrupters*. As the film finished, and it was clear he was a central figure in the film, Eddie fielded questions from persons staying at the halfway house. After the film, Eddie distributed his business card, and Marlon followed up with a phone call. Marlon, reflecting on this experience, described it not as a chance encounter but as a spiritual experience—it was "ordained to happen." Marlon said he had already wanted to involve himself in "getting back out and trying to help out the community."

Marlon said that when Eddie visited his halfway house, Marlon was oblivious to the way in which politics functioned: he did not understand funding allocation for programs for the formerly incarcerated, or the way that sentencing guidelines were shaped by law. However, through his participation in FORCE, Marlon began to learn about the legislative process, the importance of voting, and how to put pressure on politicians. Marlon eventually invited his fiancée, Trisha (also a formerly incarcerated person) to FORCE meetings. Together, they attended organizing workshops and meetings and played important roles in campaigns. As we saw earlier, Marlon gave a personal testimony for FORCE's Sealing Bill campaign; Trisha offered a personal testimony for a corporate campaign against Walgreens' hiring practices, trying to call attention to what appeared to be a "blanket" policy against hiring formerly incarcerated persons.

During the time that Marlon became involved with FORCE, he worked in construction, rehabilitating houses. He spoke proudly of the integrity he displayed and trust he earned at work; he worked independently, gutting houses, patching up walls, and painting, among other tasks. Marlon only had to take pictures and check in with his project manager daily, but otherwise had autonomy, setting his own hours and letting his project manager know what tools he needed for work. In turn,

Marlon tried to use his status at work to have a fellow FORCE member, Dennis, hired. Marlon had been mentoring Dennis at FORCE, grooming him into a leader, but also knew the importance of having paid work; he wanted to help Dennis resist returning to illicit economic activity by giving him paid work.

Marlon drew from his spirituality to make good from his drug conviction. He hosted an informal gathering of religious folks from his community, in Englewood, every Friday evening. The name of the group was God or Nuthin', and its purpose was to agitate members, asking them to defend the way they lived their faith in their everyday life; it was from this group that Marlon drew some members to FORCE. Marlon also saw himself as a mentor to others; he said he frequently asked himself, "How can I prevent someone else from experiencing . . . eighteen years in prison?" In his interview for this study, Marlon said that he hoped this research would "educate" people so that formerly incarcerated persons would be given second chances.

Marlon articulated ideas of civil religion that were rooted in the tradition of progressive, prophetic activism. Marlon said that he saw FORCE "as a voice in the community," working "on behalf of formerly incarcerated persons." Marlon saw his personal development in line with faith-based community organizing; he said that in five years he wanted to be off supervised release, to have achieved an associate's degree from Harold Washington College, to have his own construction company, and to develop his own chapter of FORCE for South Chicago. Marlon looked up to Eddie, because although Eddie had served fourteen years in prison, within four years of being released Eddie had earned a degree, got married, and done "inspiring" work in violence prevention and community organizing.

Marlon replaced Eddie as a CRS organizer and as FORCE's leader when Eddie took a job with the YMCA of Chicago. As Marlon became FORCE's leader, Alex told members that they could no longer count on Marlon to do many tasks. It was Marlon's responsibility as an organizer to train others as leaders; he continued grooming Dennis as a leader, even helping him to chair meetings. The following year, WBEZ in Chicago ran a story on Marlon trying to register voters. Using a table at a nearby McDonald's to do his work as a CRS/FORCE organizer, Marlon was visiting local reentry groups, holding one-on-ones, and encouraging formerly incarcerated persons to vote.

Jose

Jose, a forty-two-year-old Mexican American, was the Homeboys LOC's founding member. Jose had deep roots in the immigrant experience, as well as growing up in a low-income neighborhood. His parents were both undocumented immigrants from western-central Mexico, but they both received legal status and citizenship through Jose's birth. Jose proudly described them as never having been arrested or resorted to government aid. At the same time, he grew up in a neighborhood that he described as "dominated by gangs and drug sales . . . violent activity . . . [and] a lot of young men just like me dying." Jose's parents worked a lot—his father held two jobs and his mother also worked—and he attributed his socialization into gangs and drug use to this fact. Jose said, "When people come to a county they don't know, and their priority is work, sometimes those people's children also are damaged because of that."

The local school system had designated Jose as a gifted child, and he took a bus to attend a predominantly white school in a more affluent part of town. Nonetheless, Jose still felt let down by the American class system; he lacked many of the resources that other students had. Jose painfully recalled not being able to attend field trips, or other "special activities," because he didn't have the funds. Instead, he sat in a classroom all day, an experience he described with shame. Later, at the age of fifteen, as he had become involved with gangs, he recalled a teacher telling his father, "The best thing you can do for your son is send him to Mexico. He'll have a better shot over there." Jose's father promptly removed him from school and took him to Mexico for a year and a half—separated from the rest of his family.

Jose began using drugs at an early age, and at seventeen he was arrested for armed robbery. He robbed a drug dealer—an experience he bitterly recalled and for which he received five years in state prison, rather than drug treatment. Jose entered the adult prison system as a minor, was very "impressionable," and wanted to fit in and be a part of something. At the same time, Jose felt subordinated by white administrators, and the prison was segregated by race. Jose was taught to maintain control of the prison yard for the "southern Mexican" (i.e., "Mexican Mafia") prison gang by manipulating guards or making weapons. Jose developed racist attitudes. He learned to subordinate white inmates, Blacks, and Latino immigrants. For thirteen years, during two different stints, this was Jose's "world." He suffered "traumas" in prison—racism, violence, and intimidation—that "hardened" him and made him "even more of a danger" to himself and to his community upon release. Jose also experienced strained family ties over his addictions and prison stints. He was absent for the first eight years of his daughter's life, during his second stint in prison. Then, at the age of thirty-five, Jose lost his son, who was murdered in front of his house, by two Black men, in what Jose described as a race-based murder.

A few years after the murder, Jose entered twelve-step recovery, and then later joined Homeboy Industries and began to work and receive drug treatment. Jose demonstrated leadership skills, interacting with other Homeboys, and Father Greg asked him to serve as Homeboy Industries' representative with LA Voice. Jose accepted the offer, attended LA Voice events, and was soon chosen by LA Voice's executive director, Rev. Zach Hoover, to participate in community organizer trainings and "research actions." The first research action Jose worked on was for Los Angeles' Fair Chance Initiative. He met with policy makers and community leaders, such as Eric Garcetti (he was then a mayoral candidate) and renowned labor leader Maria Elena Durazo. Jose sat at a table, "full of tattoos," and discussed removal of the felony conviction question from employment application. He also moderated a mayoral candidate forum. As he spoke with leaders, he learned that his "voice did matter."

After leading and forming the Homeboys LOC, Jose was promoted to director of employment services. In his new leadership roles, Jose sought to give Homeboys and Homegirls opportunities to participate in community organizing. He felt that former gang members, drug addicts, and the formerly incarcerated had been "oppressed by the system" and faced unfair stereotypes. Jose felt that "letting people participate in some of the [community organizing] actions . . . raise[d] [their] level of hope." He said that when people participated in phone banking for Prop 47, they saw that others listened to them, which lifted up their hope.

When I asked Jose whom he looked up to or admired, he promptly answered, "Father Gregory Boyle!" Jose said he strove to embody Father Greg's "unapologetic compassion and unconditional love." Jose called him one of his "biggest heroes" as well as his "most influential mentor" and "a second father." Jose hoped to become one of the Homeboy Industries executives within five years, and felt that his experience being a "political liaison" for Father Greg, talking about "reentry" at City Hall, the state capitol, or in DC, was setting him up for such a position.

FORCE and Homeboys LOC Members

The following four case studies of members examine how they became involved with community organizing. In most cases, they had experienced recovery—and even leadership positions within the settings of recovery—prior to community organizing. However, while "reformed" street intellectuals understood and communicated the mutually constitutive importance of personal and political reform, their commitments to organizing were more tenuous. Among respondents, the desire to make good and achieve the American dream loomed larger than civic and political participation. Nonetheless, members participated in civic engagement, in part because they wished a better life for their own children, or because they looked up to organizing leaders who embodied the personal changes they wished to experience.

Olivia

Olivia, a twenty-nine-year-old second-generation Puerto Rican with a gang past but no criminal record, was one of the first persons to get involved with FORCE under Eddie—and one of the only women. Olivia was studying for a bachelor's degree in social work at Northeastern Illinois University (NIU), a midsize, private, four-year university in the Chicago area. It was at NIU that Olivia first learned about the Illinois Sealing Bill, met Eddie, and became involved with the FORCE project.

Olivia grew up with four sisters, a mother, and a father whom she described as both abusive and absent. She recalled that with her father "we weren't allowed to do anything . . . we were terrified of him all the time . . .

any little thing we would get hit or yelled at." By the time she became an adolescent, Olivia's father had left and her older sister had become pregnant. Her mother, in turn, worked two jobs. Olivia described this period as one in which "we were left to do whatever we wanted." She hung out with gangs at school, became affiliated with them, and got involved in gang activity. She cut school, sold drugs, and held guns for the gang.

Olivia became pregnant with her son at age sixteen. She described this event as life-turning: "I would always cut [school], and once I got pregnant everything changed. I started thinking, 'now I have someone else to take care of.'" Olivia's mother helped her with childcare for her son, and Olivia continued going to school. At her school, someone showed her how to apply for welfare and food stamps. Olivia reflected on this experience warmly; she wanted to give that same help to someone else. Olivia planned her educational attainment around employment in fields where she could serve youth in situations similar to her upbringing. She first took the test required to join law enforcement, but didn't pass. She considered teaching, until her college counselor discouraged her due to NIU's high unemployment among graduates trained for teaching. Instead, Olivia's counselor encouraged her to go into social work, because it was "in demand."

Olivia met Eddie while completing some community service hours for her bachelor's degree, organizing for two bills: the Illinois Sealing Bill and statewide legislation to allow undocumented immigrants to gain driver's licenses. Olivia wrote about the Sealing Bill in a policy class at NIU, which she felt was directly relevant to her personal life and professional efforts. Olivia said of her own sister's husband that he wanted to "make a difference" and "provide for his family," but that his criminal record had him "held down." He once found a job, but was fired the instant the results of a background check came back. He eventually found a job out of state, for minimum wage, but Olivia was convinced that if that had not happened he would have returned to crime.

After Eddie invited her to organizing workshops, Olivia said she began to finally understand how her clients faced obstacles that could be changed only by organizing for better laws. I attended one of these trainings, in which I sat next to Olivia and overheard her conversations during our breaks. When Michael, a fellow FORCE member who was also interested in pursuing a career in social work, asked her how she was paying for her college education, she said she was taking out loans. She advised him, "You have to invest in yourself." However, as I got up to use the restroom and returned, I found the tone of the conversation had shifted: Eddie was urging her to think about how to create social change, on a larger level, by organizing.

Olivia hoped that in five years she would be able to land a full-time job in social work and be a homeowner. Olivia did not look up to anyone, though she did say that Eddie was an inspiration to her because "he's doing so much work in his community." Although Olivia did seem to have a clear grasp of what community organizing was, she participated in it because she was guided by her need to make good from her past. She said that she was afraid that her son would become involved on the street, as a form of "punishment" for the things she did on the street during her youth. Olivia shared, "When I decided to do social work, I made a deal with God. I will help these youth change their lives if you spare my son." Olivia hoped that by making good from her past and being redeemed, she could protect her son from the dangers of the street.

Gilda

Gilda, a second-generation Mexican American woman in her early thirties, worked at Homeboy Industries as an assistant to Father Gregory Boyle's executive assistant, Norma Gillette. Jose, the Homeboys LOC lead organizer, had recruited her to become a leader. She worked on the Los Angeles Fair Hiring Ordinance and California Proposition 47 campaigns.

Gilda's family was originally from rural, mountainous Mexico—her father from Jalisco and her mother from Nayarit. Both arrived in the United States during their adolescence, and had remained for about four decades. Gilda was very open about the abuse and neglect she experienced, and how this formed a foundation for the problematic relationships she would later have with men. Gilda described her upbringing as one of "Mexican culture," in which "all they wanted to do was work, so they kind of forget what was going on at home." When issues did arise at home, Gilda said her family "always wanted to solve everything by yelling."

Gilda married at age seventeen to a much older (twenty-eight-year-old) man, and moved to Chicago with him for eight years. Gilda's husband was involved with drug trafficking at a very high level, and was very controlling. Gilda said of the experience, "He dictated everything in my life. Who I could talk to, who shouldn't I talk to. When can I visit my family, when I cannot. Who can come over." Gilda's husband was eventually kidnapped and disappeared. Investigators declared him dead after two years of failing to find information.

Gilda returned to her old neighborhood in Los Angeles, which she described as "still the same," rife with gang violence and drug abuse. Unable to cope with the kidnapping and new routines, she turned to drinking and drug use. Her home also had a lot of gang activity. Gilda's brother and sister were in gangs (though not the same one). Gilda then met and married her second husband, whom she had her first son with. However, two months after the birth of her son, Gilda's second husband was murdered in front of her house. She married yet again, but her third husband also passed away—committing suicide. Eventually her children were taken away. Gilda said she came to a point where she "gave up" and "had no hope." She continued being active with her gang, and was convicted of a gang crime and sentenced to six years.

Gilda said a turning point happened in prison. Upon release, she went to a recovery home for nine months, followed by a sober-living home for six months. At that point, she came to Homeboy Industries. Gilda started participating in LOC events, almost immediately after arriving at Homeboy Industries. She was in a supportive role, listening to the public testimonies of others, because she thought "if I'm changing my life, I want to help others so they could change their lives also." To Gilda, who described herself as "a believer of God," the stories ministered to her. She said that as she listened to people's testimonies, she felt "inspired."

One day, Gilda was surprised to find herself recruited to speak about the Los Angeles Fair Hiring Ordinance for the Homeboys LOC at a rally in front of Los Angeles City Hall. Gilda recollected:

> Jose said, "I just got a call. They need a certain individual, that looks presentable, that does not look like they've been to prison, that could just blow their minds away when you're speaking and you say you went to

prison and you want a different life. That's the kind of person—we see that in you. Are you interested in doing it?"

Gilda said she had spoken in public very few times in her life, but that she knew the importance of the legislation. Gilda said that records discrimination was "shutting the door" for people who were already on the streets, and allowed them to continue participating in street life. She used herself as an example; she said that despite her qualifications she was automatically disqualified from jobs because of her felony record and prison time. She said, "they don't even want to hear any explanation or what even led me to commit the crime." Gilda felt that she should not be automatically disqualified and wished that would-be employers would take into consideration the root causes of her participation with gang activity.

Gilda would get "really pumped up" and "all excited" because such organizing efforts were what she "had been waiting for." She described the thrilling, emotional rush as a form of personal empowerment. In fact, she compared her participation in the Homeboys LOC to a drug high—but without the remorse: "I remember it was the same rush that I used to have when I used to do things with my gang. But this one was way better, because it was a positive thing." Gilda added that community organizing was a lot of work, but that "hey, we went out of our way to get that [drug] high . . . why not [go out of your way to] make this your high?"

Gilda's participation in the LOC was grounded in a religious articulation of the compensatory model. She reasoned that God may have put her through all of her struggles because it was part of his plan, and that if this was part of God's plan, it would be her "destiny" to draw from her experiences to "change people's lives." Gilda was making good from her past crimes by participating in community organizing. She felt that if her efforts could affect just one person, she would know she had been successful in giving back to her community.

Gilda also had modest ambitions outside of the LOC. When I asked where she would like to be in five years, she mentioned that she had just graduated as a makeup artist—but that she wanted work with organizations helping people, such as cancer patients. She also wanted to travel, and to be a homeowner. When I asked whom she admired or looked up to, she replied that she didn't admire any one person—but then used Jose as an example to illustrate how she admired qualities in different people. She admired how Jose was a "strong speaker," knew "how to motivate," and could command people's attention when he walked into a room and gave a speech. She also said that she admired Father Greg because he was so compassionate and Homeboys' chief financial officer because she was so professional. Gilda stopped participating in LOC meetings, but a few months later, when I ran into her husband at Homeboy Industries, he was excited to see me and to tell me that Gilda had been promoted to a full-time, permanent position as a staff member.

Oscar

Oscar, a Mexican American former gang member in his late twenties, entered Homeboy Industries after being released from his second prison term. While there, Oscar was approached by Jose and asked to give his testimony of incarceration and reincarceration at city town hall meetings and rallies. Oscar participated, hoping that his testimony would help shed light on the barriers he experienced after incarceration, and would lead to reforms reducing recidivism. He was one of the Homeboys LOC's most visible members, but stepped away from the LOC as he earned promotions and received greater responsibilities within Homeboy Industries.

Oscar grew up in Los Angeles' Boyle Heights neighborhood, surrounded by violence. At age nine his mother threw him a birthday party only to have the house shot-up in a drive-by. In addition, Oscar had experienced abandonment from his parents. His father had left for a military career, and his mother was a drug addict who spent her money on her habit—rather than "on the kids and food for the house." Oscar saw his homeboys as a "family," filling the absence that his parents had left in his life. He looked up to older boys in his neighborhood, who also lacked father figures, as he searched for a "male role model." In particular, he looked up to his cousin. Oscar admired how he had managed to do so well with drugs, money, cars, and women. However, Oscar's behavior became self-destructive. He said that at one point he thought, "screw it, I'm gonna do drugs."

Oscar described being in a gang and going to jail as a "mentally and emotionally traumatic experience." In addition, he said that after being released from jail for the first time he did not have access to resources such as therapy and employment and claimed that this was the reason he remained involved with gang and drug activity. He reoffended quickly, committing a violent offense, and served nine years before being released.

Oscar went to Homeboy Industries after his second release from prison. It was there that he received a job in employment services, as well as therapy and anger management and drug classes. Oscar said that through that experience, he learned that gang social norms—such as beating up, robbing, and shooting others—were "not normal." He also said that therapy helped him to learn that "there's more to life" than gangs and drugs. Oscar began to see himself as "on track" with a "positive lifestyle," and wanted to be "a normal productive person." He attributed the developments in his life to the opportunities to change that Homeboys provided.

Jose approached Oscar a few months after his arrival at Homeboy Industries. He recalled Jose coaxing him into attending an LA Voice meeting by telling him, "You look like you actually want to do something and give back to the community." Oscar felt strongly about attending the LA Voice meeting, as a way of paying forward his gratitude for Homeboy Industries. Oscar felt Homeboy Industries had given him opportunities to change his life and he wanted to pay it forward by doing what he could for his community.

Attending the meeting, Oscar found that they had discussed issues directly relevant to his first experience being released from jail. Oscar had experienced, and seen others with convictions experience, rejection for job interviews due to a criminal record. Oscar said that he learned from Jose that, as formerly incarcerated persons, they did "have a voice," and could have influence in public debates. Oscar got involved with the Homeboys LOC as an advocate for Ban-the-Box initiatives, gave his testimony at actions, and was given opportunities to speak to City Council members. Oscar learned the value of community organizing and getting people involved in the political process: "We can't just wait around and see what happens in the education department . . . what happens for jobs . . . we have to go out there and show the people in the community . . . how to go about getting involved."

Figure 3.1. A Homeboy giving a testimony at the 2014 Fair Chance rally. Credit: Pocho One Fotography.

Oscar stopped attending Homeboys LOC meetings at the time of my interview with him. His work schedule conflicted with LOC meeting date/times. Although he was hoping to return to school, he did not want to forget about the Homeboys LOC. He felt that Homeboys and LA Voice had both been stepping stones for himself, and for others, giving him opportunities to change his life. Oscar hoped that in five years he would have a career, possibly go back to school, but be in a place to "give back" to Homeboys. He also wanted to give back to LA Voice by showing up to walks and protests whenever possible; he felt strongly about the passage of California Proposition 47, which he felt would improve educational funding in his community and give children better opportunities than the ones he once had.

Oscar wanted to follow in Jose's footsteps. Like Oscar, Jose had done time in prison, had lots of tattoos, and had started working at Homeboy Industries in the maintenance department; at the same time, Jose became director of Oscar's department (employment services), led LOC meetings, and generously purchased items needed for the LOC, such as materials to make signs for picketing, out of his own pocket. Jose also "spoke up" for members such as Oscar, trying to get jobs for them during meetings with private firms. Oscar said he used to think that he "didn't have a voice," until he saw Jose speaking to firms, and that his experiences with Jose showed him "we do have a voice."

Oscar moved up within Homeboy Industries. He took leadership responsibilities, under Jose in employment services, connecting contractors with employees. During one of my visits, I crossed paths with Oscar in the bakery. Beaming with a large smile that was hard to miss, he walked by me and shook my hand. I took one look at him, and impressed by how immaculately ironed his shirt and pants looked, I told him he looked great. I then asked him how he was doing. He told me proudly that a Homeboy Industries client had hired an entire graduating class, of about two dozen Homeboys, from the solar panel training program. We spent time chatting, and he also told me of other contractors that had managed to hire people who came to Homeboys looking for service-sector work. Oscar was no longer involved with the LOC, but found deeply meaningful work in job development.

Connie

Connie, a Black woman in her fifties with youthful qualities, was a member of the Homeboys LOC. When I interviewed her, she was dressed casually in a Homeboys T-shirt, with curled hair and glittered eye shadow. She was also especially kind and polite. As I searched for office space in which to interview her—a very stressful experience for me, because I didn't want to lose an interview—she remained very patient. When we found room and finally sat, our interview quickly got under way. I explained the IRB consent form and asked if she had any questions, and she softly responded that she had none.

As I started the interview, I was surprised to find out Connie was from a small community in California's Central Valley, just a few miles from where my in-laws live—a rural geography with many prisons (e.g., Gilmore 2007a). But I was also surprised to find out that Connie grew up in an "abusive, dysfunctional family" and recalled always being told that she would "never amount to nothin." This history of violence in her family contrasted with her kind, patient demeanor. As the interview continued, I found that she had also experienced corporal punishment as a child. She spoke painfully of "holding emotions in," and having to learn to cope with anger and violence. Later, as an adult, Connie experienced drug addiction, and served prison time. Under California's three-strikes law, she was given a life sentence for her third strike, stealing four DVDs. Connie spent thirteen and a half years in prison, before California Proposition 36 had passed, requiring that a third strike be a violent offense. She won her case on appeal in 2012.

To my surprise, Connie didn't seem to harbor any resentments about having been incarcerated. She calmly reflected on her experience in prison, speaking somewhat fondly of her activities while incarcerated. She took college classes and earned a degree. She took Alcoholics Anonymous and Narcotics Anonymous classes to learn about her drug addictions. She also took self-help classes such as Celebrate Recovery, Mind-Changing, and Mirror-to-Mirror. Some of the classes were faith-based; Celebrate Recovery, an addiction class, used Bible verses to teach members how to cope with addiction. She was most proud, however, of having been a facilitator. She facilitated Co-dependency, Anger Management, and Domestic Violence. She said that taking and facilitating classes was a learning experience for herself, as she tried to understand what made her do drugs. Becoming a facilitator also helped her feel empowered, that she could help others.

Connie's description of the self-help classes seemed tinged with self-blame, as well as the cult of "positive thinking" (e.g., Ehrenreich 2009). When I asked how Mind-Changing helped her, she responded, "You have to look outside the box sometimes . . . if you see things in a different light, it gives you a chance to expand your horizon and learn more." When I asked for an example of this, Connie recounted our interactions just before the interview. We had met in the lobby, and on our way to the elevator I had commented on the recent, ninety-five-degree heat. She told me that although it was hot, she had air conditioning. However, she drew from this exchange to illustrate the point that she could have said, "It wasn't that hot to me." This was an example of how the Mind-Changing course had taught her how to disregard discomforting thoughts.

Mind-Changing was held in a prison, and the prisoners were told to focus inward and to ignore their problems. Surprisingly, as I probed,

Connie's response did not suggest that she had experienced the class as oppressive. She used the example of the Prop 47 campaign to explain how the lessons in Mind-Changing had helped her to reimagine her circumstances in the outside world, and to behave differently, in ways that were empowering. Connie said,

> When I did the phone banking with Prop 47, I did it because I really wanted 47 to pass. I pushed it as much as I could. But in the back of my mind, I was sayin' to myself, "This is not gonna happen," because for me, to see victory is, like, slim to none. So when I was able to see victory, it made me see things in a different way. And if I wouldn't have never took that Mind-Changing class, I probably wouldn't even try to work on that, because I probably would have said in the back of my mind, "It's never gonna pass anyway, so why work on it?" But the Mind-Changing class lets you stop thinking one way and think in numerous different ways.

Connie had wanted Prop 47 to pass because it would downgrade many felony convictions to misdemeanors and benefit others the same way she had benefited from Prop 36. But she was fearful because she thought, pessimistically, "victory is, like, slim to none." Having faced adversity in her life, and having suffered imprisonment, Connie had trouble believing she could help pass an initiative to narrow the definition of a felony. Yet the Mind-Changing class, styled to help prisoners look inward and work on themselves, helped Connie to believe that the Prop 47 campaign could indeed be successful. It was this belief—that she was working on a winnable campaign—that Connie convinced herself of to remain motivated for phone banking.

Homeboy Industries, apart from the LOC that she participated in, also provided a setting where Connie could experience the personal healing she sought. Connie felt that if she had a problem, she had people to speak to at Homeboy Industries and that they would listen. She also took classes at Homeboy Industries. The NA and AA classes helped her understand, through interactions with newer members, how much progress she had made. Homeboy Industries' classes also taught her how to communicate. Not communicating and "holding things in" were the biggest problems she had as a child and had led to her becoming very angry and violent. Last, Connie was taking the Parenting Class to learn how to become a better grandmother and mother; as opposed to using corporal punishment, which was how she was raised, she learned about communicating, taking away toys or TV, or sitting and talking about feelings to let others know how they had hurt her.

Connie said she had ambitions in life, and simply saw Homeboys as a "stepping stone." She was a recovered addict and a formerly incarcerated person, and couldn't find work elsewhere: "You go to another job interview and they say, 'Have you ever been convicted?' and your interview is over." At the same time, Connie had a daughter with a drug problem, and needed a job to make sure her grandchildren wouldn't experience the foster system. Having work at Homeboy Industries ensured that the state wouldn't take her grandchildren away. In the long term, however, Connie aspired to a job helping people. Her "passion" was to help others make "good" decisions, and even if she felt like she couldn't help everyone, she said she just enjoyed the idea of helping change the lives of one or two people.

Connie's strong sense of moral convictions shaped whom she admired and sought to become like. When I asked her whom she admired or looked up to, she mentioned LA Voice executive director Rev. Zach Hoover as well as two other LA Voice staff members. She saw them as friendly, giving, loving, and powerful. She admired the civic activist work they did around issues affecting the formerly incarcerated: "They fight our fight. They have so much courage. I want to be like that . . . I want to one day be able to speak on the behalf of our community. I want to be able to not be ashamed, to be able to stand up and do what's right." Then, when I asked Connie where she would like to be in five years, she said she wanted to be an organizer, to go door-to-door in communities, build resistance to mass incarceration, and show Congress "we're not afraid, that we will speak up, we will fight, we know what's going on."

Conclusion

FORCE and Homeboys LOC members sought personal reform. They had experienced disadvantaged childhoods, marred by segregation, poverty, or incarceration, as well as family abandonment or domestic violence. Connie, for example, had lived through drug addiction and spent thirteen years in prison for a nonviolent third strike. Such disadvantages compounded the difficulties of an increasingly unstable labor market. Some members, such as Gilda or Connie, aspired to work in the nonprofit sector, or in professions helping others, such as social work, but faced obstacles—such as a criminal record—in landing better paying work. As a result, members sought to experience a sense of dignity by making good through violence-prevention efforts, such as taking or leading therapeutic classes, or through civic engagement that involved helping others; while Connie had led therapeutic classes in prison, Olivia had mentored gang youth in her community.

FORCE and Homeboys LOC members' efforts at personal reform took shape through redemption scripts, which emphasized making good from past crimes by becoming responsible family members and by giving back to their communities. In large part, this rested upon notions of the American dream: they wished to return to school, obtain good jobs, have careers, become homeowners, and mend strained family ties. FORCE and Homeboys LOC leaders, such as Eddie, Marlon, and Jose, had achieved some of these lofty goals. Eddie enrolled in (and later finished) a graduate program at the University of Chicago, while Jose was promoted to director of employment services. Others, such as Marlon and Gilda, landed full-time jobs in work they felt gave them a sense of dignity; Marlon enjoyed the autonomy and respect he experienced in the construction work that he did, while Gilda was glad to land a coveted staff position at Homeboy Industries. Others, such as Olivia, were in school or planning to return.

At the same time, FORCE and Homeboys LOC members' redemption scripts were compatible with collective and political action. FORCE and Homeboys LOC leaders, for example, facilitated civic and political participation by providing subjects with "vocabularies of motive" that framed community organizing as a way of "giving back." Leaders extended members' efforts to make good from violence prevention to civic activism, and compelled them to increase civic activism through community organizing. As Eddie, Marlon, and Jose engaged in collectively empowering forms of giving back, members admired how they embodied personal change and wished to follow in their footsteps.

We now turn to how CRS and LA Voice's contrasting religious displays—the insurgent and the pastoral—provided rituals of reacceptance and reabsorption that socially integrated members who sought personal reform. Chapter 4 examines how CRS was rooted in the Black church and drew from issue-based community organizing to facilitate collective action among FORCE members. Chapter 5 explores how LA Voice was rooted in Catholic teachings and drew from the relationship-based community organizing model to facilitate collective action among Homeboys LOC members; in addition, the needs of Homeboy Industries—as a large, prominent nonprofit—further shaped relationship-based community organizing. As FORCE and Homeboys LOC members learned to participate in community organizing, they reshaped it as a form of personal reform—deploying redemption scripts to make good from their past.

4

"There Is Tension in Democracy"

The FORCE Project

On a cold December morning in 2011, at the downtown Chicago offices of the Illinois Coalition for Immigrant and Refugee Rights (ICIRR), Eddie Bocanegra helped lead one of the first FORCE community organizing meetings. Eddie and Chris Moore, an activist who had previously led earlier efforts to mobilize formerly incarcerated persons (through the Muslim-based Exodus Renewal Society), co-chaired a meeting centered on "records discrimination" and employment. In attendance were about thirty persons: a few clergy, several persons with records, and several others with activist backgrounds. They were Black, white, and Latino, and represented diverse religious backgrounds—Baptist, Catholic, Eastern Orthodox Christian.

Eddie and Chris were joined by two persons with extensive experience in community organizing: CRS lead organizer Alex Wiesendanger and ICIRR director Steven Smith. Alex and Steven then guided Eddie in drawing heavily from conventional community organizing practices, such as opening and closing with a short prayer, distributing a written agenda with a goal (to start the FORCE project), restricting the meeting to a moderate length (sixty to ninety minutes), and starting and ending the meeting on time. Similar to sociologist Stephen Hart's (2001, 105) research on community organizing, in which he found that organizers limited the boundaries of democratic discussion—by sticking to the agenda and stating that participants were "people of great value whose time . . . is important"—so too did Eddie regulate discussion at times to follow the agenda closely "out of respect for everyone's time."

After distributing the agenda, Chris asked us to introduce ourselves by stating our name and organization and to answer a "relational question," a standard community organizing technique that asks participants to articulate their "self-interest" in organizing. In this case, Chris asked us to justify our presence by stating "one reason why [we] think ex-offenders need their own political voice." FORCE members responded to the relational question by voicing concern with the stigma of the criminal record they personally carried—and describing it as an unfair obstacle to employment. They felt that the work they were doing—volunteering and giving back to their communities—should have mitigated some of the negative judgment their criminal records presented.

Eddie, as a founding member of FORCE, gave a testimony illustrating how political activism for records discrimination was intimately connected to his efforts at personal reform. Dressed as usual in a sweater vest, shirt, and tie, Eddie shared heartfelt testimony, proudly recalling how the Illinois governor and the United Nations had recognized his work in violence prevention; at the same time, the stigma of his criminal record overshadowed his skills and disqualified him from many types of violence-prevention work. As he finished his testimony, several persons echoed Eddie's reflection, affirming his claims of both unfair discrimination and being a changed person.

Following the relational question and discussion, ICIRR organizer Steven Smith provided a brief training on community organizing. Steven taught us how to organize and run "house meetings" by asking about people's "problems," connecting those problems to "issues," and identifying "targets" who could be pressured to bring about change. Steven explained that house meetings should aim to increase membership, while also building a "broad," demographically diverse base. Relating his personal experience with organizing, Steven told us that a broad-based coalition would be much more difficult to attack because "the opposition" would have a more difficult time finding a way to attack so many groups. He commented on the racial and religious diversity in the room, and said this would be an asset in building support for legislative reform. As the meeting closed, Steven and Alex announced that they would be searching for a business to target for a corporate campaign. Steven asked for volunteers to help Alex, conducting research and creating a list of private employers with poor records of hiring formerly incarcerated persons.

Over the subsequent year, FORCE members compiled a list of businesses and chose to target Walgreens. Walgreens had headquarters nearby, in Deerfield, Illinois, and Alex explained that this made it more practical to hold an "action," such as protesting on the front lawn of the CEO's house. First, Alex and Eddie directed FORCE members to submit employment applications to Walgreens, and to note whether they received interview call-backs. Then, Alex and Eddie directed FORCE members to conduct research on Walgreens' board members—compiling their affiliations in education, work, religion, and associations—in order to identify powerful board members and avenues that might be used to place social pressure on them. FORCE members then targeted Walgreens' diversity officer, Steve Pemberton—who had written a rags-to-riches story about his rise through the corporate world. FORCE members held meetings with Mr. Pemberton and Walgreens officials and urged them to remove the felony conviction question from their employment application. They argued that Walgreens' diversity policy—claiming to hire people representative of the neighborhoods they served—were at odds with their hiring practices.

After several tense negotiations—some of which included lies, accusations of threats, and the use of legal counsel—CRS staged their fall 2013 worship assembly at Mr. Pemberton's church, Glenview Community Church. Eddie took to the microphone, delivering his testimony after CRS members sang and clapped to CRS's performance of "Victory Is Mine." Eddie stated that he was a graduate student at the University of Chicago, had spoken at the United Nations, and had received an award from the governor—but that Walgreens had not called him for a job interview. Eddie emphasized, "Not one call," as some members murmured as to shame Walgreens. Eddie also told the assembly that FORCE tried to get Walgreens to partner with three prominent prisoner reentry programs (Safer, Westside, and St. Leonard's), but that the company had never given a phone call to any applicant from these sites. However, Eddie also announced that FORCE had met with US congresswoman Jan Schakowsky, state representative Danny Davis, and Cook County president Toni Preckwinkle. In turn, Preckwinkle called a meeting with Walgreens to support FORCE. To this, Eddie rejoiced, and CRS members broke out singing and clapping "Victory Is Ours." By March 2014, Walgreens had conceded not only to remove the felony conviction question from employment applications, but to form a partnership with several local halfway houses that provided training and jobs for formerly incarcerated persons. In April, Walgreens hired the first trainee from their halfway house partnership.

Political scientist Heidi Swarts (2008) has argued that North American literature on social movements has tended to focus on the "moments of madness" that galvanize national social movements, but that it has ignored local social movements, such as community organizing, which tend to be much more focused on continuity and on the commitment to building organizational capacity. CRS, for example, provided an investment of time and resources into FORCE. Alex, Eddie's supervisor, helped to teach community organizing principles and practices, offering impromptu as well as formal trainings and workshops. In addition, CRS provided transportation to FORCE members for annual lobby day visits to the state capitol. Thus, CRS's efforts to build organizational capacity for local social movement activity deepened formerly incarcerated people's participation in civic and political action.

The Walgreens corporate campaign was an example of insurgent prophetic redemption. First, CRS/FORCE leaders translated Alinsky-style community organizing lessons in ways that resonated with members' lived experiences on the street and in recovery.[1] Second, FORCE leaders and members drew from recovery to reconstruct the meaning of community organizing. Third, CRS/FORCE leaders deprivatized FORCE members' efforts at personal reform for collective action in the public arena.

"Taking Power": Issue-Based Community Organizing

CRS incubated FORCE through hierarchical notions of organizational structure that hinged, partially, upon notions of combativeness; Alex presented members with faith-based community organizing's hierarchical social structure, while Eddie drew from gang and street metaphors to justify it. At one of FORCE's first meetings, Alex drew a pyramid on butcher block paper, labeling sections from top to bottom: "faith in action," "take action," "3x a year," and "pews." Alex then explained that status within the hierarchy was accorded based upon commitment; serious members put their "faith in action" regularly, attending all events, while others participated in actions once a month, only three times a year, or possibly never—showing up only to meetings. Alex then drew a second pyramid next to the first, and suggested that the organizational hierarchy—consisting of a "leadership team," "task force members," "chapter leaders," and "chapter members"—rewarded these differing levels of commitments.

Eddie related Alex's description of a community organizing hierarchy to FORCE members by likening it to the hierarchies of Chicago-based gangs, which refer to themselves as "organizations" and have leadership "boards." At a meeting, Eddie told us in a soft voice that when he saw Alex's hierarchical diagram, "I'm thinking of the streets." Eddie explained that on the streets he used to evaluate people based on their skills, and their "willingness" to commit to the gang's activities. What Alex referred to as the "base" (chapter members), Eddie referred to as "troops"; Eddie suggested these members were easily recruited, like gang members inviting their classmates to hang out on the street. Eddie then contrasted the "base" with the higher levels of the community organizing hierarchy, which he likened to higher levels of the gang, such as "enforcers" and "security." Eddie then said, of the middle-tier officers, that "you trust them with stuff," suggesting their job was to protect the leadership and carry out their orders. Last, Eddie explained that the highest level of the organization was reserved for persons involved in "making decisions." In turn, one of Eddie's first initiatives was to create a FORCE leadership board, consisting of core members with criminal records, modeled after the Almighty Latin Kings' organizational structure.

Eddie also drew from the idea of gangs as having hierarchies to communicate community organizing lessons about "base building" and "raising up leaders." At the one-day training, Eddie wrote a few names of organizations on butcher block paper: NAACP, Vice Lords, National Organization of Women. Eddie then asked, "What do these organizations all have in common?" FORCE members failed to guess Eddie's response; Marlon said that they create "some type of change," while Camron replied that they were about "bettering the community" and "bringing jobs." Eddie turned to the next sheet, revealing the words, "Recruitment, Expanded Chapters, Vision." Eddie made his point, that for FORCE to raise its public visibility it would have to grow, by comparing civil rights organizations like the NAACP and NOW with gangs such as the Vice Lords. Inherent to such growth would be the formation of distinct, local chapters each with its own leaders.

Members debated questions about the group's sustainability through analogies with gangs and advocacy groups. Eddie's departure from CRS and FORCE, eighteen months following FORCE's inaugural meeting at ICIRR, created questions about FORCE's sustainability. Alex called a special meeting and led a debate that invited questions about the group's sustainability. Alex asked the six leaders present pointed questions about their commitment and the stability of the organization: "Where do you see yourself in this leadership structure? Where do you see yourselves in the dues structure? How many members do you see yourself bringing in?" The tension was palpable, as Eddie distributed a handout with a "tentative leadership structure." Eddie described the hierarchy of chapters and a steering committee in gang terms familiar to the men in the room, but he also softened the tone by drawing parallels between FORCE, gangs, and the NAACP. Eddie claimed that he could relate to the importance of dues because he came "from the gang perspective." Eddie enticed FORCE members, telling them, "Many of the organizations, street organizations, pay dues." Eddie explained that it was important to have funds to pay for buses to lobby at the state capitol, before introducing a "pledge card." He insisted that others fill it out as a sign of their "commitment" and as a demonstration of the group's sustainability.

CRS organizers drew from religious understandings to communicate Alinsky-style community organizing principles. At the one-day training, after practicing one-on-one meetings, Alex asked us to debrief and share our self-interests; when Wesley, a member, stated that Jesus was his self-interest, Alex shot back, "That's a value, not a self-interest." Alex quoted scripture faster than I could take notes, stating that there are many parts in the body of God. Alex then probed Wesley by asking, "We're all called by God to do different things, what are those things?" Alex then drew from Wesley's answer to explain how self-interests connected with issues and issue-based community organizing.[2]

In line with Alinsky's combative tactics and zero-sum concept of power, organizers "agitated" members, contested their ideas of humility as power, and urged them to instead "take power." At the one-day training, Eddie opened a conversation by posing a question: "What are some of the strengths that we have?" Trisha responded first: "Knowledge about the criminal justice system." Camron responded second: "Survival, adversity." However, when Olivia mentioned "power," Eddie replied, "I'm gonna push back." Eddie asked, "How?" Olivia was unable to answer. Marlon offered, "Humility." Eddie, again, said, "I'm gonna push back."

Marlon responded quoting scripture, claiming that "if you are good and humble, God is gonna raise you up." Eddie again politely disagreed—this time asking FORCE members to speak about their "weaknesses," illustrating the extent to which formerly incarcerated persons were disempowered. Members remarked that their weaknesses were embarrassment, shame, fear, and doubt. Eddie affirmed their responses, stating, "Right, lack of confidence."

Later in the discussion, Eddie shared that he felt being in prison structured his food and time in such a way that made him less assertive. When Walgreens called him to discuss the corporate campaign, he was afraid to return their calls—once receiving four calls before he had the courage to return them. Eddie was afraid to speak to Walgreens because, as he said, "I lacked that ability to feel like I had the ability to talk for others." Eddie's humility, rather than being a strength, was a weakness that undermined his empowerment. Eddie explained that this was political because when he failed to speak on behalf of formerly incarcerated persons, that "let others have the power, like academics or politicians." Eddie saw one of those persons, the head of Cook County Corrections, give a talk and thought to himself, "This guy is . . . the dumbest person I've ever met. He shouldn't be making decisions for us." Eddie's Alinsky-style teachings on zero-sum power resonated with members' experiences, as Camron blurted an "uh-huh." Eddie finished the lesson by saying, "We have to take that power."

CRS organizers highlighted the importance of discourse in "taking power"; organizers not only gave members strict training to "take power" by following a discursive script—such as with "making the ask"—but also admonished "giving away" power by straying from scripted interactions. CRS organizers emphasized the importance of collectively pressuring elected officials as a way of taking power. At debriefs, following large events in which "asks" were made, CRS organizers advanced collective notions of power. At a monthly meeting, following a lobby day visit to the capitol, Eddie asked us, "What did we learn?" Robert responded as a member with experience typically would: "All of us are more powerful than one." Several members mumbled in reply, "Yup."

I learned the discursive rules of collectively "taking power" firsthand, following a FORCE meeting I organized with Illinois House representative Greg Harris (who represented my home district, district 13). Prior to the meeting, I had met with Eddie to familiarize myself with the agenda: introductions, discussion of the bill, some personal testimony, and then "the ask." We then went to Harris's district office in North Chicago, joining Jennifer Cossyleon (my graduate research assistant), Katy (a CRS organizer), and Chris Patterson (a community leader, author, and formerly incarcerated person). It had been my first experience attending a meeting with an elected official, let alone chairing one, and I—accustomed to the status and privilege I enjoyed as a college professor—was completely unprepared for Harris's abrasive style.

I had only introduced myself before Harris interjected to say, "Let's start with [group] introductions, okay?" He chastised me for arriving with a group, falsely insisting that I had scheduled only a one-on-one meeting. Then, Harris moved our discussion between items as we tried to respond to him. In end, we "made the ask" to Harris and received his support for the Sealing Bill—but not without him first patronizing us by telling us how we should have instead been building support from the business community. Immediately after the meeting, we walked to the sidewalk in front of Harris's office to "debrief."

Eddie's first question was, "What could we have done better?" As I exchanged glances with others, nervously awaiting the first response, Chris spoke and made a remark about how I allowed Harris to "take control" of our meeting because I hadn't spoken assertively enough to guide us through the agenda items. I was ashamed, and could feel my face turn red, but we were not done debriefing. In order to make sure I had understood the lesson, Eddie more succinctly reiterated Chris's remark: "Ed, you let [Harris] take the power."

The Redemption Imperative: Reshaping Issues-Based Community Organizing through Recovery

FORCE members were preoccupied with redeeming themselves, sensitive to the idea that they might be judged against the stereotype of the hardened criminal. Quintin Williams (2015, 3), a FORCE member who conducted an ethnographic study of the organization, found that members felt it necessary to continuously engage in displays of being reformed—what he termed the "redemption imperative." For example, at the one-day training in CRS's offices, I overheard Marlon and Camron talk about formerly incarcerated friends they were trying to orient away from illicit street activity. As they poured coffee and picked out donuts during a morning break between workshops, Marlon mentioned to Camron that he had a friend who was "getting out" of prison. Marlon was doing community service with this friend, but the friend asked him to do something illegal. Marlon punctuated his disbelief and disappointment by exclaiming, "I'm like, 'man!'" Marlon, in expressing some of his desire and disappointment in helping others, had countered the image of the hardened criminal. Participating in FORCE allowed members opportunities to engage in displays of reform.

FORCE members drew from displays of personal reform—particularly redemption scripts—to construct reformed identities in the settings of community organizing. At the one-day training, as I left the coffee table and went to use the bathroom, I had a conversation with a FORCE member, Ben, whom I had never met before but who was very willing to share about his personal life. Ben struck up a conversation with me as we washed our hands, side by side, telling me that he had an interest in educational psychology, specifically "transgenerational trauma." Ben expressed tragic optimism and demonstrated the compensatory model: he asserted that his incarceration was both "a curse and a blessing," and that he was "glad it happened" because "it opened [his] eyes," and helped him understand how he could be "part of the solution." By deploying a redemption script during our break, Ben deepened his participation in FORCE. As we returned to the training, he drew from the experiences he shared with me to engage with community organizing lessons and exercises on the articulation of "self-interest."

Members constructed reformed identities from meetings to bathroom breaks, public testimonies at worship assemblies, and breakfasts with elected officials. Marlon's conversation with Camron at the coffee station nurtured a bond built on making good, as did Ben's conversation with me about his educational goals. After monthly meetings, I sometimes met and interacted with FORCE members' acquaintances. Often new members had just been released from prison, and, on one occasion, Marlon approached me and asked—because I had roots in California—if I'd be willing to meet with a friend of his who had just been released from a prison there. Marlon was concerned that his friend was vulnerable to the lure of illicit activity and hoped that community organizing might be a good influence deterring him from the street.

CRS organizers taught FORCE members community organizing practices that reoriented them from the privatistic displays of personal reform to forming public relationships and advocating for political reform. For example, Alex offered a one-on-one lesson during a training. A vital tool, the one-on-one is used for intentionally evoking people's stories and revealing their commitments to public action (Swarts 2008). Alex started by reading from our training workbook, which defined a one-on-one as "a personalized meeting aimed to recruit like-minded individuals." The workbook listed the characteristics of a one-on-one: thirty to forty-five minutes, "stories," "face-to-face" interactions, "intentional," and "mutual." Alex then shared a story with us: once, during a one-on-one, an elderly woman of color asked him, "You're young and white. Why are you here?" Such direct language is not only acceptable but encouraged in one-on-ones; they are fundamentally concerned with opening "a window into the passions that animate people to act" (Chambers 2003, 45). Alex explained that as they talked, it became clear she was only asking for his "story," and that it ended up being one of the best one-on-ones he ever had.

In teaching us about one-on-ones, Alex made clear to contrast them with the private forms of social communication and action that FORCE members were familiar with. At the one-day training Alex asked, "How many of you have had one-on-ones?" When Camron responded affirmatively, Alex probed and found out that Camron thought his meetings with his drug counselor counted, to which Alex said, "That's a one-on-one, but that's a different type of one-on-one." Alex then explained that a one-on-one involved looking for "public" relationships around "shared values." Whereas private relationships entailed loyalty—irrespective of values—public relationships shape how we pursue our similar values in the world. Alex explained to FORCE members that the purpose of conducting one-on-ones was to build power by organizing people. One-on-ones are the most important tool for expanding power—recruiting new members and deepening relationships among existing members (Jacobsen 2001).

FORCE members drew from community organizing practices to express their self-interest in experiencing personal reform. When Alex invited a FORCE member, Reymundo, to join him in a one-on-one demonstration at the one-day training, Reymundo took the opportunity to perform being reformed. Reymundo casually walked to the center of the room and took a seat, face-to-face with Alex. Alex wasted no time, leaning in to Reymundo and asking how he heard about FORCE. Reymundo responded with a lengthy testimony; he was at NIU one day and asked one of his professors if—because he had a criminal record—he was wasting his time working toward a degree. Alex asked several more questions, each probing deeper into Reymundo's life. Alex asked about the contents of Reymundo's record, the "struggles" he faced, the changes he would like to see, and whether he knew anyone else who was "hungry" for change. Reymundo's responses revealed he was fighting the urge to return to illicit street activity by attempting to "make good" from his past: he wanted to create change, so that others (including himself) could remain crime-free, work hard, and support a family. By participating in a one-on-one demonstration, Reymundo engaged in a performance of reform and redeemed himself to us.

Following Alex and Reymundo's one-on-one demonstration, Alex asked us to practice one-on-ones with a partner. I conducted a one-on-one with Dennis, who told me he had been in prison for seventeen years, had two sons (ages thirty-two and seventeen), and was concerned his sons were getting into trouble. Dennis wanted to set a good example for them, didn't want them to get discouraged, and found strength in faith. Dennis shared with me that what motivated him was to help others, and for that reason he was involved with FORCE.

FORCE members' self-interest in personal reform played an important role in how they reshaped community organizing lessons, and constructed the meaning of community organizing. At the special meeting in which Alex presented the idea of paying dues, members responded affirmatively by relating the paying of dues to gangs—but also to faith-based recovery. Michael drew from street language to assert religious principles. In support, Michael said, "I'm gonna lay it flat. I feel like we're doing God's work." Marlon too expressed support, but drew from the language of recovery. Marlon said, "We should have to be self-sufficient." Robert also supported the idea of dues drawing from street tropes. Robert commented, "You get to see who's committed." Robert took out a ten-dollar bill and, with a tense demeanor, tossed the pledge card with the bill to the center of the table and said, "that's where I'm at." Oscar, a Black male in his twenties, also supported paying dues through recovery terms. Oscar mentioned "tradition," commented that one of the twelve steps is to be "self-sufficient," and made the comparison between dues and twelve-step "trips, literature, and coins." Oscar even drew from a common trope in recovery—the redirecting of his prior commitment from gangs and drugs to making good (e.g., Flores and Hondagneu-Sotelo 2013). Oscar said, "When I was getting high, I committed myself to being a lookout on the corner . . . that didn't do me no good, but this did do me good!"

Faith-based community organizing's ideas and practices "allow it to reconcile values and concepts that have frequently been irreconcilable in the logic of American political culture" (Swarts 2008, 68). Just as Swarts (2008, 68) found community organizing to link "narratives of private pain with public action" and mobilize members, so too did CRS organizers link FORCE members' private pain with public action. However, while CRS organizers sought to use "one-on-ones," "elevator speeches," and "the ask" to build organizational capacity for local social movements, FORCE members drew from their experiences in recovery, such as "ritualized verbal displays" (Flores and Hondagneu-Sotelo 2013), to reconstruct the spaces of community organizing as redemptive.

FORCE Meetings and Ritualized Displays of Recovery

FORCE meetings followed typical community organizing protocol: they always (with the lone exception being the time Alex was absent) began on time, with a prayer and with a distributed, typed agenda that clearly labeled the time—rounded to the nearest five minutes—next to each agenda item. After the prayer, we proceeded with an introduction (including a relational question) and business items (including evaluations from any prior actions), then closed with quick evaluations and a prayer. Nonetheless, FORCE members drew from their experiences in recovery to reshape interactions in such meetings.

FORCE members infused opening and closing prayers with recovery's "ritualized verbal displays" (Flores and Hondagneu-Sotelo 2013) of personal reform. As we closed our eyes, bowed our heads, and, at times, formed a circle and held hands, the member leading us in prayer gave an inspirational, stream-of-consciousness prayer. A few members would repeat some of the prayer's words or murmur call-and-response terms used in Black Protestant churches, such as "yes" and "Lord." Sometimes a member asked to read scripture in lieu of a prayer, drawing from an experience in twelve-step recovery; in one case, a member read Ecclesiastes 9 to 11, and then told us that rewards come to those not with talent but with "commitment." Others recited prayers that relied heavily on gang recovery's notions of reformed masculinity (e.g., Flores 2014); these prayers emphasized "heart," "willingness," and "family." Prayers meshed the discourse of collective action with that of faith-based recovery, asking God to use the meeting to "guide us." This latter language resembled Alcoholics Anonymous's discursive prescriptions—such as to "accept things beyond your control" and to "believe in God or a higher power" (Hoffmann 2006, 675)—which has been documented in Pentecostal restoration and clinical rehabilitation approaches to gang recovery (e.g., Flores 2014).

FORCE meetings proceeded to "introductions," at which point members took turns giving their name, and stated whether they were a FORCE leader or FORCE member or if it was their first time at a meeting. These introductions were often paired with a "relational" question, in which members articulated a reason for their participation in FORCE: "Why are you here? How did you get involved? How do you see yourself contributing to the group?" Responses were tinged with faith and recovery. At one meeting at the beginning of a campaign season, Alex asked us to state our name as well as what we felt our "purpose" would be in "launching campaigns for the new year." We went around the room, speaking individually about where we saw ourselves fitting into the campaigns of CRS and FORCE. Marlon felt his calling to be in recruitment; he said he felt his purpose was to "build a base, and momentum." Anthony, speaking quietly as if humbled by his past crimes or struggle to make good, responded that his focus would be on working and being a member of FORCE and his congregation, and that—through those things—he was hoping to give "just that much more . . . being a vessel." Three people in the room, Alex, Lisa, and Bob, who didn't have records, gave less poignant responses. However, when it was Dennis's turn to speak, he mentioned a "vision" of personal reform that included halfway houses and prisons.

FORCE members drew from recovery discourse's trope of "strength through weakness" to encourage vulnerability in responding to relational questions. Newer members, still in or fresh out of recovery, wore large, oversized clothing but made remarks that resembled confessions and suggested they were trying to accomplish personal change, such as by saying they were trying to "figure out how to be a returning citizen." Alan, a Black adult male in his thirties and a newer member of FORCE, gave a particularly heartfelt account of how he was staying involved with FORCE because it was something "positive" to serve as an inspiration to his incarcerated nephew. This member said he had been involved with "drugs, mayhem, craziness and other stuff" in the past, but suggested that he was now "trying to get back by doing something positive." As he talked, Alan said that he kept coming because every FORCE meeting was a "little bit" more of something "positive." Every time Alan's nephew asked about Alan, his family would tell him that Alan was doing good. Alan said that he wanted to keep coming to FORCE meetings because he wanted to keep being an inspiration to his incarcerated nephew.

The introductions and relational questions were akin to recovery, allowing members to rehearse a "presentation of self" centered on performances of reform. A relational question of "How did you join FORCE?" elicited responses that highlighted themes such as the desire to "give back," and emphasized the collective dimensions of reform, such as by stating "we're here for other people." At times, some members encouraged a type of civic engagement that was rooted in volunteerism, individualism, and personalism (e.g., Eliasoph 2012, 2013); members' comments, such as "we're here to give hope, and inspire others," sometimes highlighted interpersonal relationships and mentoring rather than collective political action. Nonetheless, even personalistic comments were vitally important to building capacity within FORCE; just as Marlon talked with Camron about mentoring during a break at the one-day training, FORCE members' discussions of personalism facilitated relationship building that sustained the group.

FORCE meetings ended with one-word "evaluations," always hopeful and optimistic, which provided further opportunities for members to construct community organizing as a redemptive space. The two rules Alex set forth were that our evaluations had to be "feeling" (no "thoughts") and had to be one word. As we went around the room at the end of every meeting, members routinely peppered the evaluation with uplifting comments, such as "thorough," "insightful," "efficient," "collaborative," and "intelligent." Where scholars have found evaluations to be crucial for development of community organizing strategies, Alex's rule encouraged members to offer less instrumental, more expressive words—such as "hopeful," "focused," "excited," "energized," "enlightened," and "motivated." Such expressions were rooted in displays of personal reform—providing hope and inspiration to those pursuing recovery—rather than efforts to develop community organizing strategies.

FORCE did utilize monthly meetings to evaluate events; these evaluations fit much more with scholarship on community organizing evaluations, and it was from these evaluations that meanings of community organizing were constructed as insurgent. Event evaluations were distinct from the one-word evaluation, though they also proceeded with an analysis of "What went well?" or "What could have been better?" At a monthly meeting, Eddie led an evaluation asking us about a lobby day trip in which CRS coordinated a "die-in" inside the state capitol building. Smiling, Eddie told us, "Say in one word how you felt." We responded with agreeable words such as "excited" and "good." Eddie then asked us, "What was your favorite moment?" A FORCE leader described putting pressure on a politician, hesitant to support the Sealing Bill, to support it. Many of us reacted by smiling and nodding.

"You Are the Expert": From Private Narratives to Testimonies for Collective Action

FORCE members drew from recovery displays to reshape the meanings of criminal justice "expertise," and to expand the rights of the formerly incarcerated. Law professor and sociologist David Garland (2001, 110) has argued that the "old myth of the sovereign state" and instrumental action has been displaced by expressive action around the "anger and outrage that crime provokes." This is reflected in the various studies that have examined how powerful actors and organizations have sidestepped criminal justice experts in order to expand incarceration (e.g., Gilmore 2007a; Page 2011; Simon 2007). What has received less attention

Figure 4.1. CRS and FORCE members at a 2014 Illinois House Judiciary and Restorative Justice Committee meeting. Credit: Community Renewal Society.

is how grassroots social movement activists may draw from therapeutic techniques to resist oppression and to reshape definitions of expertise (Whittier 2009). Similarly, FORCE members drew from redemption scripts as they resisted their exclusion, took the place of experts in legislative reform, and expanded the rights of the formerly incarcerated.

CRS organizers helped FORCE members turn their personal narratives into public testimonies for collective and political action (e.g., Flores and Cossyleon 2016). Similar to sociologist Ruth Braunstein's (2012) work on liberal religious storytelling, CRS provided acceptable repertoires to share stories, such as the Christian act of bearing witness, as well as the platforms necessary to enable collective and political action around members' stories. First, CRS leaders drew from traditional community organizing repertoires—such as "elevator speech" workshops—to shape FORCE members' redemption scripts from personal narrative to personal testimony. Second, FORCE members' testimonies were shared in several settings conducive to political action, such as worship assemblies, coalition meetings, meetings with elected officials, and "lobby day" trips to the state capitol. In turn, FORCE members drew from therapeutic discursive practices to both redefine "expert" knowledge and advance legislative reform expanding their own rights.

The FORCE one-day organizer training taught members community organizing principles and practices necessary for turning personal narratives into public testimonies—and, in turn, collective and political action. Activities included lessons on power and "self-interest" (mentioned earlier) but also exercises for one-on-ones and presenting testimonies. Eddie started a lesson on thirty-second "elevator speeches" by asking us how we would explain FORCE. Most members told personal stories, but failed to highlight unfair laws and how FORCE might effect legislative change. Trisha said she wanted to win change for her brother. Reymundo shared how his record was an obstacle to earning promotions at work and led him in and out of college. Olivia followed, saying that she "used to gangbang"—but avoided getting a record—and now mentors youth. Camron gave the final speech—passionate, lasting a few minutes, and emphasizing that he was reformed—in a way that seemed more suited to an evangelical or Alcoholics Anonymous setting. Camron said that he was "tired of being the problem," had previously been influenced by guys who were older than him and sought to "pass the baton," but that his "experience" being incarcerated "humbled" him. Having a record, Camron said he was in a situation where "it's more tough now than before."

Eddie responded empathetically—but urged Trisha, Olivia, Reymundo, and Camron to shorten their speeches and communicate more effectively. Eddie told Camron he had some really important words to say, but asked him, "How would you explain it in 30 seconds?" Camron appeared unfazed, and responded by speaking a little faster—but still took about a minute to conclude his speech. His last words, prose that rhymed, were more expressive than instrumental. Camron said, "All we know how to do is fight, you have to be that shining light." Eddie's response was terse: "Try to put in thirty seconds . . . because not everyone will have time to listen." To communicate the earnest nature of his request, in a way that Camron could understand, Eddie said, "If I'm out on the street, I might say I'm busy. Like, 'I gotta go around the corner, but I'll see where you're at later.' So those thirty seconds are important." Eddie looked back at the FORCE participants, who acknowledged Eddie's comment with slight nods. Eddie proceeded to turn the butcher block paper, revealing a sheet with the words: "People with Records," "Fair Chance," and "Discrimination." Eddie pointed to these themes for guidance in developing our speeches, assuring us, "This is the one thing that people struggle with the most, the thirty-second speech." Eddie then asked us to practice the thirty-second speech in groups of four, with the intention of developing the speech as a recruitment tool. Eddie asked, "How do you engage someone in an elevator speech, someone with a record?"

The thirty-second speech practice session was clumsy; one person in my group thought an "elevator speech" was literally to be given in an elevator, then tried to use an elevator as a metaphor ("you can go up or down"). With the little time that remained for practicing, my group members all struggled to keep the speech under thirty seconds. When our time was up, Eddie asked for one person from each group to volunteer giving the speech. Several attempted to give the speech, but they all had the same problems as my group members—keeping it under thirty seconds. Eddie promptly told each person that his or her speech was not under thirty seconds. The frustration was palpable; members unequivocally showed self-disappointment through gestures such as loud sighs or dropping their heads. Eddie assuaged the members' frustrations, encouraging them to persist with practicing the thirty-second speech—because they had street "skills" that were transferable to the public sphere. Eddie said, "One of the things I was good at on the streets was recruiting, and I wouldn't doubt that all of you have those skills. We know how to hustle, and this right here is the hustling game, in general. We're using that framework to do something positive and productive."

At the end of the one-day training, Alex and Eddie passed around a sheet with activist protest chants, and told us we would be going outside to do chants and take turns standing on a soapbox. FORCE members were clearly inhibited from public displays of private emotion, and expressed incredulous reluctance (e.g., "Aw man!" or "Wait—now?!") at the idea they would be going outside to chant and take turns on the soapbox. When members nervously asked what they were supposed to talk about, Alex simply told us our speech should be "something we were passionate about, that we cared about." The personal narratives we had spent that morning turning into "elevator speeches" would soon be transformed into personal testimonies outside on the soapbox. We put our sweaters on, headed down the elevators, and followed Alex and Eddie a block north of CRS's offices.

In the midst of the bustling pedestrian traffic of downtown Chicago's Michigan Avenue, and despite FORCE members' bewilderment, fear, and reluctance, Eddie and Alex led us to a tree planter where they shared their plan: we were to transform the concrete ledge to a soapbox for protesting and delivering testimonies. We looked at each other with brief glances, before Alex and Eddie told us, "Okay, let's form a circle." Alex started by clapping and rhythmically singing the first chant, "Ain't no power like the power of the people cuz the power of the people don't stop!" Eddie responded, "Say what?" Quickly, we chimed in with Eddie's responses. Alex led chants, thrusting his fist in the air, and soon his face had turned red with shouting. Every few repetitions, Alex turned to the person next to him and shouted, "Go!" One by one, FORCE members took to the concrete bench to deliver abbreviated—but heartfelt—testimonies about having a record, being discriminated against, FORCE, and the Illinois Sealing Bill. Alex kept the energy up, shouting at the top of his lungs with a growl in his voice, as he introduced chants to us. When Alex exclaimed, "We're fired up!" we learned to counter with, "Can't take it anymore!" When Alex shouted, "People with records are under attack!" we shouted back, "What do we do? Stand up fight back!" The excitement was infectious. Pedestrians and people in passing cars smiled, cheered, pumped fists, and took photos. Confronted by public expressions of encouragement, FORCE members smiled irresistibly and continued clapping and chanting. Later, many members would fondly reflect on the experience as one in which they learned that they did "have power."

CRS leaders required "prep sessions" for any member giving a public testimony. During prep sessions, CRS leaders helped members practice describing their personal experiences, how their experiences were due to existing laws, and how legislative reform would personally benefit themselves and their families. Prep sessions were held the day before a worship assembly, a coalition meeting, or a visit with an elected official. An organizer might convene with members over breakfast for small meetings, or at a member church for large events. Organizers strictly regulated the talk at these public meetings, reminding members, "If you don't prep, you don't talk." Prep sessions provided rehearsal of

several standard agenda items, such as introductions, statements of issues, testimonies, and legislative asks—though longer meetings offered
the opportunity for more comprehensive preparation, such as role-play
demonstrations, exercises, and debriefs. The largest focus was on delivering one's testimony and "making the ask."

FORCE leaders held a prep session, during a monthly meeting, for a
lobby day visit as part of the "absolute bars" campaign (to weaken legislation banning formerly incarcerated persons from employment in some
industries). Alex asked for volunteers to demonstrate a "role play" so
that we could all witness it, and four members volunteered. Lisa's role
was to play an elected official, Chip (a FORCE advocate) was to represent FORCE and "do the introductions," Marlon was to talk about the
legislative bill (HB 3061), and Quintin was to share his testimony and
"make the ask." After Quintin gave his testimony, Lisa stammered end-
lessly and wouldn't give a yes-or-no response. Lisa, playing the part of
an elected official who wouldn't support the bill, claimed that she was
undecided because she didn't "have all the [policy] details."

Leaders always debriefed from role-play exercises, evaluating "the good
and the bad," and expected a high level of participation—calling on those
who didn't speak. After the above-mentioned role-play exercise, Alex
debriefed and explained that the ambivalence Lisa performed through
her character—claiming to not know all the policy details—was to be expected: it allowed elected officials to avoid supporting a bill, while avoid-
ing encountering any resistance. In contrast, Alex encouraged FORCE
members to pressure elected officials by making the ask; he claimed that
the best way to do this was to create a transition to make the ask.

At times, FORCE leaders drew from street tropes to debrief from
demonstrations. Marlon encouraged members to participate by reminding them that they had "skills on the street" that would transfer
well—such as how to "talk really fast." This was reminiscent of Eddie's
advice at the one-day training, in which he told members they were now
"hustling" in a "positive and productive way." Similarly, during the lobby
day role-play debrief, Camron used street tropes to communicate Alex's
point about "making the ask" and creating a transition to the ask. Camron explained to the members in the room that although Lisa's character wouldn't give a yes-or-no response, they needed to "take it back . . .
because that's what we would've done in the streets." Camron encour-

aged FORCE members—despite their social status being lower than an elected official's—to use community organizing practices to reverse power relations in public. Camron framed "the ask" through Alinsky-style notions of zero-sum power (e.g., "taking power back"), and encouraged them to draw from aggressive vocal dispositions learned on the street.

Alex validated FORCE leaders' encouragement by telling FORCE members that if an elected official told them they didn't know the policy details of a bill, they should not hesitate to take control of conversations or make the ask; Alex explained them that due to their lived experiences, "you ARE the expert." Leaders often reminded everyone that by telling their stories, they were breaking stereotypes, such as by showing others that they could be "productive citizens," and presenting legislative reform as desirable. These lessons were often repeated before meetings with legislators or trips to the state capitol. Once, during a lobby day visit to the state capitol, a member quoted the book of Luke, reminding us that "the first person Jesus saved was an ex-con." On another occasion, Marlon gave the example of having had a meeting with state representative Fred Crespo, who was once been the victim of a home invasion; Marlon, through the presentation of himself and his testimony, had convinced him that not all formerly incarcerated people were the same and won Crespo's support for the Sealing Bill.

At the monthly meeting prep session for the lobby day visit for absolute bars legislation, we broke up into three groups and rotated turns at three different stations. Each station featured a FORCE member playing the part of an elected official. The purpose of the exercise was to get us accustomed to the different types of ways it would be necessary to speak to state representatives from different ideological backgrounds. Alex instructed us with our objectives for each simulated meeting. At one station, Marlon played a Democrat who was a supporter; our objective was to thank him for his support and to remind him of the constituent power in our group. At another station, Lisa played a "downstate Democrat," who wasn't initially receptive to us but might listen if we appealed to her values; our objective was to use conservative language (e.g., "I don't believe the government should determine who we should hire") to appeal to the legislator's values. Last, Alex played the part of a "Republican from DuPage County," who would not support us or even listen to us.

The role-play seemed to be an exercise in learning to use prepared, declarative statements—though it took me the duration of the exercise to realize this. As it wore on, I noticed the exercise contrasted with the long bouts of time I enjoyed, alone, conducting research with a very narrow focus. There was very little time to prep for these simulated meetings. I had to divide tasks among two other group members. It seemed overwhelming to prepare for three very different scenarios within a few minutes. However, I found that I was underprepared—just like many others in my group. While I found myself hesitating to speak, trying to find the most appropriate responses to the mock legislator's comments, others in my group made the mistake of trying to argue back and forth with Alex. We all failed to use a simple script and to stick to it.

As we ended the exercise and regrouped to debrief, Alex made it clear that many of us made the same mistake—explaining too much—and told us to stick to the same responses no matter what we were asked. Members asked about specific questions they struggled with in the role-play sessions, but Alex simply warned us "nothing good could ever come from" loaded questions. Marlon noted the time and commented that "out of respect for people's time" we needed to "move along schedule." Marlon's tabling of the discussion suggested that not only nonscripted responses but also discussions about them were discouraged. The careful policing of the language FORCE members used in public ensured that the visit to Springfield fostered collective, not individualistic, behavior.

Conclusion

CRS's theological orientation—rooted in the historically Black Protestant church—fostered prophetic redemption through insurgent displays. CRS organizers taught FORCE members Alinsky-style, issue-based community organizing principles and practices during trainings, meetings, and event debriefs. CRS organizers taught members the meanings of terms such as "problems," "issues," "self-interest," and "targets," and provided spaces to workshop practices such as "elevator speeches," "one-on-one meetings," and "house meetings."

FORCE leaders, in turn, translated lessons from the issue-based model of community organizing in ways that resonated with FORCE members' experiences on the street and in recovery. Alinsky-style concepts were often at odds with FORCE members' lived experiences, such as recovery's emphasis on "humility" rather than empowerment. FORCE leaders—such as Eddie or Marlon, who were formerly incarcerated—in turn agitated members by giving "push back" and highlighting how passivity could undermine efforts at empowerment. Eddie used his personal testimony to communicate the importance of formerly incarcerated persons' "self-interest" combating "records discrimination." Eddie further communicated the meaning of community organizing principles and practices, such as "self-interest," "elevator speeches," or "one-on-ones," through street vernacular or performances of reform.

FORCE members not only participated in an issue-based model of faith-based community organizing, but also drew from recovery to reconstruct principles and practices. Just as sociologist Francesca Polletta (1998) had found that civil rights activists' narratives of participation articulated personal and political reform, so too did FORCE members articulate personal and political reform. FORCE members drew from recovery's "ritualized verbal displays" (Flores and Hondagneu-Sotelo 2013) at FORCE monthly meetings—through introductions, relational questions, and evaluations—and emphasized personal reform as a way of deepening participation in collective action. They framed CRS and FORCE activities as a form of volunteering and "giving back," and as a way of making good from their pasts.

CRS's shaped how FORCE members experienced political and personal reform. CRS drew from highly polarizing practices—from ecstatic worship at assemblies to Alinsky-style practices—to socialize FORCE members into insurgent displays of faith-based community organizing. CRS organizers encouraged FORCE members to draw from recovery displays to displace elected officials and to assert themselves as "the expert." In addition, CRS created the platforms—from worship assemblies to coalition meetings to lobby days—for redemption scripts to foster social movement activity. Similar to sociologist Nancy Whittier's (2009) research, which suggested that grassroots activists can draw from therapeutic discourse to reshape state-citizen relationships, CRS and FORCE members drew from recovery to reshape state-citizen relationships. CRS and FORCE drew from insurgent religious displays to expand the rights of the formerly incarcerated, and to facilitate their integration into the civic and political arena.

5

"Imagine a Circle with No One Outside of It"

The Homeboys Local Organizing Committee

In August 2014, as a campaign for California Proposition 47 was under way, the Homeboys LOC held a biweekly meeting at Homeboy Industries' modern-style, $8.5 million building. Only six of us were in the room (a second-floor group therapy room), including a Homeboy Industries staff member and myself. As the meeting was about to begin, Rev. Zach Hoover, executive director of LA Voice, waited patiently with two guests: an LA Voice–affiliated pastor, Joseph, and a member of the mayor's downtown advisory council, Simon.

Hoover paid the visit in the effort to provide guidance for the LOC. LA Voice was one of many California-based PICO chapters that had become involved with the California Proposition 47 campaign, which sought to downgrade many classifications of nonviolent, nonserious offenses, involving less than $950, from felonies to misdemeanors. Hoover was undertaking efforts to foster LA Voice partners' participation in the Prop 47 campaign, because of what the campaign represented—but also because the campaign was an opportunity to deepen civic engagement among groups with historically minimal civic participation.

Peter, who in recent weeks had taken Jose's place as the Homeboys LOC leader, started the meeting by distributing an agenda. The agenda had LA Voice and Homeboy Industries' logos, with the Homeboys LOC's mission statement ("empowerment is transformational") and a list of typical agenda items: an introduction, opening prayer, discussion items, evaluation, and closing prayer. Peter asked for someone to pray, but initially no one volunteered. Finally, Pastor Joseph spoke, opening with a prayer "from the Christian tradition"; speaking clearly and softly, he asked that God work through us, and that no "unjust laws" get in the way of our work. After the prayer, Peter started the meeting by asking us to briefly give our names and affiliations, before proceeding to discuss business items. Peter, running an LOC meeting for one of the first times, tried to do this in a very matter-of-fact way. However, he initially stumbled between agenda items.

Hoover helped guide the meeting, offering details about the Prop 47 campaign. When Peter mentioned that there would be a Prop 47 training in the coming weeks, Hoover emphasized the importance of bringing "the whole team to the same training." There seemed to be some confusion at first, and Hoover helped to clarify. Peter asked each of us if we would be available Saturday or Sunday, but Hoover suggested that it would be best to ask which of those two days would work best for collectively attending. Peter asked again, the second time asking if we were available either or both days, and found that Saturday worked best for us.

The Homeboys LOC's strategy for participation in the Prop 47 campaign contrasted with many LA Voice partners, and this became a source of tension during the meeting. The Homeboys LOC had planned to gather five hundred votes for Prop 47, though they weren't planning on following LA Voice's guide. At one point Pastor Joseph asked a very pointed question. Looking confused, Joseph asked, "How are you doing it without canvassing? We are all trying to get that many with canvassing." Peter responded defensively, claiming that the LOC wasn't planning on canvassing due to concerns over members' safety; many were former gang members, and canvassing neighborhoods might place them at risk of retaliation from rival gang members. After some discussion, Hoover tried to offer an alternative. He suggested that the LOC could indeed canvass, but just not place Homeboys on the street. Homeboys took care of necessary supporting tasks, such as food, water, and planning, while members of other LA Voice–affiliated organizations went door-to-door.

Homeboys LOC members seemed intent on relying upon their own, unconventional strategy. When Hoover asked again how the Homeboys LOC could gather five hundred votes, Peter suggested that the LOC would combine Homeboy Industries' public outreach efforts with civic engagement. Peter said that they were planning to inform people of Prop 47 during Homeboy Industries' visitor tours. In addition, Peter suggested combining Homeboy Industries' social services and employment model with civic engagement; new trainees could be registered to vote during their "intake." This strategy was not in line with conventional community organizing practices, such as providing a detailed plan for contributing to the National Voter Database.

Hoover responded to the Homeboys LOC members' lack of responsiveness by providing what appeared to be an impromptu—but well-organized—workshop that drew from the principles of relationship-based community organizing. Hoover asked us first to turn the agenda over, and draw how we imagined the emotional energy of a campaign trajectory. After explaining that a campaign increases in activity as an election date nears, Hoover told us that successful campaigns spend time developing relationships in preparation for the increase in activity. Hoover also told us that face-to-face communication was far more effective than any other form of communication. He explained that the research on voting suggested that only two methods work to turn people out to vote: face-to-face conversations and phone calls. Hoover's impromptu workshop and lesson communicated to us that our greatest resource was interpersonal relationships—not social media or case management.

Hoover returned to his original question, asking us how we could increase voter turnout without canvassing. Homeboys LOC members described Homeboy tours, case management, and social media. One Homeboy Industries staff member said, with conviction, that "testimonies are powerful" and that putting a different person's testimony online every week could help people "put a face to the [legislative] bill."

Hoover replied to the LOC members' rebuttals by, again, emphasizing the importance of relationships in community organizing. He walked toward me and told the group, softly and calmly, "we know that two methods work." Leaning in to stare at me and get my full attention, Hoover said, unflinchingly, "Face-to-face conversations, and phone calls." Taking a step back and looking around the room he said, "Of the two, face-to-face conversations work the best." Hoover then asked us to identify Homeboy Industries' greatest asset. He asked, "Given that face-to-face conversations are the most effective way of getting votes, how are we gonna do it?" Peter nervously confessed, "See, that's what I wasn't sure about."

Hoover walked back to the butcher block paper and the magic marker, and again delivered an organizing lesson that communicated the importance of relationships in organizing. Hoover asked us to list out "what we have," "what we need," and "what we want." He then told us that "organizing is using what we have, and figuring out what we need, to get what we want." Hoover told us that we want to win the Prop 47 campaign, and that the Homeboys LOC is trying to get five hundred votes. Hoover implored us to think deeply about what we have. We suggested that he write under "what you have" the following words: "staff," "supporters," "trainees," "families," "1,000 in-person visitors a month," "200,000 social media visitors," "a donor list of 10,000 persons," "businesses," "an executive board," and "150 volunteers." Hoover finished by pointing to the board and telling us softly, "Here's what I see as your greatest resources: 'families,' 'trainees,' 'staff,' and 'house meetings.'" Yet, at the following LOC meeting, members again commented that the Homeboys LOC had its own model.

Hoover drew from relationship-based community organizing methods to encourage the Homeboys LOC to go from supporting Prop 47 to canvassing for it—but Homeboys LOC members reacted against such efforts. Homeboys LOC members resisted adopting relationship-based community organizing tactics, as well as straying from Homeboy Industries' single-issue focus on the at-risk and formerly incarcerated; Homeboys LOC members preferred to advocate for social services and employment rather than learn how to canvass neighborhoods, or how to enter data in the National Voter Registration database.

Homeboys LOC members engaged in pastoral displays of prophetic redemption: advocating for the expansion of the rights of the formerly incarcerated, by emphasizing development of relationships. Homeboys LOC leaders drew from LA Voice's organizing model, adopting the language of "voice" and "diversity" to help members construct the meaning of community organizing. Leaders translated the principles of relationship-based community organizing in ways that resonated with members' lived experiences on the street and in recovery. At the same time, the Homeboys LOC—deeply rooted in Homeboy Industries' identity, as the largest gang prevention program of its kind—was averse to public displays of insurgency; the LOC questioned and resisted LA Voice's relationship-based community organizing model, and, in fact, drew from the logic of LA Voice's organizing model, emphasizing diversity, to argue that the LOC should have "a different model." Leaders created platforms for members to give their personal testimonies advocating for the expansion of the rights of the formerly incarcerated, but instead of calling out elected officials, celebrated Homeboy Industries. In doing so, they constructed the civic sphere as a site for performing reform and experiencing redemption. Homeboys LOC members participated in collective and political action in ways that resonated with members' need for personal reform, and helped Homeboy Industries to protect its role in providing employment and social services.

"Your Voice Counts": PICO-Style Relationship-Based Community Organizing

Homeboy Industries and LA Voice played formative roles in shaping the Homeboys LOC—which represented Homeboy Industries' first attempt to engage its members in community organizing. Homeboy Industries, which had a long history in Los Angeles—dating back to Father Greg's work at Dolores Mission in the late 1980s—provided employment, social services, and legal services, but lacked a formally institutionalized civic engagement component. Prior to 2013, Father Greg had asked a Homeboy, associate director Hector Verdugo, to represent Homeboy Industries at LA Voice. Homeboy Industries at the time did not extend civic participation to more members. However, in 2013, Father Greg asked Jose Osuna to play a role different from Verdugo's—to "take the lead" in the group's "relationship" with LA Voice. Hoover promptly took Jose under his wing and began to teach him about community organizing, completing a PICO national leadership training and taking part in meetings with policy makers, such as Los Angeles mayoral candidate Eric Garcetti. Jose felt that his involvement with LA Voice could provide an opportunity for Homeboy Industries to become involved with community organizing, and after a mayoral forum he proposed the idea to Homeboy Industries and began to recruit for the Homeboys LOC.

Homeboy Industries' creation of an LOC was not smooth. In my interview with him, Jose recalled having to remind Father Greg that Homeboy Industries came about as a result of community organizing; Father Greg had gone to a community organizer training, led by PICO founder Father John Bauman, about the time PICO had formed in the early 1970s. Jose said he would remind Father Greg that the most effective way to influence policy makers was to say, "We control this many votes . . . you need to be on the same page with us, or we will vote you out." Jose said that because Father Greg had been trained as an organizer so long ago and because he was busy running Homeboy Industries as its executive director and co-CEO, Jose had to remind him to defend community organizing—to tell Homeboy Industries executives that their organization "came about" through community organizing. Jose described the executive body as comprising eight members, only one of whom was formerly incarcerated, the rest having "not lived the lifestyle at all." Jose sparred with the executives, telling me, "There were conflicts." However, once he started organizing, Jose felt "empowered." Jose said, "If I'm gonna organize the community outside of Homeboy Industries, then I'm gonna organize internally as well, and they're gonna hear me." Jose's internal organizing consisted of listening to other staff members who shared his concerns, such as not having adequate Homeboy representation on the executive committee, and deciding to speak out once he was sure he had the support of other Homeboys. Jose said his goal was to one day become an executive.

It was always clear that Jose was the leader of the Homeboys LOC—except for the brief period when he stepped down to allow Peter to take over (which he signaled was at Hoover's suggestion).[1] Jose had a very commanding presence. He was in his late forties, tall and broad-framed, and sported a shaved head with a thick black beard. A former "shot-caller" in a prison yard, Jose once told us there was a time in his life when he believed the only time he would ever hear from the governor of California would be for a pardon. Although he was a former gang member who used to abuse drugs and rob drug dealers, Jose had experienced recovery. He was astute and well-spoken and arrived prepared for meetings. Some Homeboys LOC members mentioned, in my semistructured interviews with them, that they admired Jose; one subject, who had sporadic problems with drinking, admired Jose for his commitment to alcohol recovery. Soon after becoming the Homeboys LOC leader, Jose was promoted to a prestigious position within Homeboy Industries: director of employment services.

Jose helped members construct the meaning of community organizing by drawing from LA Voice and Homeboy Industries' inclusive institutional missions, such as LA Voice's emphasis on diversity and voice or

Homeboy Industries' emphasis on reentry. Jose told members they could use their voice to shape a growing awareness of the importance of reentry, and that the LOC, through LA Voice, provided access to the settings that would be crucial for their voice to shape public opinion: coalition meetings with LA Voice partners, PICO organizer trainings, meetings with elected officials, testimonies during the public comment portion of hearings at City Hall, and public rallies.

Jose used the term "voice" to communicate the collective notions of power. He emphasized that large, public settings magnified one's voice. In preparation for their first action, a march to City Hall and a rally in favor of the proposed Fair Chance Ordinance, Jose told members that the purpose of the action was to "show our voice" and that our "voice counts." Jose told us this march would be "historic" because we would be advocating to implement the most comprehensive Fair Chance Ordinance in the nation. The Homeboys readily adapted the language Jose used. They incorporated terms like "voice" and "being heard" into their vernacular and spoke in awe of public action. At debriefs following organizing activities when leaders asked members what they learned, members often stated that they learned they "had a voice."

An important component of voice was multiculturalism. Homeboys contrasted their experiences in diverse public settings—with congregants from Westside Jewish synagogues to Catholic Latinos and Methodist churches—with their lived experiences in low-income East or South LA neighborhoods and in prison. They were "in awe" of whites, Blacks, and Latinas/os as well as people of different faiths—Catholic, Muslim, Jewish, and Protestant—coming together, fostering a sense of belonging that they had desired but often failed to experience as formerly incarcerated persons. The most frequent comment when members reflected on participation in LA Voice events was the "diversity." Members expressed "beauty" in "people coming together," "breaking bread," and "breaking down preconceived notions." They spoke proudly of not being intimidated to speak with someone of a different faith or race. They expressed joy in seeing so many people who were "interested" in and "cared" about mass incarceration and who wanted to be "involved with the movement" to dismantle the scourge. In turn, they experienced belonging. As they spoke to people who did not share their background about their experiences with incarceration and records discrimination, Homeboys LOC members felt that their "voice" was heard. Homeboys LOC members felt personally empowered in ways that had political implications: by sharing their stories, they could shift public opinion to attitudes more favorable toward expanding their rights as formerly incarcerated persons.

Homeboys LOC meetings created diversity and inclusion in somewhat similar ways as LA Voice. The number of Homeboys at biweekly meetings was usually small, between five and ten when no actions were planned, or ten to fifteen at biweekly meetings preceding major actions. In addition to this number, however, were Homeboy Industries staff members, interns, and volunteers who participated in the LOC. This consisted of a rotating assortment of non–gang members, such as Homeboy Industries' chief financial officer, the senior staff attorney, undergraduate students from Loyola Marymount University or Jesuit-themed programs, seminary students, and myself. Although the number of persons with non-gang backgrounds was almost as high as the number with, the LOC explicitly formed with the intent of providing leadership opportunities to the formerly incarcerated. The diversity of the Homeboys LOC and the concern that non–formerly incarcerated persons expressed about mass incarceration paralleled the displays of diversity and celebration of multiculturalism that were visible in LA Voice.

Jose used the LOC to help members construct ideas of voice, diversity, and power. In line with typical community organizing practices, LOC biweekly meetings gave time for debriefs of members' participation in organizing activities, such as organizer trainings, coalition meetings, and political actions. Members spoke about the political nature of these activities, such as the profitability of prison construction and the need to do research to target those groups profiting from prison building. At the same time, they also spoke about the personally empowering experience of being in spaces where people critiqued the prison pipeline and racism, sharing their own experiences and even crying. Jose asked pointed questions of members who debriefed, and a common refrain was the importance of "power in relationships."

Newer members often had trouble putting their experiences with civic action into words. At one debrief, following Homeboys' visit to an LA Voice–affiliated synagogue to lobby for the Fair Chance Ordinance, Jose asked two Homeboys, Alfonso and Oscar, to tell members about their experience at the synagogue. The Homeboys were nearly speechless. Oscar, who had tattoos on his head and had been incarcerated for fifteen years, seemed very nervous about speaking publicly. He used short, declarative sentences to tell us about his visit—making sure to draw deep breaths as he spoke.

Jose asked Oscar to tell us about the size of the congregation: "How many people were there?" Jose had earlier emphasized the size of the synagogue ("the third largest west of the Mississippi") and its geographic location (LA's affluent Westside), but Oscar failed to communicate very much—simply noting there were "a lot" of people. Jose implored Oscar to tell us the size of the congregation: "But, like, *how* many?" Oscar looked around our room, and with wide eyes, not only described the congregation as "a lot" but also said "the energy was *deep*." Taking a moment to reflect, Oscar said he was there to "speak power," but said he was nervous. When Jose then asked Alfonso, a very tall, broad-shouldered Homeboy in his thirties, to also share his experience, Alfonso simply told us that he got a bit overwhelmed.

Jose aided members in constructing meaning from experiences with civic action by drawing from the discourse of relationship-based community organizing. Following the Westside synagogue visit, Jose offered an informal lesson that stressed the importance of "voice" and "diversity" in "power" and drew from the organizing principle of power as collective. Jose said, "In the LOC, we're always talking about power," and proceeded to describe the visit as "powerful" because there were many people there. Jose told us that he believed Oscar and Alfonso's testimonies helped many of those in the congregation with dissimilar backgrounds understand the discrimination that formerly incarcerated people experienced, and that this would help to gain support for the Fair Chance Ordinance.

Partnerships and Hierarchies in Relationship-Based Community Organizing

Many of the Homeboys LOC's activities extended faith-based community organizing to issues concerning the formerly incarcerated. Members publicly decried mass incarceration and records discrimination. At the Ban-the-Box march to LA City Hall, members held signs proclaiming "Ban the Box," "Jobs Not Jails," and "Schools Not Prisons," and chanted the former two as slogans. During the Prop 47 campaign, Jose told Homeboys LOC members that community organizing was important because it could help them mobilize voters and shape public policy issues affecting them. Jose expressed hope at building a "powerful" voting bloc of five hundred persons that could affect the outcome of local races in a low-turnout election. Jose told the Homeboys they needed to "take it to policy makers" so that they would not just listen "to Father Greg, but collaborate with us."

At the same time, LOC leaders constructed community organizing as pastoral. The Homeboys LOC's first slogan, printed prominently on their biweekly meeting agenda, was a classic PICO organizing principle: "Empowerment is Developmental."[2] Similar to how mainstream criminology has long emphasized developmental psychology in theories of crime and desistance, the Homeboys slogan suggested that civic participation fostered recovery due to its personally empowering effects. The LOC's "purpose" reflected a concern with the pastoral as well. The LOC proclaimed its purpose was to "continue to lift up the importance of relationship-building for those within our LOC and others with the community that share our values and interests." The Homeboys LOC sought to utilize relationship-based community organizing for Homeboy Industries' broader mission to rehabilitate the formerly incarcerated. Later iterations of the LOC's principle and purpose reflected these concerns with the pastoral. The principle later changed to "the first revolution is internal," and the purpose changed as well: "To empower LOC members by offering them opportunities to step into leadership roles."[3] These changes again suggested that political reform arose from personal reform and that the LOC was to foster personal reform by expanding the boundaries of democratic inclusion.

Homeboys LOC leaders drew from gang and street metaphors to communicate meanings of partnership rooted in relationship-based community organizing. In describing LOC activities, Jose drew from street discourse to disavow publicly shaming elected officials who stood against issues important to the LOC. Jose told us, "I'm gonna say it in street terms. You know there's been times you would have murked some fool, but he might have been the guy you needed a connection through, so you didn't." Jose warned against insurgent displays that risked straining relationships with organizations or persons who funded them.

Homeboys LOC leaders were deliberate and strategic in utilizing community organizing activities and partnerships to advance Homeboy Industries' fund-raising activities and social service provision. In discussions surrounding the LOC's participation in Prop 47 voter canvassing, a member asked if we could create a partnership with Rock the Vote; Homeboy Industries' chief financial officer expressed delight, mentioning the words "Donors!" and "Money!" She only half-jokingly apologized, telling us with a grin, "I'm sorry, I always have to think development." At another meeting, Homeboy Industries' staff attorney cautioned against the LOC's planned involvement at a legal clinic—citing the long waiting list for jobs at Homeboy Industries—until a member entertained the idea of setting up a table to promote services. LOC leaders emphasized how community organizing built upon Homeboy Industries' mission of providing social services to at-risk youth and formerly incarcerated persons, and how civic engagement could advance Homeboy Industries' pastoral mission.

Homeboys LOC leaders also drew from gang metaphors to construct ideas of hierarchies within community organizing. At a lunch meeting at City Hall, Jose emphasized the importance of relationships in community organizing. He told the LOC members that Father John Bauman was a friend of Father Greg's and had contacted Father Greg urging him to get Homeboy Industries involved with LA Voice. Jose then drew from a street gang metaphor to communicate how community organizing groups and individuals existed in relation to each other. He described Homeboys as a "cliqa"—a term for a gang subunit—of LA Voice. Using wide hand gestures in an umbrella shape, Jose said Homeboy Industries was under LA Voice. Making even larger hand gestures, he then explained that LA Voice was under PICO California. Then, with the widest hand gestures, he explained that PICO California was under the PICO National Network. Jose finished his lesson, to the amusement of the LOC members, by describing PICO as the "big homies" and Homeboy Industries as the "little homies." The members laughed generously, repeating that "they're the big homies" and "we're the little homies."

The Homeboys LOC's single-issue mission at times created distance between itself and LA Voice. While Hoover claimed that the work behind Prop 47 was less about the campaign and more about mobilizing voters, Jose suggested that the Homeboys LOC was to engage in organizing only on issues related to criminal justice or immigration. In turn, LA Voice's relationship-based community organizing approach and the Homeboys LOC's single-issue focus strained their relationship. At one point Jose perceived that Hoover—in the tradition of using community organizing to build up new leaders—had expressed his support for a new LOC leader. In turn, Jose stepped down and Peter took over. Jose gave no indication he was pleased to step down. As I chatted with him outside an LA Voice leadership assembly at Homeboy Industries, Jose expressed that he felt his abilities as a leader had been questioned—both at Homeboy Industries as director of employment services, and at LA Voice as the leader of the LOC.

The LOC had indigenous leadership, being led by formerly incarcerated persons, whereas Homeboy Industries and LA Voice were led by professional, formally educated staff. This was an important distinction between the LOC and the other organizations. At the above-mentioned leadership assembly, Jose expressed to me his frustrations with Hoover, who he felt was from a more privileged background and didn't understand Homeboys and Homegirls as well as he did. Jose said he knew how to be passionate and "light a fire," claiming "I understand our population. I move people." He felt his background as a formerly incarcerated person qualified him to continue being the LOC leader. This frustration was not specific to LA Voice, but included Homeboy Industries as well. To my surprise Jose cited a page from my book, God's Gangs, in which I described how Homeboy Industries had almost no former gang members at the top of their organizational hierarchy. Jose retorted, "I think it's a problem."

The Homeboys LOC's internal hierarchy looked much different from the horizontal leadership structure that LA Voice attempted to have with its member organizations. At a training for the Prop 47 campaign, an LA Voice lead organizer presented the group's organizational structure through a diagram with interlocking circles, each representing "teams" within each LA Voice member organization; this was in contrast to another diagram that an LA Voice leader drew—a pyramid—but quickly erased after being heckled. The pyramid would have been characteristic of the Homeboys LOC, which had a clear hierarchy with Jose at the top.

The Homeboys LOC's internal hierarchy—and its distance from LA Voice—allowed leaders to exercise a high degree of discretion over how members engaged with LA Voice. Facilitators gave a detailed report after events in a way that allowed meetings to become centered on previous events. Less discussion was given to transparency, in terms of the direction of organizing strategy or future LA Voice–related actions. I personally experienced this twice, in trying to communicate with Zulema (an LA Voice organizer assigned to the Homeboys LOC toward the end of my fieldwork). In one case I offered to forward names of Homeboys to Zulema for her listening campaign at the LOC; she asked me to forward them not to her but to Jose. In another case, when we debriefed following a visit to the LA County Jail, evaluating "what went well" and "what could have been better," I commented that I would have liked to learn about the event earlier; Zulema commented that she didn't extend the invitation because she wasn't sure it would involve the LOC. Then, when I asked if I could email her directly, she replied that Jose was supposed to talk to us and that I was not to email her directly—because she was "the organizer."

The LOC created a space for members to take leadership in addressing issues pertaining to themselves, such as the decriminalization of low-level drug crimes, the use of criminal background checks in employment applications, or the minimum wage increases affecting Homeboy Industries employees' salaries. However, the sheer complexity of campaigns or proposed policy sometimes undermined the leaders' obstinate will to lead. This was true of the Prop 47 canvassing, as Harvard-educated Hoover understood voting behavior research better than the Homeboys—but faced resistance in shaping strategy. This was also true of the Fair Chance Ordinance campaign, in which Jose and Miles (a pseudonym for an LA Voice organizer, who was also a formerly incarcerated person) interacted in ways that suggested they preferred that professional advocates defer to the formerly incarcerated persons as experts on policies related to themselves.

Public actions involving partnering organizations presented situations in which representatives from regionally or nationally prominent organizations threatened to displace the formerly incarcerated as leading advocates. At the hearing for the Fair Chance Ordinance, Jose and Miles expressed concern with Lauren (a pseudonym for a senior staff member with the National Employment Law Project). Just before the hearing, Jose and Miles warmly greeted each other with a big handshake and quickly exchanged their concerns about the persons lining up to speak during the hearing's public comment section. Lauren was not the only member of a prominent partnering organization to have traveled to Los Angeles for the hearing; representatives from PICO and from Californians for Safety and Justice also attended. However, Miles felt particularly threatened by Lauren since the National Employment Law Project had published a "best practices" guide and she would be speaking on it. Miles told Jose that he "waived her off" (which I interpreted as having her removed from the list of public comment speakers). As Miles told his story, Jose agreed with him. Miles said he told Lauren, "Public comment is ours, don't take that away." Jose added that he had asked a City Council member to "double refer" the ordinance to avoid more discussion. Jose and Miles both feared that Lauren's affiliation with a prominent organization and use of public comment might displace the formerly incarcerated as experts and leaders in the campaign.

"A Different Model": Rejecting Community Organizing's Insurgent Displays

As described earlier, the Homeboys LOC's civic activities were guided by a cautious approach that sought to protect Homeboy Industries' public image and its relationships with institutions or persons that funded them. When discussing elected officials, Jose made it very clear to members that elected officials were "partners"—rather than "targets," the common term in community organizing—and that Homeboy Industries sought to preserve relationships with them. This concern led Homeboy leaders to shun insurgent displays that risked straining relationships with funders. One example of this was the LOC's participation in the LA Voice action at the LA County Jail (see chapter 2). LA Voice leaders did not participate in polarizing displays or articulate language that made elected officials "targets," but instead celebrated racial and religious diversity, social justice, and the pope's visit to the United States. Instead of shaming elected officials, the vigil ended with a foot washing—a Catholic ritual symbolizing paying forward good deeds. Similarly, Jose encouraged members to experience personal empowerment by building support with diverse partners and by making their voice heard in public. At a meeting, Jose emphasized the importance of maintaining a

Figure 5.1. Jose Osuna shaking hands with Los Angeles Councilman Gil Cedillo. Credit: Pocho One Fotography.

good relationship with the County Sheriff: "As an organization, there is sometimes support not to pursue something."

The Homeboys LOC's aversion to insurgent displays was anchored by a strong organizational identity in Homeboy Industries. Homeboy Industries, self-described as the "largest program of its kind," relied upon several public and private funding streams for its massive operations. At the core of these relationships was Father Greg's status as Los Angeles' most iconic advocate for gang outreach (e.g., Fremon [1995] 2004). LA Voice also celebrated the Homeboys LOC's strong identity in Father Greg; at an LA Voice training, Hoover borrowed Father Greg's famous quote, asking us to "imagine a circle with no one outside of it."

The campaign for California Assembly Bill 953 (the Racial Profiling Act of 2015) is one example of how PICO sought to address an issue relevant to Homeboy Industries' members but that the LOC decided to avoid lobbying for out of consideration for political partners, such as the County Sheriff. Signed into law in October 2015, AB 953 required California law enforcement agencies to collect basic information on police stops, so that such traffic data could be analyzed for racial inequalities.

A few weeks prior, Zulema had told us about an action that involved traveling by bus to the state capitol for an AB 953 lobby day; she encouraged members of Homeboys to attend and told us organizers would keep Homeboys out of any risk of trouble. However, Zulema presented the possibility of attending the action as our meeting came to a close, and the lack of any further meeting before the action ensured that no Homeboys LOC members would attend.

The AB 953 lobby day (attended by various PICO affiliates and CBOs) was an insurgent display of prophetic activism. That morning roughly one thousand persons arrived at an LA Voice–affiliated church near the capitol. We sang civil rights hymns and heard passionate, firsthand testimonies from family members who had lost loved ones to police-involved homicides. We then marched down the streets and finished with a die-in at the state capitol; several of us lay on the cement to symbolize the number of police-related killings. Two hundred of us then went inside to speak with legislators, while about one hundred staged a confrontational protest in front of the governor's office. The protest involved two hours of obstructing the hallway, locking arms, singing civil rights songs, and chanting loudly. We demanded that the governor emerge from his office and support the bill, though a representative simply told us he was out of town and could not comment. Our intense protest eventually forced the police in front of the governor's office to retreat inside, as two dozen people locked arms in the hallway and risked arrest.

I gave a report on the AB 953 lobby day trip at the following LOC meeting, but was chastised when I suggested I thought LOC members should have gone. Some members expressed concern with Homeboy Industries' image in the media. Others suggested that inviting Homeboys would have placed them at risk of getting thrown back in prison if they got in trouble with the law. As I suggested that some participants had records and that most did not risk arrest, several Homeboys responded viscerally, warning that they would be targeted by the police. Eubaldo exclaimed, "You never know what could happen!" One of the two new LOC members, a Black male in his twenties named Andrew, held up a paper with police pictures of himself with tattoos: "You don't understand. *You* can get arrested, because you've never gone through *this*." As I reminded Jose that we had participated in a similar action on the front lawn of Los Angeles City Hall, Jose pointed out one crucial difference:

we had received the mayor's approval but not the governor's. After the meeting, Jose suggested that Homeboy Industries had developed a good relationship with the County Sheriff's office, but the office was against AB 953 and publicly supporting it risked straining that relationship.

Homeboys LOC leaders taught members notions of relationship-based community organizing—such as the idea that insurgency strained relationships and prevented social change. During the previously mentioned lunch at City Hall, after Jose explained how Homeboy Industries was "under" PICO, one Homeboy asked, "If they're the big homies, and we're the little homies, then who's our enemy?" When I pointed up, to the City Council members' offices, Jose expressed shock: "Ed, no!" He then turned to the Homeboy and, correcting me, explained that the officials upstairs were "our partners." Conflating insurgency with violence, Jose asked the Homeboy what the LA riots—or throwing a rock through a window—had "ever accomplished." The Homeboy responded, shrugging and smiling, "Nothing." Jose replied, "Right." Homeboys LOC lessons suggested that adversarial relationships lacked efficaciousness, and that cooperation with elected officials was the only route to social change.

To avoid any implication that Homeboy Industries was politically radical, during the final LOC meetings in the fall of 2015 Jose changed the group's name to "Homeboys Organizing Committee," before renaming it once more at a subsequent meeting to "Homeboys Civic Engagement Committee." Jose explained to us, "the word 'organizing' has connotations." These efforts were in line with Homeboy Industries' attempts to establish its LOC as a noncombative partner with public officials for criminal justice reform efforts. Jose feared that the word "organizing" was too insurgent and risked creating distance between Homeboy Industries and the public entities and private philanthropists who funded them.

The Homeboys LOC's pastoral, cooperative approach to civic engagement shed discursive practices that were useful for members holding each other as well as elected officials "accountable." As we saw previously, in my meeting with representative Greg Harris, FORCE members chastised me for not sticking to a structured agenda and allowing him to talk over me and "take the power." In contrast, LOC meetings placed less emphasis on debriefs and evaluations as time wore on, and when employed they did not emphasize collective dimensions of power (e.g., "power in numbers"). In one case, the Homeboys LOC utilized a discursive practice—a faith reflection before a meeting—to allow elected officials to escape accountability. At an LOC meeting following one of Jose's visits to the White House, Jose used the faith reflection segment to mention his visit—and to prevent any critical discussion of it. He had visited the White House to meet with President Obama's staff over an executive order to "ban the box" for federal contractors' employment applications and insisted that Obama was going to follow through with his promise. Jose finished his faith reflection by simply telling us he didn't want to discuss the details—he just wanted us to celebrate the president's support. The omission of discussion about the trip as well as the encouragement to fully support Obama exhibited relationship-based and pastoral rather than insurgent notions of community organizing.

Elected officials graciously reciprocated Homeboy Industries' efforts to maintain close relationships with them. In return for Homeboy Industries' public support, the City Council publicly supported Homeboy Industries' pastoral mission. At the City Hall hearing on the proposed Fair Chance Ordinance, the City Council demonstrated its strong support of Homeboy Industries. Before a crowded room of fifty persons, Councilman Curren Price—flanked by fellow council members Gil Cedillo and Marqueece Harris-Dawson—started the meeting by citing Homeboy Industries' mission statement. Price then talked about the Fair Chance Ordinance in light of "the [prisoner reentry] movement" being strong and received a chuckle from the audience when he quoted Father Greg as saying, "Nothing stops a bullet like job." Acknowledging Homeboy Industries and Father Greg more for their pastoral than prophetic activities, Price drew from popular tropes, such as the idea of "social reintegration" and the term "productive citizen," to argue for criminal justice reform that would allow the formerly incarcerated to "reenter society differently." Finally, Price cited research suggesting the stigma of a record reduces hires by 50 percent and claimed that employment helps the formerly incarcerated "become active members of society again." Rather than talk about unjust laws and the morality of state actors, Price painted a picture of the state, faith-based programs, and employment as tools for shaping the morality of the formerly incarcerated.

The Homeboys LOC, rooted in a strong organizational identity in Father Greg, rejected not just insurgent displays but also LA Voice's efforts to formally train Homeboys in relationship-based community organizing. When Zulema tried to pass around a flier with the PICO model of organizing and provide a workshop using the illustration, Jose kindly tabled the workshop for a future meeting (though the flier was never revisited). Later, Jose insisted that Homeboy Industries would have a "different model" of organizing, and added that Homeboys would be teaching LA Voice to "rethink the way that they are doing organizing." Members were partially reluctant to embrace the PICO model of organizing because they perceived their backgrounds—as formerly incarcerated persons—to require different needs in community organizing. Homeboys felt that they needed to remain focused on issues directly facing the formerly incarcerated and that any civic participation would have to clearly demonstrate their path to redemption.

Ironically, Homeboys LOC members withdrew from LA Voice–related campaigns by drawing from the logic of relationship-based community organizing. Following the Prop 47 campaign, members continued to assert that the Homeboys LOC had a "different model"; they drew from the concepts of diversity and voice to justify the Homeboys LOC's narrowing focus on issues relevant to their members. While LA Voice supported the passage of a historic fifteen-dollar minimum wage ordinance in Los Angeles, partnering with an influential coalition of local labor unions and community groups, Jose led Homeboy Industries in an organizing campaign to pass an exemption—for themselves and two other similar job-training nonprofits—from the ordinance.

Jose later described the exemption campaign as a "David versus Goliath" battle in which the progressive City Council was against him fourteen votes to one and "organized labor" was a "huge powerful enemy." Jose's use of language to describe his aversion to the labor-community coalition was striking. The SEIU, the labor union that formed the backbone of the coalition that campaigned for the ordinance, has been portrayed as among the most inclusive and activist organizing groups in the nation (e.g., Gilmore 2007a; Milkman 2006, 2010; Soja 2014). LOC members had never used such polarizing language to describe an organized body—let alone one as progressive as an SEIU labor-community coalition. Yet, the incompatibilities between LA Voice's prophetic mission and the Homeboys LOC's single-issue mission fostered conflict between the two organizations, and the conflict, in turn, distanced the Homeboys LOC from participation in more militant forms of local activism.

Homeboys LOC members' use of the logic of relationship-based community organizing (e.g., "multiculturalism") to reject its very principles (e.g., expanding the rights of the most marginalized) had unintended consequences that sometimes threatened to undermine the efficacy of collective action. As mentioned earlier, Homeboys had used the Fair Chance Ordinance hearing's public comment to advocate for Ban-the-Box, highlighting their personal experiences with the postincarceration experience, the efficacy of Homeboy Industries' social programming, and the need for better policies for the formerly incarcerated. Jose and Miles had displaced Lauren, a senior staff attorney for the National Employment Law Project who was there to speak about "best practices." This almost compromised the passage and implementation of the ordinance.

While Jose urged the City Council to "immediately" pass the Los Angeles Fair Chance Ordinance, Councilwoman Nury Martinez expressed her ambivalence about its efficacy. Martinez, who also sat on the City Council's wage theft committee, claimed that the $250 fine for violating the ordinance would not be severe enough to deter businesses from violating it. Fortunately, in a dramatic turn of events, Homeboy Industries' senior staff attorney—who was much less experienced with advocacy than Lauren—graciously sacrificed her own speaking slot to allow Lauren to speak after Martinez for the final public comment. Lauren encouraged Martinez to look at the National Employment Law Project's "best practices" online resource for better Ban-the-Box ordinance enforcement language. In response to Lauren's comments, Martinez expressed her support for the ordinance and convinced her colleagues on City Council to postpone a vote while the ordinance was revised for stronger enforcement language. As the hearing ended, several Homeboy Industries members nonetheless celebrated "their" victory with LA Voice's Miles; the LOC members shook hands, hugged, and loitered around the City Council members long enough to talk and take pictures with them. (Hoover, along with AOUON, worked to pass the Fair Chance Ordinance a year later, in November 2016, with much heavier fines—up to $2,500 for repeat violations.)

In their effort to stake a claim as leaders in a campaign, LA Voice and Homeboys LOC risked having passed an ordinance that would have proven less effective. In this respect, the relationship between LA Voice and the Homeboys LOC—and the Homeboys LOC members' desire to participate in and lead civic engagement—was no different from CRS's relationship with FORCE, or FORCE members' desire to be "leaders." However, unlike the relationship between CRS and FORCE, the tense relationship between LA Voice and Homeboy Industries created confrontations that—at times—provoked Homeboys to resist the guidance of partnering organizations or formally educated advocates in ways which threatened the efficacy of such collective and political action.

As the Homeboys LOC and LA Voice drifted apart in the fall of 2015, Jose started a more radical ten-week program outside the confines of both groups. The program was developed with a Harvard doctoral student and had been inspired by Homeboys LOC members' interest in Black Panther–style community organizing. As part of the program, Jose and four other members of Homeboy Industries participated in an all-male camping retreat with a local Muslim-based nonprofit organization, ISLA (also a member of LA Voice with support from Zulema). Homeboys LOC members sought to develop more empowering, activist forms of civic engagement that spoke directly to their lived experiences, but that at the same time would not pose a threat to Homeboy Industries' public image.

"Making Amends" and Taking Credit: Pastoral Displays in the Civic Sphere

The Homeboys LOC's emphasis on voice and orientation toward building cooperative relationships rather than displaying insurgency enabled members to construct meanings of public testimonies as "giving back." The testimonies drew heavily from redemption scripts, but little from the discourse of Alinsky-style community organizing; most Homeboys/girls' testimonies were centered on Homeboy Industries, and made a weak connection between their experiences and the importance of legislative reform. Homeboys regularly deployed these redemption scripts through meetings, trainings, one-on-ones, and public testimonies.

At the Fair Chance rally, Oscar, a Latino in his late twenties who had served nine years in prison, gave a testimony in describing his experiences with Homeboy Industries rather than the implications of the proposed ordinance. Oscar praised Homeboy Industries for changing his life. He had transgressed, hit bottom, and found himself with no support, before discovering Homeboy Industries and accessing the opportunities that he needed to change: employment and mental health services. Oscar claimed that formerly incarcerated people needed opportunities to change, to become—to paraphrase Homeboy Industries' mission statement—productive members of society.

The public spaces of community organizing served primarily as a platform for the performance of making good. In my one-on-ones with members and in my tape-recorded interviews with them, LOC members praised Homeboy Industries and spoke of giving back to the organization. They did this so much that their redemption scripts often buried the importance of political activity. In my one-on-one with Peter, he articulated his participation in the LOC and LA Voice through notions of making good. Peter saw his organizing activity as giving back to Homeboy Industries because it was the place where he changed; he was also grateful to Hector Verdugo, who was the first to have become involved with LA Voice and had helped Peter quit drugs and land a job. Precisely because the time commitment made LA Voice and Homeboys LOC participation feel like a "second job" without pay, Peter viewed them as a way to "make amends" and "give back" to Homeboy Industries. Peter did not broach the subject of political empowerment during our one-on-one.

LOC one-on-ones did not foreground structural problems as much as highlight Homeboy Industries' important role as a social service provider. In my one-on-one with Efrain, a late thirties Homeboy who supervised the typing lab, he talked at length about Homeboy Industries—but not legislative reform. Efrain—speaking softly to avoid disturbing those in the computer lab—discussed Homeboy Industries' provision of services, rather than grassroots social movements. He warned that social problems like gang violence would persist if we did not invest more funding in youth social programming or in employment support for formerly incarcerated persons. Efrain also said that there should be more organizations like Homeboy Industries. Jose spoke not about the importance of "power," but rather about public service announcements.

At times testimonies centered squarely on personal reform, and not the expansion of social and economic rights. In March 2015, Jose

Figure 5.2. Fair Chance hearing at Los Angeles City Hall, 2015. Credit: Pocho One Fotography.

engaged in a campaign to exempt Homeboy Industries from the Los Angeles minimum wage increase. As Homeboy Industries' director of employment services, he opposed the increase because he claimed it would force the organization to reduce staff. This went against local progressive coalitions' efforts. Nonetheless, Jose took members of Homeboys to lobby City Council members to speak about the need for an exemption for nonprofits. The Homeboys and Homegirls gave testimonies explaining that if the minimum wage went up they might lose their jobs and the social services they received at Homeboy Industries, such as free mental health treatment. One Homeboy shared with me after the visit that he didn't know the purpose of their lobbying until he was at City Hall and didn't agree with the exemption proposed; for this Homeboy, public testimonies focused on personal reform worked against the expanding of social and economic rights.

Homeboys LOC members were eager to celebrate accomplishments that cemented Homeboy Industries' status as an exemplary organization. At the Homeboys LOC meeting before the Fair Chance Ordinance rally, Jose emphasized the historic nature of the march to highlight the importance of what it would do for Homeboy Industries' institutional profile. In addition, following one of Jose's first meetings with Hoover over the Prop 47 campaign, Jose enthusiastically told us that we were the only organization in LA Voice to be classified as a "number one": we were complete, with a leader, team leaders, and teams.

The LOC's celebration of Homeboy Industries at times obscured the contributions of other LA Voice–affiliated groups. At a meeting for the Fair Chance Ordinance, Jose insisted that Homeboys take the lead in writing the ordinance, even though A New Way of Life was also involved. At another meeting, Jose gave credit to Father Greg for the Ban-the-Box campaign; he told us that Father Greg had been "doing this for over 30 years" and that "now it's time to take it out of this place [Homeboy Industries]." Jose even insisted, "We need to thank him . . . he paved the road for us back when reentry wasn't sexy." However, AOUON had been recognized for the national Ban-the-Box movement, and A New Way of Life had been involved with starting the fight for the Los Angeles Fair Chance Ordinance.

Homeboys LOC members often used public testimonies to honor Father Greg and Homeboy Industries for the role they had played in their personal reform. At the hearing for the Fair Chance Ordinance, after thirteen persons (many with representatives from other organizations, such as the International Brotherhood of Electrical Workers union) offered public comments, eight Homeboys and Homegirls spoke about their personal experiences with unemployment. They spoke about being rejected from work due to their criminal histories and celebrated Homeboy Industries for giving them an opportunity. Such comments didn't always strengthen their argument for the Fair Chance Ordinance. Three members who celebrated Homeboy Industries did so to applaud their own success—being a "success" to their families and finally being able to "redirect" their lives—but without discussion of political reform.

Jose Osuna gave a testimony as part of the Fair Chance hearing's public comment session that celebrated Homeboy Industries and his personal reform—but failed to acknowledge the LOC's partners. Jose opened his testimony formally, thanking the City Council for the opportunity to speak. He then introduced himself using his job title, director of employment services at Homeboy Industries, rather than as a member of LA Voice or leader of the Homeboys LOC. Jose proceeded to

Figure 5.3. Jose Osuna giving public comment at the Los Angeles Fair Chance hearing. Credit: Pocho One Fotography.

voice support for the ordinance by speaking about his personal experiences as well as his professional experiences as a Homeboy Industries director. Just as he did during the LOC meeting prior to the hearing, Jose gave credit to Father Greg and Homeboy Industries. He reminded the council members that Father Greg founded Homeboy Industries as a response to labor market discrimination and that the Fair Chance Ordinance was in line with Father Greg's vision; he did not give credit to the organizations that had already been involved with Ban-the-Box efforts, such as LA Voice, the National Employment Law Project, AOUON, or A New Way of Life. Jose finished with an impassioned plea, urging the council to "move quickly" in passing the ordinance. After he finished, he stood up and walked to the back of the room with an intense, straight face as several Homeboys and Homegirls clapped and cheered loudly for him.

The LOC recognized individuals for their efforts and contributions in ways that detracted from community organizing's emphasis on collective and political action. In contrast to CRS, where pastors were annually given awards—such as the City on a Hill award—in recognition of civic engagement "for the greater good," Jose regularly "lifted up" individual members of the Homeboys LOC in much less ceremonial ways. For example, at an LOC meeting, Jose celebrated the efforts of Cristina, the Homeboy Industries senior staff attorney, by asking her to recount how she attempted to expand—and finally succeeded in expanding—the pool of persons Homeboy Industries was targeting for Prop 47 services. Cristina said she had pushed the coalition group she worked with to try to get a statewide list of persons who qualified, and eventually a Los Angeles County supervisor came to Homeboy Industries asking how to expand Prop 47 outreach. Jose praised Cristina because she had worked so hard for social change and because it was all the more remarkable that a supervisor came to Homeboys rather than Homeboys having to go to the supervisor.

The LOC sometimes celebrated Homeboy Industries at the expense of realizing the weaknesses of the group. During the Prop 47 campaign, Homeboys LOC leaders reported to LA Voice that we all had the characteristics necessary for a "team" to do phone banking and voter canvassing; we were subsequently categorized as a "number one," this despite the fact that Homeboys LOC team leaders' only experience with organizing was limited to the Fair Chance campaign and LOC meetings sometimes had fewer than five members. Rather, it seemed that our leaders were eager to categorize us as a "number one" given that this fit with Homeboy Industries' identity as the largest program of its kind. LOC leaders did not appreciate the difference between the resources necessary to mobilize for phone banking or voter canvassing and the resources Homeboy Industries was rich in: persons willing to volunteer time to tell their own stories. As a result, Homeboys LOC phone banking for Prop 47 fell short of initial expectations.

Conclusion

LA Voice's theological orientation—rooted in PICO's Vatican II–inspired Catholic teachings—fostered prophetic redemption through pastoral displays. LA Voice leaders drew from Catholic notions of dignity and ecumenism to extend faith-based community organizing to the formerly incarcerated. LA Voice leaders drew from PICO's relationship-based model of faith-based community organizing to teach members terms

such as "voice," "diversity," "power" and "partnerships," and to bring formerly incarcerated persons together with others in public spaces and
build meaningful relationships. LA Voice trainings further emphasized
the importance of members' stories, "one-on-one meetings," and public
testimonies for legislative reform.

Homeboys LOC leaders, in turn, drew from Homeboys LOC members' experiences and Homeboy Industries' institutional mission to
facilitate faith-based community organizing through the relationship-
based model. Homeboys LOC leaders drew from members' experiences
with recovery—such as their ability to give testimonies and their desire to make good by giving back to the community—in order to solicit
members' participation in political campaigns. Leaders also drew from
notions of gang hierarchies to socialize members into faith-based community organizing; Jose used the terms "big homies" and "little homies"
to legitimate PICO and LA Voice's hierarchical relationship with the
LOC. Last, leaders drew from notions of adversarial street politics—such
as resisting the urge to exact revenge against a rival so as to work toward
a common goal—in order to quell any public expressions of insurgency
against elected officials. For example, Jose encouraged Homeboys LOC
members to perform personal testimonies in order to build cooperative
relationships with elected officials rather than publicly shame officials
and risk Homeboy Industries' public funding streams.

Homeboys LOC leaders drew from concepts such as "diversity" not
just to translate the meaning of the relationship-based model, but to
reconstitute how Homeboys LOC members participated in collective
action. Homeboys LOC leaders sought to protect members from participation in PICO or LA Voice's more militant displays of prophetic
redemption. Jose claimed that shaming elected officials could strain relationships with them, and have consequences for Homeboy Industries'
public streams of funding and ability to provide social services. In turn,
LOC leaders rejected LA Voice's efforts to organize its members into
voter canvassing teams. They first claimed that Homeboys/girls were
not suitable for door knocking, but then ultimately fell back on notions
of "diversity"—claiming that Homeboys simply followed a "different
model" of community organizing. The relationship between the Homeboys LOC and LA Voice became further strained as Jose—Homeboy
Industries' director of employment services—sought to protect Home-

boy Industries from a historic fifteen-dollar-an-hour minimum wage ordinance. While LA Voice organized for the minimum wage increase, Jose led Homeboys LOC members in organizing for an exemption for Homeboy Industries.

LA Voice and the Homeboys LOC's reliance on Catholic teachings and relationship-based community organizing shaped how Homeboys LOC members experienced political and personal reform. LA Voice's notions of human dignity, diversity, and ecumenism—such as the presentation of testimonies—socialized Homeboys LOC members into pastoral displays of faith-based community organizing. However, while LA Voice created platforms for Homeboys LOC members to perform personal testimonies, members often failed to highlight campaign issues. Thus, while LA Voice sought to engage LOC members in prophetic redemption, LOC members principally performed testimonies to celebrate Homeboy Industries, elevate its visibility over other local nonprofits, and ensure that Homeboy Industries maintained its position within the local penal field as a provider of prisoner reentry. Nonetheless, Homeboys LOC members ultimately drew from pastoral religious displays to expand the rights of the formerly incarcerated and to facilitate their social integration into the civic and political arena.

6

Returning Citizenship

WITH JENNIFER ELENA COSSYLEON

> Organizing has brought me two of the most beautiful moments in my life, both having to do with my children—one who's passed on and one I still have in my life. There's no way that I can minimize the impact that organizing has had on me on a personal level.
> —Jose, Homeboys LOC

Prophetic redemption constructed a sense of belonging and kinship. As Jose's vignette suggests, his involvement in the Homeboys LOC was both political and personal. He felt that the campaigns were important, that the actions were powerful, and that he had created shared experiences and memories with those in the LOC. Jose held a sense of pride over accomplishments such as the Ban-the-Box march and rally.

Jose's personal experiences in the LOC extended to his family; his daughter had participated in LOC actions and witnessed him act as a leader. When he was meeting people to form the LOC, he was asked to have "one-on-ones" with several individuals. Jose chose to meet with his daughter for a one-on-one. She was sixteen years old, and he had asked her to get involved with the LOC. She attended the mayoral forum where Jose served as a moderator and the Ban-the-Box march and rally.

The LOC actions afforded Jose the ability to make good from his past and redeem himself in his daughter's eyes. He proudly recalled that she saw "her dad go in and come out of Mayor Garcetti's office with the mayor." Jose then trembled and his voice cracked when I asked what the experience meant to him. His eyes teared up as he told me, "It means that my daughter could see that her dad did thirteen years in prison and was this gang member, and now he put on a suit and his voice was heard." Jose took a deep breath before he continued:

It's brought me many moments of redemption with that child. The first eight years of her life I was incarcerated, because her mother was pregnant when I got locked up. This is a child who by all rights could have hated me. But she hasn't. She's seen both sides of me. The LOC and organizing has allowed her to see this other side of me that makes her proud. I really value those memories and that experience that we share.

Jose faulted himself for having a drug problem, having been incarcerated, and having been absent the first eight years of his daughter's life. He had nearly cried and was overtaken by emotion, describing how he was redefined from "gang member" to community organizer. As he participated in the LOC, Jose felt he was repairing his relationship with his daughter.

FORCE and Homeboys LOC members constructed the meaning of being "formerly incarcerated" or an "ex-offender" through notions of citizenship. Anthropologist James Holston (2009, 6) has argued that Brazilian favela dwellers—having participated in the making of self-constructed homes and neighborhoods, from the "autoconstructed" urban peripheries—redefined citizenship from being exclusively elite to reclaiming property, political rights, and democratic participation. Similarly, FORCE and Homeboys LOC members drew from recovery and community organizing discourses to rearticulate conventional notions of citizenship; they rejected labels of second-class citizenship and made claims for greater social and economic citizenship rights. Through these efforts they constructed the notion of the "returning citizen": one who has experienced incarceration, but has made good by being "positive" and "productive"—and deserves to regain civil, political, and social rights lost to the stigma of a criminal record.

Shortly following World War II, British social theorist T. H. Marshall (1950) falsely predicted that the emergence of the postwar welfare state would increase social rights and thereby access to civic and political rights, further reducing social inequalities. In the United States, the federal expansion of substantive citizenship rights has often faced resistance; this is rooted in the United States' history of racism, slavery, and state-centered federalism (e.g., Alexander 2010; Du Bois [1935] 2007). For example, as described earlier, the CSG was founded precisely as a

Figure 6.1. Jose Osuna holding National Voter Registration Day scrolls, following Los Angeles County's recognition of Homeboy Industries. Credit: Pocho One Fotography.

means of mounting racist resistance to progressive New Deal reforms expanding social citizenship.

Sociologist Evelyn Nakano Glenn (2002), in her comparative study of nineteenth-century racism and labor, contended that institutional racism marginalized people of color but also fostered resistance, created community among the oppressed, and redefined civic participation. Similarly, today, even though records discrimination risks running afoul of Title VII's Disparate Impact Provision (Smith 2014), persons with records face discrimination in housing and labor markets (e.g., Alexander 2010; Lageson, Vuolo, and Uggen 2015; Pager 2003; Smith 2014). FORCE and Homeboys LOC members' criminal records subjected them to such discrimination and in turn made it difficult for them to access affordable housing and stable jobs and to participate in civic and political action. Some FORCE and Homeboys LOC members had stable work, but were forced to choose between going to work and taking a day off work to take a bus to the state capitol and lobby legislators. Others struggled to find ways to repair personal relationships—especially in the absence of financially providing for partners or children. Nonetheless, Jose's experience demonstrated how such exclusion encouraged resistance that built personal relationships, created a sense of community and kinship, and ultimately challenged such exclusion.

Formerly incarcerated persons who participated in community organizing created the notion of being "returning citizens" in ways that resonated with "cultural citizenship" (Rosaldo 1994, 57): the right to maintain cultural distinctiveness while retaining civic, political, and social citizenship rights. Members' narratives of participation—their redemption scripts—were central to the development of returning citizenship. Respondents drew from two types of narratives to participate in community organizing: cultural deficit narratives, which emphasized a lack of household- and neighborhood-level collective efficacy, and structural barrier narratives, which emphasized poverty, marginality, and records discrimination.

FORCE and Homeboys LOC members further challenged the gendered distinctions in the field of community organizing. FORCE and Homeboys LOC members' narratives of participation—from cultural deficit to structural barrier narratives—challenged conventional notions of manhood by repairing their personal relationships and resisting their exclusion. Whereas FORCE and Homeboys LOC members lacked resources for achieving conventional expressions of manhood, they drew from narratives of participation to make good and build personal relationships—as well as kin ties with each other. In turn, they drew from the conventional notions of the "positive" and "productive" citizen to rearticulate returning citizenship—and to refashion dominant notions of citizenship and manhood as rooted in expressive displays and collective action.

Blurring the Public-Private Distinction

Practitioners in the field of community organizing have often made the distinction between public and private (Alinsky 1971; Chambers 2003; Jacobsen 2001). Saul Alinsky, for example, famously suggested that in community organizing one has "no permanent friends and no permanent enemies." The Alinsky view of community organizing rested on conflict-oriented approaches to attacking bureaucratic institutions, such as public actions at local town hall meetings. Similarly, recent changes in the field of community organizing—as we have seen, emphasizing relationships rather than issues—have further advanced a public-private distinction. Gamaliel National Network director Dennis Jacobsen, for example, admonished community organizers to separate private, household relations from community organizing. Jacobsen (2001, 52) warned of the "habitual 'self-denial'" that often prevents pastors from building "truly intimate relationships" at home—such as spending time with one's spouse.

Popular notions in community organizing, however, not only draw from a public-private distinction but also build upon the idea of the lower worth of women's unpaid household labor. Edward Chambers's *Roots for Radicals* (2003, 72), a primer for community organizers, constructed the meaning of the public-private distinction through a chapter titled "Relationships: Private and Public." In the chapter, Chambers (2003, 78–79) illustrated the distinction between private and public by drawing from a story with deeply masculinist tones. Chambers recounted that a female organizer's husband once called IAF headquarters, angrily asking for Chambers. The man, upset that his wife returned from an IAF training refusing to cook, asked Chambers, "What the hell are you guys up to, anyway?" Chambers promptly got on the phone with the man's wife and found out she was staging an action against her husband. Chambers explained to her that actions were to be used only against "the opposition, not your husband." The woman quickly apologized to Chambers and promised not to repeat the mistake.

Chambers's story of the woman who accidentally staged an action at home suggests that an Alinsky-influenced community organizing public-private distinction rests on men's institutional privileges. Chambers, a leader in community organizing, advanced not only a public-private distinction, but implicitly sexist notions as well: that women should carry a larger burden of household labor, that organizing leaders will not interfere with gendered divisions of labor, and that women won't (or shouldn't) reject such gendered arrangements. Community organizing practitioners, insofar as they draw from and build upon such public-private distinctions, advance sexist, gendered divisions of labor.

Jose's description of the meaning of community organizing, however, reveals that notions of public and private and gendered expressions may be far more complex than those communicated through Chambers's story. As a formerly incarcerated person, Jose displayed a masculine identity that contrasted with modern notions of breadwinning males and subservient wives. He was born to undocumented immigrants, had joined gangs, and had become addicted to drugs. He served two stints in prison, rose up as a shot-caller, and had been released from prison with little social support. Jose's gendered expressions were developed not within a position of privilege, but rather as an expression of "marginalized masculinity" (Connell [1995] 2005, 81).

As we have seen, Jose drew from community organizing practices to rearticulate conventional notions of manhood. Jose sought to recover from drug addiction and to participate in the formal labor market. For this, Homeboy Industries provided him employment and mental health services. However, he also sought to repair his personal relationships—namely, getting to know his youngest daughter, whom he had not known for the first eight years of her life. The LOC provided opportunities for this. Jose conducted a one-on-one with his daughter and brought her to a mayoral forum he moderated and the march and rally he led. Jose demonstrated that he was no longer a gang member, and built a closer relationship with his daughter.

The personal significance of community organizing in Jose's life became clearer to me as I interviewed him. It was close to nightfall, and I had visited the modest duplex he rented. He shared a unit with another Homeboy in an urban neighborhood off a major freeway, and after a busy day at Homeboy Industries, Jose had been gracious enough to give me an hour and a half of his time. As I thought we completed the interview, Jose asked to talk about something he felt we hadn't covered enough: the impact of organizing on his personal life. Jose mentioned, again, the beauty of the relationship he had formed with his daughter. But then he also mentioned another, more painful wound that organizing had helped to heal.

As we saw earlier, Jose's son had died seven years before—killed by two Black men in front of Jose's house in a race-related murder. The event had weighed heavily on Jose—who had spent years as a shot-caller for a Mexican prison gang, learning to hate Blacks. Years later, Jose visited the Martin Luther King Center in Atlanta for a PICO National organizer training. It was a weeklong training, and Jose visited Ebenezer Baptist Church, where Dr. King and others had shared deeply personal experiences. The significance was not lost on Jose, who at that moment was able to finally able to shed his racist views and the grief over his son's murder:

> I realized when I walked in, I realized where I was at, and it broke me. . . . What happened is that I left that last piece of hatred there. I realized that we were in the same struggle together, whether it be Latinos, African Americans, white people who saw the value in being part of the struggle. I realized that we all were deeply wounded, and we all needed healing, and I found healing there. It became a moment of redemption for me. I think that's the moment where I was able to lay my son to rest internally. It was a beautiful experience. I wouldn't have had it if I wasn't part of the LOC, if I wasn't part of LA Voice, a member of the community at Homeboy Industries, if I hadn't been impassioned around community organizing. So it brought me that great moment of redemption, too, to walk out of there free.

Not all FORCE and Homeboys LOC members experienced Jose's cathartic release of pain at Ebenezer, however. Some still dealt with strained family relationships. Some were still in the process of redeeming themselves by trying to give back to their communities. Some built close, meaningful kin ties with others who also struggled to rebuild family ties. In the process, FORCE and Homeboys LOC members fashioned the "returning citizen" as a form of insurgent citizenship—creating belonging for marginalized formerly incarcerated persons.

Members' narratives drew from racist, victim-blaming tropes that characterized communities of color as culturally pathological and as having an inertia of their own. But members' narratives also identified structural problems and the importance of collective and political action. In turn, FORCE and the Homeboys LOC bridged public and private in ways that didn't completely roll back racist/sexist notions, but rather rearticulated them in novel ways. Members framed collective and political action as empowering, as redeeming, and as a solution to the cultural pathologies of disadvantaged neighborhoods.

Cultural Deficit Narratives

Most respondents utilized *cultural deficit narratives* to contrast their current efforts—to become better, more nurturing people and to improve their homes and communities—against the backdrop of what they perceived as a lack of household-level and neighborhood-level collective efficacy. They described their households as having been marked by absentee parents, who were gang members or worked long hours and had poor communication with their children. They portrayed their communities as marked by poverty, gangs, drugs, and high rates of teenage pregnancy, crime, and violence. They emphasized a lack of community collective efficacy and negative mentorship from older males in the community in describing a "cycle" of poverty or violence. (A few FORCE respondents even claimed that neighborhood collective efficacy was *further* declining and compounding social problems—while no respondents from the Homeboys LOC made such claims.) By drawing from these tropes, respondents suggested that there was a social inertia within their communities that was responsible for widespread disadvantage.

Reymundo, a twenty-eight-year-old Mexican American FORCE member, grew up in Chicago's West Town neighborhood in the 1990s, when there were five to six gangs within a two-block radius. Reymundo remembered experiencing middle school fearfully, being bullied and later being forced to affiliate with a group he and his friends befriended to fend off their bullies. Reymundo described his experience with gang socialization as a thirteen-year-old child as a period of marginality ("we had to just figure things out") and masculine socialization ("[we] were forced into a false sense of manhood"). His involvement with gangs deepened. He got "jumped in," and was "gang-banging . . . running with the wrong people, doing the wrong things." There were shootings in his neighborhood, and rival gang members threatened his life. Reymundo harbored these feelings of fear privately; he never told his family because he was afraid to burden them with the same fears.

Many FORCE and Homeboys LOC members blamed themselves—and their own parents—for having been absentee parents or for having participated in masculinist street gang culture. As Reymundo became a father, he recalled, "I didn't know how to be a father." He reflected on how his experiences as a father had been shaped by his own experiences being raised by his father: "My dad was there but he wasn't there as well . . . and the responsibility that fathers have to take is to step up, break that cycle. . . . I think that would break that cycle of [gang] violence."

Similarly, Oscar, a former gang member who had been addicted to drugs, described absentee parents and drugs as the biggest problems in his community. He had an absent father and a mother who was addicted to drugs, and had once searched for a sense of family on the streets. The street gang became his family, including his older cousin—who sold drugs, had nice cars, and proved popular with women. Oscar emulated his cousin, followed in his footsteps, and had influenced younger males to also follow him into a life of gangs and drugs:

> And now kids that are in that area, like I said, that only have a mother, and I know a few, they seen what I was doing, they seen me with the money, the drugs, my guns, the women. So I just repeated the cycle. Now a lot of those little kids I knew in the past before I went to prison are from the same gang as me. The cycle's just getting repeated.

Some respondents suggested that community social problems were not just due to the absence of one or both parents but also due to parental neglect stemming from a "lack of education." Gilda, a Homeboys LOC member whose parents were from rural, mountainous Mexico, described her parents in this way. Like many other parents from her community, hers were too work-oriented. She lamented that they yelled instead of communicating through reason, and didn't pay nearly enough attention to "what's going on at home." Instead of talking about how immigration laws, racism, or economic uncertainty shaped her difficult childhood, Gilda simply said that her parents didn't "know how to be parents."

Some respondents drew from the tropes of "cultural racism," suggesting that neighborhood-level social problems were self-inflicted wounds. For example, instead of talking about his experience with incarceration as an outcome of harsh drug laws, Oscar instead blamed himself because he had "repeated the cycle" from his cousin and influenced younger men. Similarly, Camron, a FORCE member with a criminal record, said that persons in his community lacked "financial management" and "create[d] poverty" for themselves. He attributed this to absent men, failing to act as breadwinners. Instead of lamenting the lack of stable, well-paying employment in his community, Camron blamed such men for their under/unemployment, saying that they were not "doing their part as being male figures . . . not being proper fathers . . . not being proper sons . . . not being proper brothers." He implied that most were "out for themselves," suggesting that Black and Latino households remained poor due to men's continued poor decisions.

Some respondents extended the logic of "cultural racism" (e.g., Bonilla-Silva 2003) by framing issues of gangs, violence, and drugs around Black or Latino masculinity. Most respondents claimed that older men in their neighborhoods were a negative influence on younger men and boys. Olivia, a woman in FORCE with a gang past—but no criminal record—who was also finishing a social work bachelor of arts program, blamed African Americans and Latinos for their high incarceration rates. Olivia claimed that in African American and Latino cultures parents inculcated patriarchal ideas of "being a man." However, because Black and Latino men faced obstacles in the labor market, such discrimination served to "tak[e] their manhood away" and force them into illicit economic activity. Olivia said that even with her own son she taught him that being a man meant not crying, having responsibility, and being a provider. Similar to President Obama's comments about Black and Latino men, Olivia drew from a "controlling image" (Collins 1990, 72) of Black and Latino men as hypermasculine to explain their higher incarceration rates.

Against these depictions of neighborhoods as lacking collective efficacy, some respondents said their only option to remove themselves from their environment was to leave. Mary, a FORCE member in her early thirties and a female minister active in local politics, suggested that she managed to remove herself from illegal activity simply by moving out of the neighborhood. Mary's father was absent, her mother always worked, and, being surrounded by gang and drug activity, she eventually bagged and sold drugs. Fortunate that she had never been arrested ("by the grace of God"), Mary claims to have made a conscious decision to "get away" and moved out.

Structural Barrier Narratives

Not all respondents involved with faith-based community organizing articulated views of absentee fathers as the root of inner-city problems. Many respondents also drew from *structural barrier narratives.*

Structural barrier narratives utilized a structural critique, blaming social problems, such as illicit economic activity, on institutional inequalities, such as records discrimination, education, employment, poverty, housing, immigration, and incarceration. Most respondents viewed these institutional inequalities as rooted in poverty (at the same time they almost never spoke of racism). One FORCE leader, Rachael, suggested that mass incarceration was a system of oppression that took certain men out of communities to "weaken the household." She then explained that although women became the nurturers and the breadwinners, they too were now being incarcerated at high rates.

Structural barrier narratives centered on records discrimination—that the formerly incarcerated were systematically excluded from employment or housing due to a "prior mistake." Respondents reasoned that because they faced barriers in the labor market, the formerly incarcerated were at a higher risk of committing crime. Members frequently evoked the trope of the marginal young adult man who has to commit crime because he has no other economic opportunities to provide for his family.

Olivia illustrated her concerns over records discrimination by talking about one of her clients. She explained that a young man, whom she was trying to guide out of street life and crime, could not leave because, as a formerly incarcerated person, the only economic opportunities open to him were illicit:

> He broke into a car, stole a car, and his girlfriend is pregnant now, and he cannot find work. And I mean . . . you can tell genuinely somebody who wants to change . . . he's looked for work, he's done good, he's went to classes for resumes. He's done everything he can to try to change his life. And he was just tired of getting denied. Everywhere he would apply: denied, denied, denied.

Olivia's story of a young person who "wants to change" and has been "denied, denied, denied" was emblematic of the way members talked about the struggle of persistent marginalization. Postincarceration records discrimination was the second act of an urban drama in which marginality, poverty, and crime remained tightly bound together. In this act, the protagonist had "done everything he can" to leave street life and reinsert himself or herself into conventional social spheres, but—due to the stigma of a conviction and joblessness—remained with one foot in illicit street activity. FORCE members claimed that records discrimination, through the denial of the opportunity to work or interview for work, amounted to a "life sentence" and compounded the likelihood of gang activity.

Most respondents combined structural barrier and cultural pathology narratives, critiquing institutional practices. For example, Luis, a Homeboys LOC leader and former gang member with a criminal record, claimed that "poverty breeds drugs and gang violence." He asserted that records discrimination almost ensured that the formerly incarcerated would turn to crime. In turn, Luis—like every Homeboys LOC member—voiced support for initiatives to increase formerly incarcerated people's access to jobs as an effort to reduce crime. This reflected Bonilla-Silva's (2003) research on racism, which found that Blacks were more likely than whites to see institutional practices as responsible for social inequality.

At the same time, structural barrier narratives still fell back on the discourse of cultural racism. David, a Latino FORCE member and former gang member with a criminal record, described how poverty, crime, and labor market exclusion were cyclical due to culture; he explained that "generation upon generation of criminals" were "having children" and that he found it "absolutely disgusting." Clarence, a Black Homeboys LOC member and former gang member with a criminal record, discussed how the practices of slave master Willie Lynch—who sought to break Black families down by emasculating men—transmitted cultural pathologies from slavery-era Black families to the present.

Building Collective Efficacy through Collective Action

FORCE and Homeboys LOC members sought to create "change" in communities they once "helped destroy." Many respondents saw community organizing as having the potential to change "negative" cultural pathologies—such as masculine street culture—driving community poverty and crime. As Maruna (2001, 87) has suggested, through making good, former prisoners "[rewrite] a shameful past into . . . a productive and worthy life." Victor, for example, paraphrased Charles's quote in the FORCE informational video: "Don't judge me by my previous record, judge me by the record I'm making now because this one is much more powerful."

Reymundo joined FORCE to create social change at the household and neighborhood levels. At the time of our interview he was enrolled in a social work program, but knew his felony drug conviction would bar him from any occupations that involved working with children or the elderly. One of his professors knew Eddie was recruiting for FORCE and, aware of Reymundo's situation, passed along Eddie's contact information. Reymundo immediately felt connected with FORCE. Whereas broader society treated the formerly incarcerated as "the garbage of society," FORCE had a prophetic mission. Reymundo claimed they were "trying to create equal opportunities for people who have been in jail, have been rehabilitated, have turned their lives around and are now trying to do good." By becoming involved with FORCE, Reymundo was attempting to change his family and his community, to "break that cycle of [gang] violence."

Although some members talked about how legislative reform could build collective efficacy, more often respondents spoke of building collective efficacy *through* faith-based community organizing. David drew from racist tropes in talking about community issues, but suggested that FORCE members could build collective efficacy, leadership, and mentoring through the experience of organizing. Similarly, Clarence, who made comments about emasculated Black men and broken Black families, said that he saw the Homeboys LOC not as part of a political movement but rather as a therapeutic program. He sought to use experiences with the Homeboys LOC to learn how to change himself and his community—and then to use such knowledge to "break the cycle": educating his own kids on how to become empowered and passing that knowledge down to future generations.

Luis, a leader in the Homeboys LOC, narrated how he came to participate with faith-based community organizing. He drew from both cultural deficit and structural barrier narratives and highlighted how collective efficacy could be improved *through* organizing:

> It wasn't a tough decision to make . . . I felt like anything that was positive I wanted to attend, anything good. And they said, basically, "We're gonna be talkin' about issues that affect our community," and that kind of stood out to me. And then I just decided to go.

Luis cited gang activity as the major issue in his community; he had experienced gangs and incarceration and had regretted engaging in such "negative" expressions of manhood. Through participation in faith-based community organizing, he was able to absolve himself of his previous behavior and pay good deeds forward; he had the chance to attend a meeting where "issues that affect the community" would be discussed, and where he could expect to help create social change. After sharing his testimony as an ex-offender, Luis promptly got involved with the Homeboys LOC and became a leader in a major campaign.

Building Kinship through Collective Action

In the absence of strong family ties, FORCE members used community organizing to make good and build meaningful personal relationships with each other.[1] FORCE and Homeboys LOC members, like many formerly incarcerated persons, looked to family for emotional and material support (e.g., Fader 2013). At the same time, as formerly incarcerated persons, many members also lacked social support; oftentimes, their experiences with incarceration had strained family or kin relationships, and their criminal records had created new obstacles (e.g., Cossyleon 2012). In turn, members sought to build a kinship-like support system.

FORCE members referred to the organization as a group of people who could "relate to each other's struggle" and found a sense of belonging within the group. Becky described how other FORCE leaders could be supportive of her experiences because they've been there and they "got it." She explained how her support system was "failing" and they didn't "get the reentry issues."

Community organizing activities enabled members to help and to nurture one another and to build personal relationships. As mentioned in chapter 4, monthly meetings were instituted to foster relationships and to deepen involvement in collective action. Members drew from familiar, recovery-style interactions for community organizing practices, such as using "check-ins" during the introduction and "relational questions." In addition, as mentioned in chapter 2, organizers trained members how to conduct one-on-ones to build relationships, deepen participation, and mobilize members.

The purpose of a one-on-one was to "turn a private relationship into a public one" through a short and purposeful meeting—though some were still learning how to build private relationships and used one-on-ones for such means. The formal objectives were to articulate shared experiences, ask about each other's needs and wants, and identify individual and collective goals. Rosemary explained, "We sit down, like you and I are doing, and we have a one-on-one. We find out, 'What is it that you want? What is your passion? What can we do for you to help you reach your potential, your goal?'" However, some, such as Philip, a FORCE member in his twenties, learned about one-on-ones and used them to build personal relationships. While Philip stated the formal objectives of community organizing trainings and one-on-ones as learning to identify others' self-interests and to be a "good listener and a good speaker at the same time," Philip also used one-on-ones to identify people whom he could call on. Similarly, Theresa, a Black woman in her thirties, said that the one-on-one became the start of her friendship with another member: "When Marlon and I had a one-on-one that is when our relationship started, when we [became] truly sister and brother." The personal nature of a one-on-one created an opportunity for members to build personal relationships with one another.

Members' development of close, kin-like relationships filled unmet personal needs caused by family strain. David described his close relationship with one member: "He's been a good part of my support network. I've called him a few times when I've been at the edge about to jump off." Philip, a member of FORCE seeking to go back to school, claimed that FORCE members provided a "good foundation" of social support. Ron said, "If I have any problems, they're quick to help you out. They're there to mentor you, to be supportive." Thus, while community organizing's relationship-building activities were designed to deprivatize members' narratives for the public arena, formerly incarcerated persons used one-on-ones to create needed kin relationships.

For some members, development of kin relationships fostered yet deeper participation in volunteering and community organizing. Rachael, a Black woman in her early fifties, credited other members for their desistance from the street. Rachael had difficulties feeling connected with her family, particularly her kids, who blamed her for being absent for many years of their lives. Rachael coped with these discouragements by connecting with other FORCE members—many who had also experienced such family conflicts. She referred to FORCE as a "surrogate" and "blended family" who looked out for one another. Rachael volunteered at a local food pantry, but through FORCE met Camron, who was helping to start restorative justice peace hubs in his community. Like Rachel, Camron had strained family relationships. He had lost custody of his five-year-old daughter after going to prison, and after a nine-year prison stint was trying to build a relationship with his daughter. Rachel said, "If it wasn't for my surrogate family which I call FORCE, it what just be so simple for me to go back to doing what I was doing because I'd be like hey what the heck, nobody cares." Rachael described FORCE as "a true support team" that asked "how you feelin' today?" when no one else did. Rachel and Camron were mutually supportive of each other's efforts to mend family relationships and make good from their past.

Collective Action as "Positivity"

Homeboys LOC and FORCE members drew from collective subjectivity to construct returning citizenship as "positive" and "productive." Members' cultural deficit narratives framed social problems—drugs, gangs, the street, and prisons—as "negative," but being with family and setting a better example for younger men in the community as "positive." In addition, members' structural barrier narratives framed institutional inequalities—such as records discrimination in the labor or housing market—as "negative," and giving a voice to the disadvantaged, changing laws, and reforming institutional practices as "positive."

FORCE and Homeboys LOC members drew from both cultural deficit and structural barrier narratives to make sense of their own "negative" experiences, and to use that knowledge to "help others" and give back to their communities. A crucial facet of positivity involved contrasting past and present—what respondents saw as a difficult situation in the present, with a much more difficult situation in the past. Positivity was akin to a recovery testimony, containing a linear trajectory of a transgressive past, hitting bottom, and a clean future.

Dennis, a Black FORCE member in his forties and a former gang member who had served twenty years in prison, revealed that he felt dismayed at first when he was unemployed and then later when he was working for thirteen dollars an hour. He found inspiration to "overcome and overpower" his difficulties with employment, and remain committed in attempting to live a conventional lifestyle, by comparing his situation with his past and that of others less fortunate. Dennis found inspiration in thinking about a friend he had been incarcerated with:

> Yeah, there's this young man, he's like twenty-seven years old. . . . He had seven life sentences, and all the years I was locked up with him I never seen him disappointed. . . . I think about some of the things that he's around every day and he got joy. If I can change my ways and think and feel like him, [and turn] all the negatives turn into a positive, I think that's great.

A postincarceration "positive" recovery narrative involved articulating self-examination, comparing one's current situation to past struggles, and finding contentment in modest progress. For example, Marco said, "I made other people into addicts . . . didn't have food on their table . . . got shot on the streets because of me. . . . [W]hat did I get out of that? Prison life, I got shot at." However, Marco felt that his life had changed and that he no longer struggled with the same issues of violence and incarceration: "I don't wanna be all religious. But you know, it seems like if I stay away from certain things, I get a lot of blessings. I do, I get a lot of blessings and I get a lot of blessings and basically, and if you do right, right only comes back to you." Such positivity begat more positivity. Marco added, "So, now I don't do that no more and now I'm pretty positive. . . . Guess what? Positive is coming back."

Barbara Ehrenreich (2009), in a historical overview of "positive thinking" in America, asserted that early colonial American religious character undergirded the rise of twentieth-century movements in positive thinking and self-help (Ehrenreich 2009). What Max Weber ([1905] 2005, 113) once called the "frost" of Calvinist Puritanism—obsessive self-loathing, self-examining behavior—was transformed in the nineteenth century through the "New Thought Movement," and later through Norman Vincent Peale's 1952 book, *The Power of Positive Thinking* (Ehren-reich 2009, 77). Like Calvinist Puritanism, positive thinking and therapy have centered the individual through "the constant internal work of self-monitoring," although this may do little more than to blame the individual for deep, structural problems such as financial deregulation and the rise of precarious labor (Ehrenreich 2009, 90).

Formerly incarcerated persons did not simply construct "being positive," or "positivity," by looking inward, but used positivity to build relationships, challenge their exclusion, and ultimately engage in collective action. Members referred to various relationship-building activities in reentry as positive: mental health programs, therapy classes, participation with CBOs, and volunteering for the probation department. Juan claimed that Homeboy Industries, by offering rehabilitation and work opportunities, gave hope to such persons to engage in "positive" activities and leave gang life. In turn, the relationships within recovery or volunteerism formed a foundation for civic and political relationships to flourish.

FORCE and Homeboys LOC members narrated their involvement with community organizing—often for lack of stable work or stronger family ties—as an effort to do something positive. Daniel, a Black FORCE member, said, "I was a heroin user for over twenty years. Back in 2008, I made a decision to stop being high. Try to change my life and do something positive, and turn it around. That's how kinda I end up hooking up with FORCE." Daniel saw community organizing as "positive" because it did not involve drugs, gangs, or the street. Clarence—who referred to the Homeboys LOC as "a class"—got involved with the group because a friend spoke positively about it: "We were just talkin' about the classes. . . . I had gone to a [Criminals and Gang Members Anonymous] class at Homeboys . . . just havin' positive talk . . . some of the things that he was talkin' about was pretty cool. So, I got involved. I went to the class and I actually enjoyed it." FORCE and Homeboys LOC members became involved with community organizing precisely because they found community and kinship with people similarly dealing with the postincarceration experience.

Community organizing expanded the reach of "positivity" in the civic sphere, beyond members' efforts at volunteering and personal reform, to the spaces of civic activism: politicized monthly civic association meetings, community organizer trainings, worship assemblies, meet-ings with elected officials, and lobby days. For example, Daniel's experi-ences, learning to speak with elected officials—with no background in or understanding of politics—convinced him that FORCE was "posi-tive." In turn, as members became more deeply involved in community organizing, they adopted and incorporated civic and political discourse into their discussions of positivity and personal reform. In describing how FORCE could help his community, Camron emphasized the role of the formerly incarcerated, and their efforts at self-reform, in civic and political action. When asked how FORCE could help the community, Camron said,

> Well, FORCE is gonna help the community by continuing to involve re-entering citizens and ex-offenders in positive units, and positive ways, and giving them information about what they can do to break that cycle of constantly going in and out of prison . . . building up these units to rope politicians in, because, who gonna do something for us in these neighborhoods?

Conclusion

The construction of returning citizenship highlights how racist exclusion and marginality may foster collective subjectivity and empowerment. FORCE and Homeboys LOC members carried the stigma of a criminal record and experienced second-class citizenship in securing housing, employment, and education. At the same time, they sought to contest such exclusion. They participated in civic engagement, from volunteer-ing to community organizing, and drew from the dominant notion of the productive citizen to redefine themselves. A returning citizen had a checkered past, but sought to be "positive" and "productive" by making good—such as by repairing strained relationships and "giving back" to the community. Thus, FORCE and Homeboys LOC members reformu-lated dominant notions of citizenship from individualistic to collective and experienced empowering social integration.

Formerly incarcerated persons constructed returning citizenship as a form of cultural citizenship; their efforts to expand civic, political, and social citizenship were based upon cultural distinctiveness. Jose's work with the Homeboys LOC illustrates how they sought to make good more than they tried to erase the past. Jose had grieved the terrible loss of one son to a race-related murder; however, a PICO event at a Black church afforded him an opportunity to organize with and embrace Black Americans and to forgive his son's murderers. In other cases, such as with Rachel and Camron, members built kinship by bonding over strained family ties.

FORCE and Homeboys LOC members drew from many ideas popularized by the Chicago School. They explained past mistakes by drawing from structural barrier narratives, which blamed crime on social ecology. At the same time, they also drew from cultural deficit narratives, which blamed crime on a lack of neighborhood-level collective efficacy. Nonetheless, members reacted against these ideas by constructing new meanings.

FORCE and Homeboys LOC members constructed returning citizenship by defining themselves against the dominant tropes of inefficacious inner-city community members and parents. FORCE and Homeboys LOC members articulated wanting to be the hardworking, emotionally available parents and the good neighbors that they sometimes felt they had lacked or failed to become earlier in life. Furthermore, as they challenged the Chicago School's narrow, top-down conceptualization of inner-city residents, FORCE and Homeboys LOC members demonstrated that they cared about not only good parenting and neighborhood collective efficacy, but grassroots civic activism.

Conclusion

In December 2013 I spoke at the Chicago-based Business and Professional People for the Public Interest (BPI), a prominent public interest law and policy center. BPI had received the prestigious MacArthur Award for Creative and Effective Institutions the previous year and was hosting a series of "knowledge exchanges" intended to shape its focus on future substantive issues.[1] The talk took place at the group's offices, with roughly two dozen participants: BPI staff and board members and directors of prominent Chicago-based nonprofits—many of which served formerly incarcerated populations, such as the homeless.

I shared findings from my book *God's Gangs*, as well as some preliminary findings on my research with FORCE. I offered the observation that former gang members sought to make good from their past and experience social integration—but that social integration might encompass much more than work, family, and church. The mood in the room changed quickly as I went from making statements about formerly incarcerated people and rehabilitation to speaking about their civic and political participation. Sensing their disbelief, I tried to frame civic and political activity—such as learning how to conduct one-on-ones, host meetings, or meet with elected officials—as facilitating social integration.

The directors of the nonprofits did not react as I had hoped. There were frowns, shocked expressions, and uncomfortable smiles (one person even seemed unaware of how much she stared at me in disbelief). Several attendees spoke hesitantly, unsure of how to engage with the idea of political empowerment. One did not hold back: she stated that I simply did not "understand" that there was no way to make children who had been raised in gang-infested neighborhoods care about the democratic process. She even went as far as to suggest that "they" were not like us because all they saw and cared about were the colors that other children wore.

The BPI talk provided an example of how, a century after the rise of the Chicago School, criminal justice reform discourse still heavily relies on paternalistic notions of inequality, crime, and change. I faced resistance, at an organization with a storied civil rights history, for having articulated the idea that we should politically empower former gang members and formerly incarcerated people as a means of reducing crime. The BPI talk suggested that many civic leaders still hold reservations about trying to empower formerly incarcerated persons.

At the same time, a myopic view of the BPI talk ignores an equally pressing reality: that formerly incarcerated persons have in fact become increasingly involved in civic and political participation. As discussed earlier, since 2004 campaigns have increasingly been waged to reduce incarceration and to expand the rights of the formerly incarcerated in every region of the United States—from Connecticut to Texas and from Ohio to Georgia. And since 2013 these campaigns have become much more visible.

The cases of FORCE and the Homeboys LOC present us with a picture of what formerly incarcerated persons' civic and political participation looks like in the twenty-first century. CRS and FORCE's campaigns included the Illinois Sealing Bill to expand the list of sealable offenses; a Walgreens corporate campaign to remove the felony conviction question and to hire formerly incarcerated persons; an "absolute bars" campaign to remove lifetime bans against persons with records from employment in Illinois parks, health care, and schools; and the Reclaim Campaign to release all persons awaiting trial for nonviolent offenses and to shut down a wing of Cook County Jail. LA Voice and the Homeboys LOC waged campaigns for the Los Angeles Fair Chance Ordinance, to remove the felony conviction question from private employment applications and to regulate how and at what stage employers used background checks; and California Proposition 47, reclassifying nonserious, nonviolent felony crimes into misdemeanors and redirecting savings into a state fund for schools, victim services, and mental health treatment.

CRS and LA Voice fostered what I have termed prophetic redemption, expanding the boundaries of democratic inclusion to facilitate the social integration of the formerly incarcerated. They drew from faith-based community organizing practices that utilized "rituals of reacceptance and reabsorption" to enable displays of solidarity with formerly incarcerated persons. They deployed "prefigurative prayers" and "enact[ed] relationships" (Braunstein, Fulton, and Wood 2014, 713–14) at monthly meetings, organizer trainings, leadership assemblies, coalition meetings, and trips to lobby elected officials. As they portrayed the formerly incarcerated as "the other," leaders urged members to embrace them and to support campaigns that expanded their rights.

CRS and LA Voice's efforts were influenced by W. E. B. Du Bois's new abolitionism, as well as Saul Alinsky's rejection of the apolitical Chicago School social ecological perspective. CRS drew from the insurgent displays of issue-based community organizing; they took a much more militant approach to social change, targeting structural issues such as racism and poverty and shaming elected officials who didn't support their platform. LA Voice drew from the pastoral displays of relationship-based community organizing; they emphasized human dignity and taught those furthest on the margins how to engage in the public arena. While Chicago School–influenced research on crime has suggested that high-crime neighborhoods lack collective efficacy, in this book I suggest that this notion is misguided. CRS and LA Voice drew from long-standing religious traditions—very much present in inner-city communities—to facilitate social integration. CRS's insurgent displays of prophetic redemption were drawn from a history rooted deeply in the historically Black Protestant church, while LA Voice's pastoral displays of prophetic redemption were drawn from a history rooted in PICO and the Catholic Church.

As discussed earlier, elite civic organizations (such as the APPA and the CSG) have indeed been aware of the efficacious potential of urban CBOs and FBOs—enough that they responded to 1990s-era privatization contests by building partnerships with these organizations for criminal justice reform. They sought to extend controversial top-down forms of criminal justice reform—such as the broken windows policing model—into urban neighborhoods through CBOs and FBOs. Federal initiatives, particularly those that reframed broken windows probation as prisoner reentry, further protected elite civic organizations' position by deepening the role of CBOs and FBOs. However, while elites explicitly aimed to exclude community leaders from becoming empowered, FBO interpellation into criminal justice reform had unanticipated consequences.

CRS/FORCE and LA Voice/Homeboys LOC present examples of how, as CBOs and FBOs became more deeply drawn into the penal field, top-down criminal justice reform enabled grassroots activism. As regionally and locally prominent civic organizations institutionalized prisoner reentry, formerly incarcerated persons and activist clergy drew from prophetic teachings to rearticulate the meaning of reentry from individualistic to collective and political. As the California Endowment funded the PICO-affiliated Oakland Community Organizations, pastor Ben McBride participated in Black Lives Matter protests and gave a platform to Hands Up United at a 2016 PICO symposium. In Chicago, Exodus Renewal Society's Chris Moore and Eddie Bocanegra (formerly of CeaseFire) led FORCE's first meeting, which then led to a corporate campaign against Walgreens. Instead of simply supporting state-sanctioned social programming, some community and faith leaders reacted to CBO and FBO interpellation by rearticulating the meanings of prisoner reentry—from top-down criminal justice reform to prophetic redemption.

FORCE and Homeboys LOC members' activism has been further sustained by broader shifts in American civic and political engagement. In recent decades, public affairs consultants—heavily employed by business and industry groups—have risen in prominence, reshaping civic participation by drawing from 1960s and 1970s advocacy groups' tactics of mobilizing grassroots support (Walker 2014). Consultants with experience in advocacy, lobbying, and campaign strategy now apply increasingly available communication technologies for "grasstops" mobilization strategies that convene influential advocacy groups and facilitate top-down social reform. Similarly, members of the organizations mentioned in this book—AOUON, A New Way of Life, FORCE, and the Homeboys LOC—have gained experience in advocacy and lobbying and can now convene influential groups for top-down reform. The Obama administration's efforts to bring prominent formerly incarcerated persons to the White House—such as Susan Burton and Jose Osuna—suggest that formerly incarcerated persons now occupy a place in the field of criminal justice reform next to contemporary public relations consultants.[2]

Despite formerly incarcerated persons' ascending role in shaping criminal justice reform, however, elite civic organizations—such as neoliberal think tanks and civic groups—have remained influential in such efforts. In May 2015, the IPI hosted a panel near the state capitol centered on the "problems that currently plague Illinois' criminal justice system and reforms needed in the state" (IPI 2015). The IPI, as we have seen, was the target of a CRS action in 2014 over tax reform; CRS mobilized voters to lobby state representatives for progressive tax reform and accused the IPI—which was opposed to progressive tax reform—of publishing lies. IPI's panel brought together representatives from right-of-center organizations, such as the Charles Koch Institute and the IPI, with representatives with left-of-center organizations, such as Families Against Mandatory Minimums, the Justice Fellowship, and the Shriver Center (which had partnered with FORCE).

The shifting institutional arrangements between elite civic organizations and grassroots activists, in criminal justice reform, are demonstrated by Koch Industries' entrée into the field. Although Koch Industries had previously expressed little interest in criminal justice reform, the Charles Koch Institute held a summit the same year as the IPI. Eighty speakers at the summit represented several of the major organizations involved in criminal justice reform, elite civic organizations that had pioneered reentry (e.g., the CSG, the OSF, and the Urban Institute), as well as organizations providing reentry services. Only one organization comprised formerly incarcerated persons and engaged in civic and political activity (Voice of the Ex-Offender), yet representatives from libertarian think tanks tied to prison privatization and the rise of mass incarceration—such as the Heritage Foundation, the Manhattan Institute, and the Cato Institute—were there. Nonetheless, the Charles Koch Institute's meeting had the stated intention of building a "broad coalition."

Elite civic organizations' interest in criminal justice reform may have very little to do with meaningful reform. New Yorker journalist Jane Mayer suggested that Koch Industries' interest in criminal justice reform—which started in 2014—had been self-serving. Mayer (2016) cited leaked audio recordings of Koch Industries' private biannual donor summit in June 2014, suggesting that their "grand strategist," Richard Fink, took an interest in criminal justice reform for dishonest reasons. Fink spoke about winning over the "middle third" of America, despite critics' negative perceptions of Koch Industries—"they don't care about the underprivileged"—admittedly being accurate (Mayer 2016). In fact,

Koch Industries' interest in criminal justice reform stemmed from an incident in Texas in which they were hit with a twenty-million-dollar lawsuit over environmental violations. In December 2015, at a White House meeting organized by the CSG, Koch Industries' legal counsel expressed support for sentencing reform—but also for reinstating *mens rea* (i.e., intent) back into criminal proceedings, which would have granted Koch Industries more flexibility in evading criminal charges for environmental violations (Caldwell 2015).

This book has endeavored to show that elites do not have a monopoly over criminal justice reform. Even as elites may seek out members of FBOs and CBOs with experience in criminal justice reform, formerly incarcerated people construct meaning from their lived experiences. FORCE and Homeboys LOC members participated in CRS and LA Voice's spaces by reconstructing the meaning of community organizing. FORCE members used monthly meeting introductions, relational questions, and evaluations to emphasize volunteerism and "giving back," and reconstructed community organizing as a space in which to make good and experience personal reform. Likewise, Homeboys LOC members relied heavily on the use of public testimonies as a form of making good and experiencing personal reform; they regularly deployed testimonies in trainings, one-on-ones, meetings with elected officials, and, occasionally, public rallies. Then, through their participation in community organizing, FORCE and Homeboys LOC members also reconstructed the experience of being formerly incarcerated. They drew from the dominant tropes of being "positive" and "productive" to refashion citizenship as collective and political, and to regain the social and economic rights lost by a criminal record. In essence, they resisted elite civic organizations' efforts to interpellate FBOs and CBOs for top-down criminal justice reform.

Elites' cooptation of FBOs and CBOs may suggest a bleak outlook. As mentioned previously, scholarship thus far has yielded limited insight into the rise of prisoner reentry and its implications for civic and political engagement. Some have effortlessly slapped the label of "movement" on contemporary prison reform, falsely assuming it has led to wholesale reductions in incarceration. Others have challenged the label "movement," instead suggesting prison reform has been a result of top-down policy—neglecting that movements may very much emerge from instability among elites. Yet others have attempted to give credit to post-2000 conservatives, when processes in question actually emerged during the 1990s. However, some of the most damaging assessments have come from progressive scholars studying policing and incarceration; these have assumed—in a somewhat deterministic manner—that only a massive social movement to obliterate racism in all its forms can substantively reduce incarceration.

The concept of prophetic redemption, however, brings us back to the work of W. E. B. Du Bois, whose conceptualizations of racial oppression and resistance suggested that political and personal reform were mutually constitutive. Du Bois once famously predicted that the most significant problem of the twentieth century would be that of the color line—not because he had deterministic tendencies (he was, after all, deeply religious and spoke the language of prophetic spirituality)—but because he appreciated the fact that several groups had actively worked to undermine the reconstruction. It was from this perspective that Du Bois conceptualized the importance of political empowerment in social change. At the same time, Du Bois did not simply celebrate the social gospel wing of the Black church but defended "the conservative majority that opposed protest activism" (Dorrien 2015, 295).

In the era of the new Jim Crow, it will be necessary to understand the role of political empowerment among those furthest on the margins—the undocumented, the disenfranchised, the formerly incarcerated—as well as the role of personal reform. As this book has suggested, the voices of the formerly incarcerated articulate a desire for both political and personal reform. While damaging caricatures of inner-city residents—such as the absentee parent or the uncaring neighbor—circulate, former gang members and formerly incarcerated persons strive to demonstrate that they are hard workers, good parents and neighbors, people of faith, and activists. While the Chicago School aggressively pursued top-down social reform and sought to willfully ignore the role of political empowerment in personal and social reform, the greatest potential for change may lie among the civil religious institutions that focus on the personal and the political. In turn, by virtue of their relationship with civil religious institutions, formerly incarcerated people may wield substantial resistance against the conditions under which they live—striving not simply for inward-focused rehabilitation, but to make good through personal and political reform.

ACKNOWLEDGMENTS

I thank the members of FORCE and the Homeboys Local Organizing Committee for allowing me the privilege to participate in and research their activities. My participation began when Reuben Miller, then a graduate student at Loyola University Chicago, invited me to serve as a panelist at a film screening of *The Interrupters*. Reuben subsequently introduced me to Eddie Bocanegra, who would go on to help found FORCE. I had just arrived in Chicago for my first job, but Eddie lost no time in having a one-on-one with me, inviting me to FORCE's "launch" meeting, and introducing me to many good people.

I thank colleagues affiliated with institutions in California. At the University of California, Merced, Bryan Amos and Maria Mora took a graduate-level critical criminology seminar with me, and helped to advance my understanding of social movements literature. Paul Almeida, Sharla Alegria, and Kyle Dodson provided helpful comments on a chapter that I presented at a department workshop. At the University of Southern California, Pierrette Hondagneu-Sotelo and Michael Messner asked about my book and—when we lived within walking distance of each other—provided a place where, on a nice afternoon, I could walk over with my infant twins in a double stroller and talk about the ideas in this book.

Special thanks go to colleagues at Loyola University Chicago. Jennifer Elena Cossyleon, my co-author in chapters 1 and 6, was indispensable to the development of this book. Jennifer joined me in doing fieldwork during the first few FORCE meetings, conducted and transcribed virtually every FORCE interview, helped me code for themes, and offered me valuable input about existing literature in the field. I shared many great conversations about FORCE with Jennifer, as well as with Quintin Williams, a Loyola graduate student who joined FORCE and produced a master's thesis involving his experiences. Last, Lucas Sharma, who left Loyola to enter the seminary, read the manuscript thoroughly and provided sharp, detailed comments—a jolt of clarity—when I needed it most.

I am grateful for the feedback I received from important practitioners in the field of faith-based community organizing and violence prevention. Rev. Zach Hoover provided me written comments, discussed his thoughts on the book, and then connected me with PICO National Network founder Father John Baumann, S.J. My conversation with Father John helped me to better understand what is often buried beneath the dominant narratives of Alinsky-influenced community organizing: the role of faith and spirituality. Kathryn Bocanegra, an expert in the violence-prevention field, was also gracious in providing feedback on parts of this book that involved FORCE.

This book benefited from several types of institutional support. The University of California, Social Science and Law Consortium (UC-SSL) provided a collaborative research working group grant, funding research examining the development of prisoner reentry—which eventually became chapter 1 in this book. In addition, I presented some of the material in this book at a Race and the Punitive State panel at the University of Southern California Department of Sociology's centennial anniversary symposium. Last, some of the material in this book was presented at an Ethnographer's Circle workshop, organized by BlackHawk Hancock, at the Pacific Sociological Association's annual meeting in 2015. Both BlackHawk and Sharon Oselin provided me with useful feedback at the workshop.

I acknowledge that portions of this book were adapted from the following previously published works: "'I Went Through it so You Don't Have To'" (with Jennifer Elena Cossyleon), in *Journal for the Scientific Study of Religion* (2016); "Prisoner Reentry Profits: Neoliberal, Public-Private Partnerships and Colorblind Racism," in *Challenging the Status Quo: Diversity, Democracy and Equality in the 21st Century*, edited by David G. Embrick, Sharon S. Collins, and Michelle Dodson (Brill Press, forthcoming); and "Thinking Outside the Box," in *Sojourners: Faith in Action for Social Justice* (2015).

Profound gratitude goes to my parents, Alberto Flores Jimenez and Maria Elena Orozco. My parents arrived in this country with very little but the hope that my life would be better than theirs. I have them to thank for my material well-being, but also for helping me to appreciate the importance of carrying such hope. I am also appreciative of my mother-in-law, Maggie Padilla. Apart from always recognizing moments in our lives that merit a good family celebration, Maggie helped take care of Rodrigo and Julian—especially when I was deep into writing this book.

My deepest appreciation goes to my spouse, Ana Maria Padilla, whom this book would not have been possible without. Ana has a background in community organizing and social movement unionism, and has never shied away from asking me about my research or telling me her thoughts on my work. It is for this reason that I immediately appreciated the significance of CRS and FORCE, began to research their activities, and decided to learn more about the field of local social movements. The many conversations we have had were instrumental in the development of this book. Ana also helped will this book into existence by doing far more than her share of childcare, entertaining our boys for countless evenings and weekends as the final manuscript came down the stretch.

This book is dedicated to Rodrigo and Julian, who are each a blessing and have brought tremendous laughter, joy, and peace into our lives. Since their birth, I have begun to better understand the importance of compassion, as well as many of the lessons emphasized by clergy in this book. I think of these lessons from time to time, together with my earliest childhood memories: having parents who were undocumented, and the fear and uncertainty that loomed as the state threatened to separate us. I dedicate this book to Rodrigo and Julian because I hope that one day they will bear witness not just to the injustices of the world but to the inspiring actions of those who dare to make a change.

NOTES

INTRODUCTION

1 Returning citizenship falls into James Holston's (2009, 9) category of "insurgent citizenship," which refers to marginalized groups expanding their citizenship rights. However, I use the narrower term "cultural citizenship" (Rosaldo 1994, 57) because whereas insurgent citizenship is not necessarily cultural citizenship, the formation of cultural citizenship necessitates some degree of insurgency (e.g., Glenn 2002, 2011).

2 My analysis suggests thirty-eight of ninety-five ALA board members had clear ties to the eugenics movement.

3 Author's interview with Father John Baumann, November 16, 2017.

4 Du Bois's large influence on twentieth-century American sociology and civic activism is again noticeable through Saul Alinsky's work with Chicago School sociologist Louis Wirth. Sociologist Marshall Ganz (2009) noted that Alinsky had organized the Community Services Organization—and Cesar Chavez's mentor, Fred Ross—with the help of Louis Wirth, who had been involved with the postwar American Council on Race Relations. In addition, sociologist Marcus Hunter (2015) traced Du Bois's intellectual legacy on twentieth-century American sociology through Louis Wirth's research on urban neighborhoods and diversity.

5 Quintin Williams (2015) had more exposure to behind-the-scenes organizing than I did, and his well-written master's thesis reflects this level of ethnographic depth.

6 To protect subjects' anonymity, I used pseudonyms for all persons who were not clergy or lead organizers; I did not use pseudonyms for clergy (e.g., Rev. Zach Hoover) or lead organizers (e.g., Eddie, Marlon, or Jose), as they were public figures with no expectation of privacy. This was reflected in my institutional review board (IRB) protocol that I shared with all primary subjects. I did not share the IRB protocol with secondary subjects; in many cases, secondary subjects knew that I was a professor doing research—or if they did not know I was doing research, I recorded only interactions in public spaces.

CHAPTER 1. THE INCORPORATION OF FAITH-BASED ORGANIZATIONS INTO CRIMINAL JUSTICE REFORM

1 It is worth noting that this first initiative was funded through the Department of Justice's appropriation of Community Oriented Policing Services funding. (This

information was received through an FOIA request submitted to the Department of Justice by the author).

2 Based on analysis by the chapter's co-author of information obtained by an FOIA request submitted by the author.

3 Data obtained from the California Endowment 2018 grantee database.

4 Data obtained from the California Endowment 2018 grantee database.

5 Data obtained from the California Endowment 2018 grantee database.

6 Data obtained from the California Endowment 2018 grantee database.

CHAPTER 2. PROPHETIC REDEMPTION

1 Author's interview with Father John Baumann, November 16, 2017.

2 LA Voice was exceptional, even within PICO, in this regard. Baumann claimed that LA Voice was exemplary; its relationships with congregations of diverse faiths was "the way [community organizing] should be" (personal interview with Baumann).

CHAPTER 3. MAKING GOOD THROUGH PROPHETIC REDEMPTION

1 David Brotherton (2007, 258) extended social movement scholarship's emphasis on "cognitive liberation" (McAdam 1982) and on indigenously trained activists (Morris 1984) to gangs.

2 See Rodriguez (2003) and Rodriguez (2011).

CHAPTER 4. "THERE IS TENSION IN DEMOCRACY"

1 CRS's model for community organizing was rooted in Alinsky's teachings, though the form of it may very well resonate with other forms of community organizing—such as that utilized by Ella Baker during the civil rights movement. Here I simply aim to emphasize that CRS lead organizer Alex Wiesendanger communicated meanings that drew from Alinsky-influenced polarizing discourse in ways that other modern groups have consciously moved away from. See Braunstein, Fulton, and Wood (2014) for a discussion of the ways in which modern faith-based community organizing groups have generally moved away from the militancy of issue-based community organizing.

2 I frame CRS's approach to community organizing as "issue-based," whereas CRS described itself as "issue-focused" and "relationship-based," because Alex, as the CRS lead organizer supporting FORCE, described CRS's approach as "issue-based"—especially during trainings.

CHAPTER 5. "IMAGINE A CIRCLE WITH NO ONE OUTSIDE OF IT"

1 It is common in community organizing for leaders to train less experienced members by giving them leadership opportunities. Jose signaled that he felt pressured to do so, however. The dynamic behind these tensions is unclear, as little research on community organizing has explored these types of tensions. Quintin Williams's (2015) research on FORCE might suggest, however, that the setting of

community organizing—as prophetic as it may be—still reproduces marginality among formerly incarcerated members, as the latter seek to find redemption in all things while leaders are less sensitive to such positionality.

2 Rev. Zach Hoover commented to me that this is a "classic PICO organizing principle."

3 Again, Rev. Hoover commented to me that this is a "classic PICO organizing principle."

CHAPTER 6. RETURNING CITIZENSHIP

1 Homeboys LOC members did not refer to their group as a community of kinship because Homeboy Industries was the larger group within which Homeboys LOC members shared experiences. See Flores (2014) for a discussion of how Homeboy Industries members built relationships with each other through clinical rehabilitation and twelve-step recovery groups.

CONCLUSION

1 A colleague from Loyola University Chicago had invited me to speak about *God's Gangs*, which had just been published.

2 Susan Burton's experience visiting the White House was deeply meaningful (Burton and Lynn 2017). Jose was mentioned earlier as having talked about his experience with visiting the White House through a faith reflection.

BIBLIOGRAPHY

Advisory Commission on Intergovernmental Relations. 1970. "Making the Safe Streets
    Act Work: An Intergovernmental Challenge." Commission Report A-36. Washing-
    ton, DC: Advisory Commission on Intergovernmental Relations.
Alexander, Michelle. 2010. *The New Jim Crow: Mass Incarceration in the Age of Color-
    blindness*. New York: New Press.
———. 2017. "Foreword." In Burton and Lynn, *Becoming Ms. Burton*, xi–xviii.
Alinsky, Saul D. 1941. "Community Analysis and Organizations." *American Journal of
    Sociology* 46(6):797–808.
———. 1957. "From Citizen Apathy to Participation." Paper presented at the Association
    of Community Councils of Chicago Sixth Annual Conference, Chicago.
———. 1971. *Rules for Radicals*. New York: Random House.
———. 1972. "Playboy Interview: Saul Alinsky." *Playboy*, March, 59–178.
Almeida, Paul D. 2003. "Opportunity Organizations and Threat Induced Conten-
    tion: Protest Waves in Authoritarian Settings." *American Journal of Sociology*
    109(2):345–400.
American Probation and Parole Association. 1987. "APPA Organizational Position
    Statements." *Perspectives*, Summer, 6–7.
Ammerman, Nancy T. 1997. *Congregation and Community*. New Brunswick, NJ: Rut-
    gers University Press.
Anderson, Elijah. 1990. *Streetwise: Race, Class, and Change in an Urban Community*.
    Chicago: University of Chicago Press.
Austin, Ernest. 2003. "Comments to the Little Hoover Commission." January 23. www.
    lhc.ca.gov.
Beckford, James A. 2012. "Public Religions and the Postsecular: Critical Reflections."
    Journal for the Scientific Study of Religion 51(1):1–19.
Bellah, Robert N. 1967. "Civil Religion in America." *Daedalus* 96:1–21.
Bellah, Robert N., Richard Madsen, William M. Sullivan, Ann Swidler, and Steven M.
    Tipton. 1985. *Habits of the Heart: Individualism and Commitment in Public Life*.
    Berkeley: University of California Press.
Bennett, William J., John J. DiIulio, and John P. Walters. 1996. *Body Count: Moral Pov-
    erty . . . and How to Win America's War against Crime and Drugs*. New York: Simon
    & Schuster.
Bentz, W. Kenneth. 1970. "The Clergyman's Role in Community Mental Health." *Jour-
    nal of Religion and Health* 9(1):7–15.

Berger, Dan. 2014. *Captive Nation: Black Prison Organizing in the Civil Rights Era.* Chapel Hill: University of North Carolina Press.

Biebricher, Thomas. 2011. "Faith-Based Initiatives and the Challenges of Governance." *Public Administration* 89(3):1001–14.

Billson, Janet Mancini. 1984. "Saul Alinsky: The Contributions of a Pioneer Clinical Sociologist." *Clinical Sociology Review* 2(1):7–11.

Bonilla-Silva, Eduardo. 2003. *Racism without Racists: Color-Blind Racism and the Persistence of Racial Inequality.* Lanham, MD: Rowman & Littlefield.

Bosco, Robert J. 1998. "Connecticut Probation's Partnership with the Private Sector." In National Institute of Corrections, US Department of Justice (ed.), *Topics in Community Corrections, Annual Issue 1998: Privatizing Community Supervision,* 8–12. Longmont, CO: NIC Information Center.

Bourgois, Philippe, and Jeff Schonberg. 2009. *Righteous Dopefiend.* Berkeley: University of California Press.

Braithwaite, John. 1989. *Crime, Shame and Reintegration.* New York: Cambridge University Press.

Braunstein, Ruth. 2012. "Storytelling in Liberal Religious Advocacy." *Journal for the Scientific Study of Religion* 51(1):110–27.

———. 2017. *Prophets and Patriots: Faith in Democracy across the Political Divide.* Berkeley: University of California Press.

Braunstein, Ruth, Brad R. Fulton, and Richard L. Wood. 2014. "The Role of Bridging Cultural Practices in Racially and Socioeconomically Diverse Civic Organizations." *American Sociological Review* 79(4):705–25.

Brenneman, Robert. 2011. *Homies and Hermanos: God and Gangs in Central America.* New York: Oxford University Press.

Briggs, Xavier de Souza, Elizabeth Mueller, and Mercer Sullivan. 1997. *From Neighborhood to Community: Evidence on the Social Effects of Community Development Corporations.* New York: Community Development Research Center.

Brotherton, David C. 2007. "Toward the Gang as a Social Movement." In Hagedorn (ed.), *Gangs in the Global City,* 251–72.

———. 2008. "Youth Subcultures, Resistance, and the Street Organization in Late Modern New York." In Michael Flynn and David C. Brotherton (eds.), *Globalizing the Streets: Cross-Cultural Perspectives on Youth, Social Control and Empowerment,* 114–32. New York: Columbia University Press.

Brotherton, David C., and Luis Barrios. 2004. *The Almighty Latin King and Queen Nation: Street Politics and the Transformation of a New York City Gang.* New York: Columbia University Press.

Burawoy, Michael, Alice Burton, Ann Arnett Ferguson, Kathryn J. Fox, Joshua Gamson, Nadine Gartrell, Leslie Hurst, Charles Kurzman, Leslie Salzinger, Josepha Schiffman, and Shiori Ui. 1991. *Ethnography Unbound: Power and Resistance in the Modern Metropolis.* Berkeley: University of California Press.

Bureau of Justice Assistance. 2018. "Second Chance Act." Washington, DC: US Department of Justice. www.bja.gov.

Burgess, Ernest W., Joseph Lohman, and Clifford Shaw. 1937. "The Chicago Area Project." In Marjorie Bell (ed.), *Coping with Crime: Yearbook of the National Probation Association*, 8–28. New York: National Probation Association.

Burton, Susan, and Cari Lynn. 2017. *Becoming Ms. Burton: From Prison to Recovery to Leading the Fight for Incarcerated Women*. New York: New Press.

Caldwell, Leigh Ann. 2015. "Koch Brothers, White House Seize Momentum on Criminal Justice Reform." *NBC News*, December 16. www.nbcnews.com.

Caputo, Angela. 2013. "Cell Blocks." *Chicago Reporter*, March 1. http://chicagoreporter.com.

Carr, Summerson E. 2010. *Scripting Addiction: The Politics of Therapeutic Talk and American Sobriety*. Princeton, NJ: Princeton University Press.

Chambers, Edward. 2003. *Roots for Radicals: Organizing for Power, Action, and Justice*. New York: Bloomsbury.

Clark, Michael D. 2005. "Motivational Interviewing for Probation Staff: Increasing the Readiness for Change." *Federal Probation* 69(2):22–28.

Cnaan, Ram A., and Stephanie C. Boddie. 2001. "Philadelphia Census of Congregations and Their Involvement in Social Service Delivery." *Social Service Review* 75(4):559–80.

Collins, Patricia Hill. 1990. *Black Feminist Thought: Knowledge, Consciousness, and the Politics of Empowerment*. Boston: Unwin Hyman.

Community Renewal Society. 2012. "The FORCE (Fighting to Overcome Records and Create Equality) Project." www.youtube.com/watch?v=njnGXR4dQUw.

Connell, R. W. [1995] 2005. *Masculinities*. Berkeley: University of California Press.

Conquergood, Dwight. 1994. "Homeboys and Hoods: Gang Communication and Cultural Space." In Lawrence R. Frey (ed.), *Group Communication in Context: Studies of Natural Groups*, 23–56. Hillsdale, NJ: Lawrence Erlbaum.

Cossyleon, Jennifer Elena. 2012. "Family in Context: (Re)entry Narratives of Formerly Incarcerated Individuals." Master's thesis, Department of Sociology, Loyola University Chicago.

Council of State Governments. 1935a. "Chapter XIII: Entente Cordiale: Relationships of the American Legislators' Association to Other Organizations of Public Officials." In *Book of States*, 140–48. Chicago: Council of State Governments and American Legislator's Association.

———. 1935b. "Saturday Morning Session." In *Book of States*, 453–59. Chicago: Council of State Governments and American Legislator's Association.

———. 1968. "State Services for Children and Youth." In *Book of the States 1968*, 384–91. Lexington, KY: Council of State Governments.

———. 1972. "Cumulative Index to Suggested State Legislation 1941–1973." Lexington, KY: Council of State Governments.

———. 1976. "Suggested State Legislation on Criminal Justice Standards and Goals." Lexington, KY: Council of State Governments.

Crittenden, Ann. 2001. *The Price of Motherhood*. New York: Henry Holt.

Dagan, David, and Steven Teles. 2016. *Prison Break: Why Conservatives Turned against Mass Incarceration*. New York: Oxford University Press.

Davis, Angela. 2004. "Interview: The Challenge of Prison Abolition." *History Is a Weapon*, n.d. www.historyisaweapon.com.

Decker, Scott H., and Janet L. Lauritsen. 1996. "Breaking the Bonds of Membership: Leaving the Gang." In C. Ronald Huff (ed.), *Gangs in America*, 103–22. Thousand Oaks, CA: Sage.

Decker, Scott H., David C. Pyrooz, and Richard K. Moule Jr. 2014. "Disengagement from Gangs as Role Transitions." *Journal of Research on Adolescence* 24(2):268–83.

Dodson, Kimberly D., Leann N. Cabage, and Paul M. Klenowski. 2011. "An Evidence-Based Assessment of Faith-Based Programs: Do Faith-Based Programs 'Work' to Reduce Recidivism?" *Journal of Offender Rehabilitation* 50(6):367–83.

Dorrien, Gary. 2015. *The New Abolition: W. E. B. Du Bois and the Black Social Gospel.* New Haven, CT: Yale University Press.

Du Bois, W. E. B. 1899. *Philadelphia Negro: A Social Study.* Philadelphia: University of Pennsylvania Press.

———. [1903] 2007. *The Souls of Black Folk.* New York: Oxford University Press.

———. [1935] 2007. *Black Reconstruction in America.* New York: Oxford University Press.

Ebaugh, Helen Rose. 1988. *Becoming an Ex: The Process of Role Exit.* Chicago: University of Chicago Press.

Ehrenreich, Barbara. 2009. *Bright-Sided: How the Relentless Promotion of Positive Thinking Has Undermined America.* New York: Metropolitan Books.

Eliasoph, Nina. 2012. *The Politics of Volunteering.* Cambridge: Polity Press.

———. 2013. "'Plug-in Volunteering' Doesn't Cut It." *Los Angeles Times*, January 21. http://articles.latimes.com.

Emerson, Michael O. 2008. *People of the Dream: Multiracial Congregations in the United States.* Princeton, NJ: Princeton University Press.

Espiritu, Yen Le. 1997. *Asian American Women and Men: Labor, Laws, and Love.* Thousand Oaks, CA: Sage.

Fader, Jamie J. 2013. *Falling Back: Incarceration and Transitions to Adulthood among Urban Youth.* New Brunswick, NJ: Rutgers University Press.

Fairbanks, Robert P. 2009. *How It Works: Recovering Citizens in a Post-welfare Philadelphia.* Chicago: University of Chicago Press.

Fendrich, James M. 1993. *Ideal Citizens: The Legacy of the Civil Rights Movement.* Albany: State University of New York Press.

Flores, Edward Orozco. 2014. *God's Gangs: Barrio Ministry, Masculinity and Gang Recovery.* New York: New York University Press.

———. 2015. "Thinking Outside the Box." *Sojourners*, November.

———. Forthcoming. "Prisoner Reentry Profits: Neoliberal, Public-Private Partnerships and Colorblind Racism." In David G. Embrick, Sharon S. Collins, and Michelle Dodson (eds.), *Challenging the Status Quo: Diversity, Democracy and Equality in the 21st Century.* Leiden, Netherlands: Brill Press.

Flores, Edward Orozco, and Jennifer Elena Cossyleon. 2016. "'I Went through It So You Don't Have To': Faith-Based Community Organizing for the Formerly Incarcerated." *Journal for the Scientific Study of Religion* 55(4):662–76.

Flores, Edward Orozco, and Pierrette Hondagneu-Sotelo. 2013. "Chicano Gang Members in Recovery: The Public Talk of Negotiating Chicano Masculinities." *Social Problems* 60(4):476–90.

Fox, Cybelle. 2012. *Three Worlds of Relief: Race, Immigration, and the American Welfare State from the Progressive Era to the New Deal.* Princeton, NJ: Princeton University Press.

Fremon, Celeste. [1995] 2004. *G-Dog and the Homeboys: Father Greg Boyle and the Gangs of East Los Angeles.* Albuquerque: University of New Mexico Press.

Gans, Herbert J. 1962. *The Urban Villagers: Group and Class in the Life of Italian-Americans.* New York: Free Press.

Ganz, Marshall. 2009. *Why David Sometimes Wins: Leadership, Organization, and Strategy in the California Farm Worker Movement.* New York: Oxford University Press.

Garland, David. 2001. *The Culture of Control: Crime and Social Order in Contemporary Society.* Chicago: University of Chicago Press.

Garot, Robert. 2010. *Who You Claim: Performing Gang Identity in School and on the Streets.* New York: New York University Press.

Gilmore, Ruth Wilson. 2007a. *Golden Gulag: Prisons, Surplus, Crisis, and Opposition in Globalizing California.* Berkeley: University of California Press.

———. 2007b. "In the Shadow of the Shadow State." In INCITE! Women of Color Against Violence (ed.), *Revolution Will Not Be Funded,* 41–52.

Giorgi, Simona, Jean M. Bartunek, and Brayden G. King. 2017. "A Saul Alinsky Primer for the 21st Century: The Roles of Cultural Competence and Cultural Brokerage in Fostering Mobilization in Support of Change." *Research in Organizational Behavior* 37:125–42.

Glenn, Evelyn Nakano. 2002. *Unequal Freedom: How Race and Gender Shaped American Citizenship and Labor.* Cambridge, MA: Harvard University Press.

———. 2011. "Constructing Citizenship: Exclusion, Subordination, and Resistance." *American Sociological Review* 76(1):1–24.

Goodman, Philip, Joshua Page, and Michelle Phelps. 2017. *Breaking the Pendulum: The Long Struggle over Criminal Justice.* New York: Oxford University Press.

Gottschalk, Marie. 2015. *Caught: The Prison State and the Lockdown of American Politics.* Princeton, NJ: Princeton University Press.

Gowan, Teresa, and Sarah Whetstone. 2012. "Making the Criminal Addict: Subjectivity and Social Control in a Strong-Arm Rehab." *Punishment & Society* 14(1): 69–93.

Gravante, Tommaso, and Alice Poma. 2016. "Environmental Self-Organized Activism: Emotion, Organization and Collective Identity in Mexico." *International Journal of Sociology and Social Policy* 36(9–10):647–61.

Gutterman, David. 2005. *Prophetic Politics: Christian Social Movements and American Democracy.* Ithaca, NY: Cornell University Press.

Hacket, Judith C., Harry Hatry, Robert Levison, Joan Allen, Keon Chi, and Edward Feigenbaum. 1986. "Issues in Contracting for the Private Operation of Prisons and Jails." Lexington, KY: Council of State Governments.

Hagan, John. 2010. *Who Are the Criminals? The Politics of Crime Policy from the Age of Roosevelt to the Age of Reagan*. Princeton, NJ: Princeton University Press.

Hagan, John, and Bill McCarthy. 1997. *Mean Streets: Youth Crime and the Homeless*. New York: Cambridge University Press.

Hagedorn, John M. 1994. *A World of Gangs: Armed Young Men and Gangsta Culture*. Minneapolis: University of Minnesota Press.

——, ed. 2007a. *Gangs in the Global City: Alternatives to Traditional Criminology*. Chicago: University of Illinois Press.

——. 2007b. "Gangs, Institutions, Race, and Space: The Chicago School Revisited." In Hagedorn (ed.), *Gangs in the Global City*, 13–33.

Haney, Lynne. 2010. *Offending Women: Power, Punishment, and the Regulation of Desire*. Berkeley: University of California Press.

Hart, Stephen. 2001. *Cultural Dilemmas of Progressive Politics: Styles of Engagement among Grassroots Activists*. Chicago: University of Chicago Press.

Heath, Melanie. 2005. "Soft-Boiled Masculinity: Renegotiating Gender and Racial Ideologies in the Promise Keepers Movement." *Gender & Society* 17(3):423–44.

Hoffmann, Heath C. 2006. "Criticism as Deviance and Social Control in Alcoholics Anonymous." *Journal of Contemporary Ethnography* 35(6):669–95.

Holston, James. 2009. *Insurgent Citizenship: Disjunctions of Modernity in Brazil*. Princeton, NJ: Princeton University Press.

Hondagneu-Sotelo, Pierrette. 2008. *God's Heart Has No Borders: How Religious Activists Are Working for Immigrant Rights*. Berkeley: University of California Press.

Horowitz, Ruth. 1983. *Honor and the American Dream: Culture and Identity in a Chicano Community*. New Brunswick, NJ: Rutgers University Press.

Hunter, Marcus Anthony. 2015. "W. E. B. Du Bois and Black Heterogeneity: How *The Philadelphia Negro* Shaped American Sociology." *American Sociologist* 46(2):219–33.

Illinois Policy Institute. 2015. "May 20: Panel on Criminal Justice Reform in Illinois." Press Release, May 19. www.illinoispolicy.org.

Immergluck, Daniel. 2004. "Saul Alinsky." In George R. Goethals, Georgia Jones Sorenson, and James Macgregor Burns (eds.), *Encyclopedia of Leadership: A–E*, vol. 1, 25–29. Thousand Oaks, CA: Sage.

INCITE! Women of Color Against Violence, ed. 2007. *The Revolution Will Not Be Funded: Beyond the Non-profit Industrial Complex*. Cambridge, MA: South End Press.

Jacobsen, Dennis A. 2001. *Doing Justice: Congregations and Community Organizing*. Minneapolis: Fortress Press.

Jensen, Kenneth D., and Stephen G. Gibbons. 2002. "Shame and Religion as Factors in the Rehabilitation of Serious Offenders." *Journal of Offender Rehabilitation* 35(3–4):209–24.

Joel, Dana. 1988. "A Guide to Prison Privatization." Washington, DC: Heritage Foundation.

Johnson, Byron. 2004. "Religious Programs and Recidivism among Former Inmates in Prison Fellowship Programs." *Justice Quarterly* 21(2):329–54.

Johnson, Perry M. 1993. "Corrections Should Take the Lead in Changing Sentencing Practices." Keynote address to the American Correctional Association's 123rd Congress of Correction, Nashville, January 11.

Kane, R. Keith. 1942. "The O.F.F." *Public Opinion Quarterly* 6(2):204–20.

Kapor Center. 2014. "Inside the White House: My Brother's Keeper Initiative." www.kaporcenter.org.

Kaye, Kerwin. 2013. "Rehabilitating the 'Drugs Lifestyle': Criminal Justice, Social Control, and the Cultivation of Agency." *Ethnography* 14(2):207–32.

Kelling, George L., and James Q. Wilson. 1982. "Broken Windows: The Police and Neighborhood Safety." *Atlantic Monthly* 249(3):29–38. www.theatlantic.com.

Kimmel, Michael. 1996. *Manhood in America: A Cultural History.* New York: Free Press.

Lageson, Sarah Esther, Mike Vuolo, and Christopher Uggen. 2015. "Legal Ambiguity in Managerial Assessments of Criminal Records." *Law and Social Inquiry* 40(1):175–204.

Landesco, John. 1934. "The Story of the Gang." In *The Proceedings of the Attorney General's Conference on Crime, 424–34.* Washington, DC: Department of Justice.

Lattimore, Pamela K., Susan Brumbaugh, Christy Visher, Christine Lindquist, Laura Winterfield, Meghan Salas, and Janine Zweig. 2004. "National Portrait of SVORI: Serious and Violent Offender Reentry Initiative." Research report. Washington, DC: Urban Institute.

Laub, John H., and Robert J. Sampson. 2003. *Shared Beginnings, Divergent Lives: Delinquent Boys to Age 70.* Cambridge, MA: Harvard University Press.

León, Luis D. 1998. "Born Again in East LA: The Congregation as Border Space." In R. S. Warner and Judith G. Wittner (eds.), *Gatherings in Diaspora*, 163–96. Philadelphia: Temple University Press.

Lewis, Anthony. 1963. "10 States Ask Amendment to Gain Districting Rights." *New York Times*, April 13.

Lurigio, Arthur. 2005. "Safer Foundation Recidivism Study." Presentation at the American Correctional Association's 135th Congress of Correction, Baltimore, August 8.

Marshall, T. H. 1950. *Citizenship and Social Class, and Other Essays.* Cambridge: Cambridge University Press.

Maruna, Shadd. 2001. *Making Good: How Ex-Convicts Reform and Rebuild Their Lives.* Washington, DC: American Psychological Association.

Marwell, Nicole P. 2007. *Bargaining for Brooklyn: Community Organizations in the Entrepreneurial City.* Chicago: University of Chicago Press.

Mayer, Jane. 2016. "New Koch." *New Yorker*, January 25. www.newyorker.com.

McAdam, Doug. 1982. *Political Process and the Development of Black Insurgency 1930–1970.* Chicago: University of Chicago Press.

———. 1990. *Freedom Summer.* New York: Oxford University Press.

———. 1996. "Conceptual Origins, Current Problems, Future Directions." In Doug McAdam, John D. McCarthy, and Mayer N. Zald (eds.), *Comparative Perspectives on Social Movements: Political Opportunities, Mobilizing Structures, and Cultural Framings*, 23–40. New York: Cambridge University Press.

McAdam, Doug, Sidney Tarrow, and Charles Tilly. 2001. *Dynamics of Contention*. New York: Cambridge University Press.

McCarthy, John D., and Edward T. Walker. 2004. "Alternative Organizational Repertoires of Poor People's Social Movement Organizations." *Nonprofit and Voluntary Sector Quarterly* 33(3, suppl.):97s–119s.

McDonald, Kevin. 2003. "Marginal Youth, Personal Identity, and the Contemporary Gang: Reconstructing the Social World?" In Louis Kontos, David C. Brotherton, and Luis Barrios (eds.), *Gangs and Society: Alternative Perspectives*, 62–74. New York: Columbia University Press.

McRoberts, Omar M. 2002. "Religion, Reform, Community: Examining the Idea of Church-Based Prisoner Reentry." Roundtable at Prisoner Reentry and the Institutions of Civil Society: Bridges and Barriers to Successful Reintegration, Washington, DC, March 20–21.

———. 2003. *Streets of Glory: Church and Community in a Black Urban Neighborhood*. Chicago: University of Chicago Press.

Milkman, Ruth. 2006. *L.A. Story: Immigrant Workers and the Future of the U.S. Labor Movement*. New York: Russell Sage Foundation.

———. 2010. "Introduction." In Ruth Milkman, Joshua Bloom, and Victor Narro (eds.), *Working for Justice: The L.A. Model of Organizing and Advocacy*, 1–22. Ithaca, NY: Cornell University Press.

Miller, Reuben Jonathan. 2014. "Devolving the Carceral State: Race, Prisoner Reentry, and the Micro-politics of Urban Poverty Management." *Punishment & Society* 16(3):305–35.

Mills, C. Wright. 1940. "Situated Actions and Vocabularies of Motive." *American Sociological Review* 5(6):904–13.

Moloney, Deirdre M. 2002. *American Catholic Lay Groups and Transatlantic Social Reform in the Progressive Era*. Chapel Hill: University of North Carolina Press.

Moore, Joan W. 1978. *Homeboys: Gangs, Drugs and Prison in the Barrios of Los Angeles*. Philadelphia: Temple University Press.

———. 1991. *Going Down to the Barrio: Homeboys and Homegirls in Change*. Philadelphia: Temple University Press.

Morris, Aldon. 1984. *The Origins of the Civil Rights Movement*. New York: Free Press.

———. 2016. *The Scholar Denied: W. E. B. Du Bois and the Birth of Modern Sociology*. Los Angeles: University of California Press.

Moser, Whet. 2013. "The Small Social Networks at the Heart of Chicago Violence." *Chicago Magazine*, December 9. www.chicagomag.com.

Nagel, Joane. 1995. "American Indian Ethnic Renewal: Politics and the Resurgence of Identity." *American Sociological Review* 60(6):947–65.

Nolan, James, Jr. 1988. *The Therapeutic State: Justifying Government at Century's End*. New York: New York University Press.

Oberst, Paul. 1964. "Genesis of the Three States-Rights Amendments of 1963." *Notre Dame Law Review* 39(6):644–58.

O'Connor, Thomas, and Michael Perreyclear. 2002. "Prison Religion in Action and Its Influence on Offender Rehabilitation." *Journal of Offender Rehabilitation* 35(3–4):11–33.

O'Connor, Thomas, Patricia Ryan, and Crystal Parikh. 1998. "A Model Program for Churches and Ex-offender Reintegration." *Journal of Offender Rehabilitation* 28(1–2):107–26.

Omi, Michael, and Howard Winant. [1986] 1994. *Racial Formation in the United States. From the 1960's to the 1990's.* New York: Routledge.

O'Neill, Kevin Lewis. 2015. *Secure the Soul: Christian Piety and Gang Prevention in Guatemala.* Berkeley: University of California Press.

Open Society Institute. 2001. "U.S. Programs: 2000 Annual Report." New York: Open Society Institute.

———. 2002. "U.S. Programs: Soros Foundations Network 2001 Annual Report." New York: Open Society Institute.

———. 2003. "Building Open Societies: Soros Foundations Network 2002 Report." New York: Open Society Institute.

Oselin, Sharon. 2014. *Leaving Prostitution: Getting Out and Staying Out of Sex Work.* New York: New York University Press.

Owens, Michael Leo. 2014. "Ex-felons' Organization-Based Political Work for Carceral Reforms." *Annals of the American Academy of Political and Social Sciences* 651:256–65.

Owens, Michael Leo, and Hannah Walker. 2017. "Civic Voluntarism of 'Custodial Citizens': Involuntary Criminal Justice Contact, Associational Life and Political Participation." Manuscript invited to resubmit.

Padilla, Felix. 1992. *The Gang as an American Enterprise.* New Brunswick, NJ: Rutgers University Press.

Page, Joshua. 2011. *The Toughest Beat: Politics, Punishment, and the Prison Officers Union in California.* Oxford: Oxford University Press.

Pager, Devah. 2003. "The Mark of a Criminal Record." *American Journal of Sociology* 108(5):937–75.

Papachristos, Andrew V. 2009. "Murder by Structure: Dominance Relations and the Social Structure of Gang Homicide." *American Journal of Sociology* 115(1):74–128.

Park, Robert E., and Ernest W. Burgess. 1921. *Introduction to the Science of Sociology.* Chicago: University of Chicago Press.

Pattillo-McCoy, Mary. 1999. *Black Picket Fences: Privilege and Peril among the Black Middle Class.* Chicago: University of Chicago Press.

Peck, Jamie, and Nik Theodore. 2008. "Carceral Chicago: Making the Ex-offender Employability Crisis." *International Journal of Urban and Regional Research* 32(2):251–81.

PICO National Network. 2014a. "Faith Leaders Renew Resolve to Be Their Brother's Keeper; Expand Opportunity by Reducing Violence and Ending Mass Incarceration." Press release, February 26. www.piconetwork.org.

———. 2014b. "PICO Reacts to President's CHCI Speech: We Need More Than Words. We Need Action." October 2. www.piconetwork.org.

———. 2014c. "PICO Reacts to Unacceptable Delay of Administrative Action on Immigration Reform." Press release, September 5. www.piconetwork.org.

Polletta, Francesca. 1998. "'It Was Like a Fever . . .': Narrative and Identity in Social Protest." *Social Problems* 45(2):137–59.

Polsky, Andrew J. 1991. *The Rise of the Therapeutic State*. Princeton, NJ: Princeton University Press.

Prieto, Greg. 2016. "Opportunity, Threat, and Tactics: Collaboration and Confrontation by Latino Immigrant Challengers." In Landon E. Hancock (ed.), *Narratives of Identity in Social Movements, Conflicts and Change*, 123–54. Bingley, UK: Emerald.

Pyrooz, David C., and Scott H. Decker. 2011. "Motives and Methods for Leaving the Gang: Understanding the Process of Gang Desistance." *Journal of Criminal Justice* 39:417–25.

Reese, Ellen, Vincent Giedraitis, and Eric Vega. 2005. "Mobilization and Threat: Campaigns against Welfare Privatization in Four Cities." *Sociological Focus* 38(4):287–307.

Reinventing Probation Council. 1999. "'Broken Windows' Probation: The Next Step in Fighting Crime." Civic Report No. 7. New York: Manhattan Institute, Center for Civic Innovation.

———. 2000. "'Transforming Probation through Leadership: The 'Broken Windows' Model." New York: Manhattan Institute, Center for Civic Innovation.

Reitzes, Donald C., and Dietrich C. Reitzes. 1986. "Alinsky in the 1980s: Two Contemporary Chicago Community Organizations." *Sociological Quarterly* 28(2):265–83.

Reynolds, Morgan O. 2000. "Privatizing Probation and Parole." Policy Report No. 233. Dallas, TX: National Center for Policy Analysis.

Rhine, Edward E., Gary Hinzman, Ronald P. Corbett, Dan Richard Beto, and Mario Paparozzi. 2001. "'The Broken Windows Model for Probation': A Call for Transforming Community Supervision." *Perspectives* 25(2):30–33.

Rios, Victor M. 2011. *Punished: Policing the Lives of Black and Latino Boys*. New York: New York University Press.

Rodriguez, Dylan. 2004. "Interview: The Challenge of Prison Abolition." *History Is a Weapon*, n.d. www.historyisaweapon.com.

———. 2007. "The Political Logic of the Non-profit Industrial Complex." In INCITE! Women of Color Against Violence (ed.), *Revolution Will Not Be Funded*, 21–40.

Rodriguez, Luis J. 2003. *Hearts and Hands: Creating Community in Violent Times*. New York: Seven Stories Press.

———. 2011. *It Calls You Back: An Odyssey through Love, Addiction, Revolutions, and Healing*. New York: Simon & Schuster.

Rodriguez, Michelle Natividad, and Beth Avery. 2017. "Ban the Box: U.S. Cities, Counties, and States Adopt Fair-Chance Policies to Advance Employment Opportunities for People with Past Convictions." Resource guide. San Francisco: National Employment Law Project.

Romney, Lee. 2015. "Formerly Incarcerated Activist Fights to Give People a Chance to Change." *Los Angeles Times*, March 13. www.latimes.com.

Rosaldo, Renato. 1994. "Cultural Citizenship in San Jose, California." *Political and Legal Anthropology Review* 17(2):57–64.

Rose, Nikolas. 1990. *Governing the Soul: The Shaping of the Private Self.* London: Routledge.

Sampson, Robert, Stephen W. Raudenbush, and Felton Earls. 1997. "Neighborhood and Violent Crime: A Multilevel Study of Collective Efficacy." *Science* 277(5328):918–24.

Sanchez-Walsh, Arlene. 2003. *Latino Pentecostal Identity: Evangelical Faith, Self, and Society.* New York: Columbia University Press.

Schoenfeld, Heather. 2016. "A Research Agenda on Reform: Penal Policy and Politics across the States." *Annals of the American Academy of Political and Social Sciences* 664:155–74.

Sharkey, Patrick, Gerard Torrats-Espinosa, and Delaram Takyar. 2017. "Community and the Crime Decline: The Causal Effect of Local Nonprofits on Violent Crime." *American Sociological Review* 82(6):1214–40.

Simon, Jonathan. 2007. *Governing through Crime: How the War on Crime Transformed American Democracy and Created a Culture of Fear.* New York: Oxford University Press.

Slessarev-Jamir, Helene. 2010. "Prophetic Activism in an Age of Empire." *Political Theology* 11:674–90.

———. 2011. *Prophetic Activism: Progressive Religious Justice Movements in Contemporary America.* New York: New York University Press.

Smith, Andrea. 2007. "Introduction: The Revolution Will Not Be Funded." In INCITE! Women of Color Against Violence (ed.), *Revolution Will Not Be Funded*, 1–20.

Smith, Christian. 1996. *Disruptive Religion: The Force of Faith in Social Movement Activism.* New York: Routledge.

Smith, Johnathan J. 2014. "Banning the Box but Keeping the Discrimination? Disparate Impact and Employers' Overreliance on Criminal Background Checks." *Harvard Civil Rights-Civil Liberties Law Review* 49:197–228.

Soja, Edward. 2014. *My Los Angeles: From Urban Restructuring to Regional Urbanization.* Berkeley: University of California Press.

Stacey, Judith. 1990. *Brave New Families: Stories of Domestic Upheaval in Late-Twentieth-Century America.* New York: Basic Books.

Stanley, Eric A. 2014. "Interview: The Carceral State." *New Inquiry*, November 12. https://thenewinquiry.com.

Stanley, Jay. 2014. "Chicago Police 'Heat List' Renews Old Fears about Government Flagging and Tagging." *Free Future*, February 25. www.aclu.org.

Stuart, Forrest. 2016. *Down, Out and Under Arrest: Policing and Everyday Life in Skid Row.* Chicago: University of Chicago Press.

Swarts, Heidi. 2008. *Organizing Urban America: Secular and Faith-Based Progressive Movements.* Minneapolis: University of Minnesota Press.

Taylor, Robert Joseph, Christopher G. Ellison, Linda M. Chatters, Jeffrey S. Levin, and Karen D. Lincoln. 2000. "Mental Health Services in Faith Communities: The Role of Clergy in Black Churches." *Social Work* 45(1):73–87.

Thomas, Robert C., Kathy Gookin, Beth Keating, and Valerie Whitener. 1999. "Lessons Learned from Evaluating the Feasibility of Privatizing Government Services." *New Directions for Evaluations* 81:23–31.

Thomas, William Isaac, and Florian Znaniecki. 1918. *The Polish Peasant in Europe and America: Monograph of an Immigrant Group.* Chicago: University of Chicago Press.

Thrasher, Frederic. 1927. *The Gang: A Study of 1,313 Gangs in Chicago.* Chicago: University of Chicago Press.

———. [1927] 1936. *The Gang: A Study of 1,313 Gangs in Chicago.* 2nd ed. Chicago: University of Chicago Press.

Tilly, Charles. 1978. *From Mobilization to Revolution.* Reading, MA: Addison-Wesley.

Toll, Henry W. 1928. "The Work of the American Legislators' Association." *American Political Science Review* 22(1):127–29.

———. 1934. "State Legislation in the Field of Criminal Law." In *The Proceedings of the Attorney General's Conference on Crime,* 366–80. Washington, DC: Department of Justice.

Toney, Mark Warren. 2007. "A Second Chance—For the First Time: Movement Formation among Formerly Incarcerated People." Doctoral dissertation, University of California, Berkeley.

Travis, Jeremy. 2003. "Testimony before Little Hoover Commission." February 27. www.lhc.ca.gov.

———. 2005. *But They All Come Back: Facing the Challenges of Prisoner Reentry.* Washington, DC: Urban Institute Press.

———. 2007. "Reflections on the Reentry Movement." *Federal Sentencing Reporter* 20(2):1–4.

Turner, Victor. 1966. *The Ritual Process: Structure and Anti-structure.* Ithaca, NY: Cornell University Press.

University of Chicago Crime Lab. 2012. "BAM—Sports Edition." Chicago: University of Chicago Crime Lab.

Urban Institute. 2013. "Bureau of Justice Assistance. 2013. The Justice Reinvestment Initiative: Experiences from the States." Brief, July. Washington, DC: Urban Institute.

US Department of Justice. 2008. "Federal Funding & Services for Prisoner Reentry." Task Force for Faith-Based & Community Initiatives, April 25. Washington, DC: US Department of Justice.

Van Dyke, Nella, and Marc Dixon. 2013. "Activist Human Capital: Skills Acquisition and the Development of Commitment to Social Movement Activism." *Mobilization* 18(2):197–212.

Van Dyke, Nella, and Sarah A. Soule. 2002. "Structural Social Change and the Mobilizing Effect of Threat: Explaining Levels of Patriot and Militia Organizing in the United States." *Social Problems* 49(4):497–520.

Vargas, Robert. 2016. *Wounded City: Violent Turf Wars in a Chicago Barrio.* New York: Oxford University Press.

Vigil, James Diego. 1988. *Barrio Gangs: Street Life and Identity in Southern California.* Austin: University of Texas Press.

Wacquant, Loïc. 2010. "Prisoner Reentry as Myth and Ceremony." *Dialectical Anthropology* 34(4):605–20.

Walker, Edward T. 2014. *Grassroots for Hire: Public Affairs Consultants in American Democracy.* New York: Cambridge University Press.

Warner, R. Stephen. 1993. "Work in Progress toward a New Paradigm for the Sociological Study of Religion in the United States." *American Journal of Sociology* 98(5):1044–93.

Warren, Mark R., and Karen L. Mapp. 2011. *A Match on Dry Grass: Community Organizing as a Catalyst for School Reform.* New York: Oxford University Press.

Warren, Mark R., Karen L. Mapp, and Paul J. Kuttner. 2015. "From Private Citizens to Public Actors: The Development of Parent Leaders through Community Organizing." In Michael P. Evans and Diana B. Hiatt-Michael (eds.), *The Power of Community Engagement for Educational Change*, 21–40. Charlotte, NC: Information Age.

Watkins-Hayes, Celeste, LaShawnDa Pittman-Gay, and Jean Beaman. 2012. "'Dying From' to 'Living With': Framing Institutions and the Coping Processes of African American Women Living with HIV/AIDS." *Social Science & Medicine* 74(12):2028–36.

Weber, Max. [1905] 2005. *The Protestant Ethic and the Spirit of Capitalism.* New York: Routledge.

Western, Bruce, Leonard M. Lopoo, and Sara McLanahan. 2004. "Incarceration and the Bonds between Parents in Fragile Families." In Mary Patillo, David Weiman, and Bruce Western (eds.), *Imprisoning America: The Social Effects of Mass Incarceration*, 21–45. New York: Russell Sage.

White House. 2008. "Innovations in Compassion. The Faith-Based and Community Initiative: A Final Report to the Armies of Compassion." White House Office of Faith-Based and Community Initiatives, December. http://digitalcommons.ilr. cornell.edu.

———. 2014. "Remarks by the President on 'My Brother's Keeper' Initiative." White House Office of the Press Secretary, February 27. http://obamawhitehouse.archives.gov

Whittier, Nancy. 2009. *The Politics of Child Sexual Abuse: Emotion, Social Movements, and the State.* New York: Oxford University Press.

———. 2013. "Gender and Social Movements." In David A. Snow, Donatella Della Porta, Bert Klandermans, and Doug McAdam (eds.), *Wiley-Blackwell Encyclopedia of Social and Political Movements*, vol. 2, 503–7. Hoboken, NJ: Wiley-Blackwell.

Whyte, William F. 1943. *Street Corner Society: The Social Structure of an Italian Slum.* Boulder, CO: Westview.

Williams, Quintin. 2015. "Returning Citizens? The Path from Prison to Politics among the Formerly Incarcerated." Master's thesis, Department of Sociology, Loyola University Chicago.

Williams, Rhys, and N. J. Demerath III. 1991. "Religion and Political Process in an American City." *American Sociological Review* 56:417–31.

Wilson, William J. 1987. *The Truly Disadvantaged*. Chicago: University of Chicago Press.

Wineburg, Robert J., Brian L. Coleman, Stephanie C. Boddie, and Ram A. Cnaan. 2008. "Leveling the Playing Field: Epitomizing Devolution through Faith-Based Organizations." *Journal of Sociology & Social Welfare* 35(1):17–42.

Wood, Richard. 1999. "Religious Culture and Political Action." *Sociological Theory* 17(3):307–32.

———. 2002. *Faith in Action: Religion, Race and Democratic Organizing in America*. Chicago: University of Chicago Press.

Wood, Richard, and Brad Fulton. 2015. *A Shared Future: Faith-Based Organizing for Racial Equity and Ethical Democracy*. Chicago: University of Chicago Press.

Wood, Richard, Brad Fulton, and Kathryn Partridge. 2012. "Building Bridges, Building Power: Developments in Institution-Based Community Organizing." Denver, CO: Interfaith Funders.

INDEX

AB 953. *See* California Assembly Bill 953

abolitionism, 8–9, 10, 165

absolute bars legislation, 111, 112, 164

Age of Reagan: Hagan on, 6; public service privatization in, 30–31

Age of Roosevelt, 6, 11–12

Alinsky, Saul, 12, 13, 23, 95, 98, 112, 114, 146–47; *Rules for Radicals* by, 51. *See also* issue-based community organizing

ALKQN. *See* Almighty Latin King and Queen Nation

All of Us or None (AOUON), 6, 7, 52

Almighty Latin King and Queen Nation (ALKQN), 69, 71

American Probation and Parole Association (APPA), 22; broken windows probation and, 33; for-profit privatization and, 31, 41; legislation and, 32, 41; public-private partnerships and, 29–30

AOUON. *See* All of Us or None

APPA. *See* American Probation and Parole Association

Ban-the-Box movement, 7, 39, 52–53, 138; Homeboys LOC and, 123–24; PICO and, 14; prophetic redemption and, 5–6

Baumann, John, 125; on community organizing, 53–54; PICO founded by, 13–14, 53

Beckford, James, 28

Black Panthers, 8; community organizing of, 135. *See also* Davis, Angela

Black Protestant church: CRS and, 7, 18, 23, 43, 55, 113; prophetic redemption and, 9; Reconstruction-era, 9–10

Bocanegra, Eduardo "Eddie," 48–49, 79, 90, 92–98, 106, 108–9, 114; CeaseFire and, 68–69; FORCE founded by, 18–19, 68; *The Interrupters* and, 68, 71–72, 74; at YMCA Chicago, 73

Boston Strategy to Prevent Youth Violence, 32

Boyle, Gregory "Father Greg," 65, 78, 125, 132–33, 139; community organizing and, 119–20; identity of Homeboy Industries and, 129

BPI. *See* Business and Professional People for the Public Interest

broken windows policing, 33

broken windows probation, 41; APPA and, 33; OFBCI and, 35–36; OSF and, 34; Reinventing Probation Council and, 33

Brown, Michael, 38

Burton, Susan, 6, 52–54; A New Way of Life and, 7, 52

Bush, George W.: OFBCI and, 35; Prisoner Reentry Initiative of, 36

Business and Professional People for the Public Interest (BPI), 163–64

California Assembly Bill 953 (AB 953), 129–31; LA Voice and, 130; PICO and, 129–30

California Endowment, 36–38, 41

California prisoner reentry: California Endowment and, 36–38; California Proposition 47 and, 37; Ceasefire program for, 38; PICO and, 37–38

California Proposition 36 (Prop 36), 87

California Proposition 47 (Prop 47), 37, 88, 125, 140; canvassing and, 116, 117, 118, 127; civic engagement and, 116–17; LA Voice and, 47–48, 115, 116; meeting for, 115–17; relationship-based community organizing for, 118

Calvinist Puritanism, 159–60

CAP. *See* Chicago Area Project

career criminal, 6

Catholic church, 18; Homeboys LOC and, 142; LA Voice and, 7, 19, 23, 61, 91, 140, 142; PICO and, 17, 140

CBOs. *See* community-based organizations

CeaseFire, 2, 38; Bocanegra and, 68–69

Chamberlin, Marlon, 43, 46, 49–50, 75, 90, 100, 104, 111, 113; Bocanegra and, 48–49; FORCE and, 74–75; Sealing Bill and, 44–45, 74; voter registration and, 75–76

Chambers, Edward, 53, 147

Chicago Area Project (CAP), 10

Chicago Mayor's Reentry Initiative (2006), 39

Chicago prisoner reentry, 36; Chicago Mayor's Reentry Initiative for, 39; public-private partnerships and, 39

Chicago School of sociology, 16, 162; Age of Roosevelt and, 12; CSG and, 11–12; Du Bois and, 10; on gangs, 69; in late twentieth-century, 14; top-down reform and, 169. *See also* Alinsky, Saul

church. *See* Black Protestant church; Catholic Church; Los Angeles Metropolitan Churches (LAM)

citizenship: cultural citizenship, 24, 160; racism and, 144–45; social citizenship, 144–45; substantive rights of, 144. *See also* returning citizenship

civic engagement, 8, 19–20, 23, 29, 105, 163; of Chamberlin, 46; FORCE and, 1–2, 166; Homeboys LOC and, 166;

issues of, 21; of LA Voice, 45; Prop 47 and, 116–17; volunteerism and, 54

civil religion, 14, 16, 21, 25; Chamberlin and, 75; LA Voice and CRS and, 22, 66

collective action, 69, 154–56, 163; FORCE and, 67, 71, 107–11; of Homeboys LOC, 67, 71, 119; kinship and, 156–58; as positivity, 158–61; therapeutic discourse and, 70, 114

collective efficacy, 154–56

community-based organizations (CBOs), 16, 22, 29–30, 40, 165–66; criminal justice reform and, 41; elite civic organizations and, 41; former gang members and, 50; grassroots resistance, 41; prisoner reentry and, 34, 36

community organizing, faith-based: activities of, 20; Baumann on, 53–54; of Black Panthers, 135; Boyle and, 119–20; campaigns and, 66; Chambers on, 53; critical race scholars on, 8; cultural brokerage and, 71; cultural deficit narratives, 24, 146, 149, 150–52, 156; democratic inclusion and, 21, 66; diverse religions shaping, 13; FORCE and, 2, 8, 92–93, 101, 103; Gilda and, 80–83, 90; hierarchy in, 96; Homeboy Industries and, 19–20; Homeboys LOC and LA Voice model of, 120–21; Olivia and, 78–80; Oscar and, 83–86; PICO principles of, 124, 133; progressive prophetic activism and, 3; prophetic redemption and, 8–9, 45; public-private distinction and, 146–47; recovery and, 8, 95; relationship-based model of, 13–14, 23, 53–54, 62; sexism and, 147; Smith on, 93; social integration and, 22, 67; strategies of, 8; structural barrier narratives in, 146, 152–54, 156, 158; vocabularies of motive for, 71, 90. *See also* Bocanegra, Eduardo "Eddie"; Chamberlin, Marlon; issue-based community organiz-

ing; Osuna, Jose; relationship-based community organizing
community-probation partnerships, 29, 30
Community Renewal Society (CRS), 2–3, 4, 8, 60, 107; Black Catholic Church and, 18; Black Protestant church and, 7, 18, 23, 43, 55, 113; campaigns of, 21, 57; civil religion and, 22, 66; Congregational Church founding, 17; elected official accountability, 57, 58, 59, 66; elevator speeches of, 107–9, 113; faith in action message of, 43, 44; FORCE relationship with, 135; house meetings of, 44, 93, 113; insurgent prophetic redemption and, 45, 51, 55–56, 59, 114, 165; issue-based community organizing principles of, 52, 97, 113, 176n1; Knox and, 43, 56–57; legislative campaigns of, 47; lobbying of, 59; mission of, 17–18; personal and political reform and, 24; personal reform and, 24, 90–91; polarizing practices of, 114; political activism of, 98–99; power for, 97–99, 108, 114; prep sessions for, 110–13; progressive prophetic activism and, 43, 56; prophetic activism and, 39, 45; prophetic redemption and, 113, 164–65; ritualized displays for, 50; social integration for, 50–51; social movements and, 95; tax reforms of, 167; Wiesendanger and, 92; worship assemblies of, 57. See also FORCE; Sealing Bill (Illinois); Wiesendanger, Alex
compensatory model, 82
Congregational Church, 17
corporal punishment, 87, 89
corporate campaign, 46–47, 74, 93–94, 95, 164
Cortes, Ernie: IAF and, 13–14; relationship-based model of, 53–54
Council of State Governments (CSG): Chicago School of sociology and,

11–12; prisoner reentry and, 34, 35–36; prison privatization and, 31; Reentry Policy Council of, 35; surveillance and, 11; top-down policy reform and, 29
Crime Act (1994), 29, 32, 41
criminal justice experts, 106, 112
criminal justice reform: CBOs and FBOs shaping, 41; as movement, 42; prophetic redemption and, 24–25; religion in, 29. See also prisoner reentry; prison reform
criminology, 22–23
Critical Resistance, 34
CRS. See Community Renewal Society
CSG. See Council of State Governments
cultural citizenship, 24, 160
cultural deficit narratives, 24, 146, 149–50, 156; cultural racism in, 151–52
cultural racism: in cultural deficit narratives, 151–52; structural barrier narratives and, 154

Davis, Angela, 8
democratic inclusion, 21, 66
desistance, 49–50; life course model and, 50, 67; role exit and, 67
DiIulio, John, 32–33, 35
Direct Action Resource Network, 13
discrimination: AOUON and, 6; in FORCE film, 1–2; records, 145, 153–54, 158
Dorrien, Gary, 9–10
Du Bois, W. E. B., 165, 169, 175n4; Chicago School of sociology and, 10; Philadelphia Negro by, 9

EAN. See Ex-Offender Action Network
Ehrenreich, Barbara, 159
elected official accountability: CRS and, 57, 58, 59, 66; Homeboy Industries and, 24; Homeboys LOC and, 132, 141; LA Voice and, 66, 128
elevator speeches: of CRS, 107–9, 113

elite civic organizations, 22, 29, 42; CBOs and, 41; FBOs and, 38–39, 41; Koch Industries as, 167–68; prisoner reentry and, 37; social movements and, 30

Ella Baker Center for Human Rights, 34

Ex-Offender Action Network (EAN), 5, 36, 37

extended case method, 21

Fair Chance Ordinance, 52–53, 137, 164; Homeboys LOC and, 123, 127–28, 134, 138; march for, 62–63; Osuna at, 139; prayer vigil and, 64–65; progressive prophetic activism and, 62–63

Fair Sentencing Act, 48

faith, 49–50

faith-based organizations (FBOs), 16, 22, 29–30, 40, 165–66; criminal justice reform and, 41; dress for, 63; elite civic organizations and, 38–39, 41; gang exit and, 19–20; government funding of, 28; grassroots resistance of, 41; legislation and, 32; OFBCI and, 35; pastoral prophetic redemption and, 54; prayer forms for, 50; prisoner reentry and, 35, 36, 37, 42; prophetic redemption and, 30, 42. See also Community Renewal Society (CRS); LA Voice; public-private partnerships

Family Life Center, 34; voting rights and, 5

FBOs. See faith-based organizations

fieldwork and interviews, 17–18

Fight for 15 campaign, 40

FORCE (Fighting to Overcome Records and Create Equality), 3, 17, 107, 149; absolute bars legislation and, 111, 112, 164; Alinsky concepts and, 114; Chamberlin and, 74–75; civic engagement of, 1–2, 166; collective action and, 67, 71, 107–11; community organizing of, 2, 8, 92–93, 101, 103; CRS relationship with, 135; as ex-offender-led, 18; faith and, 2; film of, 1–2, 44; insurgent prophetic redemption of, 7, 23–24, 114; issue-based model of, 23, 113, 114; legislative campaigns of, 47; making good for, 2, 7, 70, 71, 78; meetings, 103–4; Olivia and, 78–80; one-on-one for, 101–3, 113; organizational structure of, 95–96; paying dues at, 102–3; personal reform and, 87, 90, 91, 95, 100, 101–2, 114; political activism and, 67, 71, 93, 94, 111, 114; prophetic activism and, 39–40; recovery and, 22; recovery to reconstruct principles and practices of, 114; redemption imperative of, 99–103, 105; redemption scripts and, 70, 100, 107; relational questions at, 105; ritualized recovery and, 103–5, 114; sustainability of, 96–97; testimonies for collective action of, 107–11; Walgreens corporate campaign and, 46–47, 74, 93–94, 95, 164. See also Bocanegra, Eduardo "Eddie"; Chamberlin, Marlon; Sealing Bill (Illinois)

former gang members, 16–17, 23; CBOs and, 50; role exit and, 49

for-profit privatization: APPA resisting, 31, 41; as threat, 29–30, 41

Gamaliel Foundation, 13

Garcetti, Eric, 119

Garland, David, 106

Gaytan, Francisco, 72–73

generativity, 69

Hagan, John, 6

Harris, Greg, 98–99

Hart, Stephen, 92

Heritage Foundation, 31, 41

Holston, James, 144

Homeboy Industries, 5, 85; Boyle identity and, 129; Catholic-Jesuit priests founding, 17; community organizing and,

19–20; elected official accountability and, 24; Gilda and, 80–83, 90; history of, 119; LA Voice and, 40; Oscar in, 83–86; pastoral prophetic redemption and, 6; relationship-based model of, 14; testimonies of, 135–39. *See also* Boyle, Gregory "Father Greg"

Homeboys Local Organizing Committee (LOC), 3, 19, 149, 177n1; AB 953 and, 129–31; Ban-the-Box movement and, 123–24; Boyle identity in, 132–33; Catholic church and, 142; civic engagement and, 166; collective and political action of, 67, 71, 119; community organizing of, 8; Connie in, 86–89, 90; creation of, 119–20; elected official accountability and, 132, 141; experience of new members of, 122–23; Fair Chance Ordinance and, 123, 127–28, 134, 138; gang metaphors of, 125; individual recognition at, 139–40; insurgent prophetic redemption and, 128–29, 131; LA Voice community organizing model and, 120–21; LA Voice tension with, 116, 125–27, 133–35, 141–42; leadership of, 126, 127; making good and, 70, 71, 78; meetings of, 122; member issues for, 127, 133; minimum wage increase and, 136–37, 141–42; multiculturalism and diversity and, 121, 122, 133, 134, 141; one-on-one of, 136, 143; organizational culture of, 125, 126–27, 141; pastoral prophetic redemption of, 118, 124, 125, 131, 142; personal reform and, 87, 90, 91, 119; recovery and, 22; redemption scripts of, 70, 135–36; relationship-based model and, 23, 91, 118, 122, 124, 131, 133–34, 141; testimonies of, 142, 168; voice for, 121–23, 135. *See also* California Proposition 47; Osuna, Jose

Hoover, Zach, 62, 115–18, 125, 129
house meetings, 93, 113, 118; CRS and, 44

IAF. *See* Industrial Areas Foundation
IBCO. *See* institution-based community organizing
Illinois Coalition for Immigrant and Refugee Rights (ICIRR), 92
Illinois HB 5723. *See* Sealing Bill (Illinois)
Illinois House Bill 3061. *See* Sealing Bill (Illinois)
immigration: anti-immigrant deportations, 14; PICO and reform for, 38
Industrial Areas Foundation (IAF), 13–14
institution-based community organizing (IBCO) coalitions, 14
insurgent prophetic redemption, 21; AOUON as, 7; CRS and, 45, 51, 55–56, 59, 114, 165; of FORCE, 7, 23–24, 114; Homeboys LOC and, 128–29, 131; issue-based model and, 23; punishment and, 7; Walgreens campaign as, 95
Interfaith Funders, 14
The Interrupters: Bocanegra and, 68, 71–72, 74
issue-based community organizing, 51, 53, 54; of CRS, 52, 97, 113, 176n1; FORCE and, 23, 113, 114

Jacobsen, Dennis, 51–52
Johnson, Perry M., 31
Justice Not Jails, 40
Justice Reinvestment Initiative, 41

kinship, 24, 160; collective action and, 156–58; one-on-ones and, 157; prophetic redemption and, 143
Knox, Eddie, 43, 56–57
Koch Industries, 167–68

LAM. *See* Los Angeles Metropolitan Churches

LA Voice, 8, 63, 176n2; AB 953 and, 130; canvassing for, 141; Catholic church and, 7, 19, 23, 61, 91, 140, 142; civic engagement of, 45; civil religion and, 22, 66; ecumenism and human dignity for, 61, 64; elected official targeting of, 66, 128; founding of, 61; Homeboy Industries and, 40; Homeboys LOC and community organizing model of, 120–21; Homeboys LOC tension with, 116, 125–27, 133–35, 141–42; labor-community coalitions and, 40; LA County prayer vigil of, 64–66; leadership assemblies of, 62; Marcus and, 50, 61–62; organizational structure of, 126; organizing model of, 118; Oscar at, 84, 85; Osuna and, 77; pastoral prophetic redemption of, 45, 54–55, 61–66, 140; personal reform for, 24, 90–91; PICO National Network and, 3, 17; Prop 47 and, 47–48, 115, 116; prophetic redemption of, 164–65; relationship-based model of, 14, 23, 54, 62, 91, 118, 140–41; religious diversity of, 61; ritualized displays for, 50; social integration for, 50–51; trainings of, 141. See also Homeboys LOC

legislation: absolute bars, 111, 112, 164; APPA and, 32, 41; Crime Act as, 29, 32, 41; CRS and FORCE campaigns for, 47; Prop 36 as, 87; Prop 47 as, 37, 47–48, 88, 115, 125, 140; Welfare Reform Act as, 29, 32, 41. See also California Assembly Bill 953; Sealing Bill (Illinois)

life course model, 50, 67

Lifelines to Healing campaign, 38

LOC. See Homeboys Local Organizing Committee

Los Angeles Metropolitan Churches (LAM): prison phone calls and, 5

making good, 1, 23, 49, 68, 73–74, 102, 136, 143, 168, 169; FORCE and, 2, 7, 70, 71, 78; Homeboys LOC and, 70, 71, 78; prophetic redemption and, 25; redemption scripts and, 91

Marcus, Imam, 50, 61–62

Marshall, T. H., 144

million-dollar blocks, 37, 39

Mind-Changing course, 87–88

Moore, Chris, 39, 92–93

My Brother's Keeper: Obama and, 27–28, 38; pastoral prophetic redemption and, 27; PICO and, 29; school-to-prison pipeline and, 27; as top-down prisoner reentry initiative, 28

National Employment Law Project, 127–28, 134

A New Way of Life: Burton founding, 7, 52

Nunn, Dorsey, 5, 6–7, 10

Obama, Barack, 132, 166; Fair Sentencing Act of, 48; faith leaders and, 28–29; My Brother's Keeper initiative of, 27–28, 38; pastoral religion and, 28

OFBCI. See White House Office of Faith-Based and Community Initiatives

one-on-one: FORCE and, 101–3, 113; of Homeboys LOC, 136, 143; kinship and, 157

Open Doors. See Family Life Center

Open Society Foundation (OSF), 29; broken windows probation and, 34; funding by, 34–35; prisoner reentry and, 33–35

Operation Night Lights, 32

organizational structure: of FORCE, 95–96; Homeboys LOC and, 125, 126–27, 141; of LA Voice, 126

OSF. See Open Society Foundation

Osuna, Jose, 19, 20, 63, 76–78, 85, 90, 119–21, 123, 124, 126, 129, 135–39, 143–44, 145, 148–49, 161–62, 176n1; at Fair Chance hearing, 139; immigration and, 76; individual recognition by, 139–40; LA Voice and, 77

Park, Robert, 10

pastoral prophetic redemption, 6, 21; Burton and, 52, 54; FBOs and, 54; Homeboys LOC and, 118, 124, 125, 131, 142; of LA Voice, 45, 54–55, 61–66, 140; My Brother's Keeper and, 27

People Improving Communities through Organizing (PICO), 119; AB 953 and, 129–30; Ban-the-Box movement and, 14; Baumann founding, 13–14, 53; Catholic church and, 17, 140; community organizing principles of, 124, 133; My Brother's Keeper and, 29; National Network of, 3, 17, 125; relationship-based model of, 13–14, 53–54, 140–41

personal reform, 69, 71–74, 76–78; Ban-the-Box movement and, 7; for CRS and LA Voice, 24, 90–91; faith-based, 25; FORCE and, 87, 90, 91, 95, 100, 101–2, 114; Homeboys LOC and, 87, 90, 91, 119; making good and, 73–74; political reform and, 8–9, 15, 16, 24; redemption scripts in, 69–70, 71, 100; rehabilitation and, 23; ritualized recovery and, 103; testimonies on, 136–37. *See also* making good

Philadelphia Negro (Du Bois), 9

PICO. *See* People Improving Communities through Organizing

PICO California: Brown and, 38; immigration reform and, 38; Los Angeles prisoner reentry and, 37–38

political activism, 163; of Bocanegra, 69; of CRS, 98–99, 110–13; FORCE and, 67, 71, 93, 94, 111, 114; of Homeboys LOC, 67, 71, 119; prep sessions for, 110–13; therapeutic discourse and, 70, 114

political opportunity theory, 29; social movements and, 30

political reform, 169; Bocanegra and, 73–74; CRS and, 24; personal reform and, 8–9, 15, 16, 24

Polletta, Francesca, 15–16

positivity, 158–61

posttraumatic stress disorder, 68

power: CRS and, 97–99, 108, 114; voice as, 121; zero-sum power, 98, 112

prayer vigil, LA County: of LA Voice, 64–66; prophetic activism and, 65

prep sessions, 110–13

Price, Curren, 132

prison: phone calls, 5; privatization, 31. *See also* prison reform

prisoner reentry, 166; California Endowment and, 36–38, 41; CBOs and, 34, 36; CSG and, 34, 35–36; elite civic organizations and, 37; FBOs and, 35, 36, 37, 42; OFBCI and, 35; OSF and, 33–35; public-private partnerships and, 37; regional and local, 36–41; as social movement, 34; state social programming and, 70; Travis on, 34. *See also* California prisoner reentry; Chicago prisoner reentry; top-down reentry initiatives

Prisoner Reentry Initiative, 28, 36, 41

prison privatization. *See* probation privatization

prison reform: as movement, 29; prison building and, 8

probation. *See* broken windows probation

probation privatization, 29, 40; in Age of Reagan, 30–31; Boston Strategy to Prevent Youth Violence and, 32; Kentucky as first, 31; legislation for, 32; Reinventing Probation Council and, 32–33. *See also* American Probation and Parole Association (APPA)

progressive prophetic activism: Chamberlin and, 75; community organizing and, 3; CRS and, 43, 56; Fair Chance Ordinance march and, 62–63; Israel and, 4

Prop 36. *See* California Proposition 36

Prop 47. *See* California Proposition 47

prophetic activism: AB 953 and, 130; CRS and, 39, 45; FORCE and, 39–40; prayer vigil and, 65; Slessarev-Jamir on, 37, 43–44

prophetic redemption, 67; agonistic perspective of, 9; Alinsky and, 13; Ban-the-Box movement and, 5–6; Black Protestant church and, 9; Chicago School of sociology and, 12; community organizing and, 8–9, 45; cosmopolitans and, 51; criminal justice reform and, 24–25; CRS and, 113, 164–65; FBOs and, 30, 42; IBCO coalitions and, 14; kinship and, 143; of LA Voice, 164–65; making good and, 25; punishment and, 6–7; rehabilitation and, 6; social integration and, 45–46; sociology of religion and, 16; theodicy and, 4. See also insurgent prophetic redemption; pastoral prophetic redemption

public-private distinction: community organizing and, 146–47; sexism and racism and, 149

public-private partnerships, 28; APPA and, 29–30; Boston Strategy to Prevent Youth Violence and, 32; Chicago prisoner reentry and, 39; reentry and, 37. See also community-based organizations; faith-based organizations

punishment: insurgent prophetic redemption and, 7; prophetic redemption and, 6–7

Racial Profiling Act of 2015. See California Assembly Bill 953

racial segregation, 9; in prison, 76–77

racism, 148–49, 153, 161–62; citizenship and, 144–45; cultural, 151–52, 154; public-private distinction and, 149; returning citizenship and, 160; social movement and, 169

Reclaim Campaign, 47

records discrimination, 145; in structural barrier narratives, 153–54, 158

redemption imperative, 99–103, 105

redemption scripts, 71; of Bocanegra, 69–70; FORCE and, 70, 100, 107; generativity in, 69; of Homeboys LOC, 70, 135–36; making good and, 91; returning citizenship and, 146

reentry initiatives. See top-down reentry initiatives

rehabilitation: pastoral prophetic redemption and, 6; personal reform and, 23; prophetic redemption and, 6

Reinventing Probation Council, 32, 35; broken windows probation and, 33

relational questions, 105

relationship-based community organizing, 13; of Homeboy Industries, 14; Homeboys LOC and, 23, 91, 118, 122, 124, 131, 133–34, 141; LA Voice and, 14, 23, 54, 62, 91, 118, 140–41; of PICO, 13–14, 53–54, 140–41; for Prop 47, 118

religion: empowerment and, 2; resistance and, 3

returning citizenship, 8, 143, 162, 175n1; collective subjectivity and, 24, 146; cultural citizenship and, 24, 160; cultural deficit narratives and, 24, 146, 149, 150–52, 156; insurgent citizenship as, 149; racist exclusion and, 160; redemption scripts and, 146; structural barrier narratives and, 146, 152–54, 156, 158. See also collective action

Rhode Island. See Family Life Center

ritualized recovery: FORCE and, 103–5, 114; personal reform and, 103

role exit, 49; desistance and, 67

Rules for Radicals (Alinsky), 51

Safer Foundation, 41

school-to-prison pipeline, 27

Sealing Bill (Illinois), 2, 39, 79, 111, 164; Chamberlin and, 44, 45, 74; lobbying for, 46; passing of, 45
Second Chance Act, 41
SEIU. *See* Service Employees International Union
Serious and Violent Offender Reentry Initiative, 28, 41
Service Employees International Union (SEIU), 40
sexism: community organizing and, 147; masculine street culture and, 154; public-private distinction and, 149
Shaw, Clifford, 10
Slessarev-Jamir, Helene, 3; on Israel, 4; on prophetic activism, 37, 43–44
Smith, Steven, 92, 93
social citizenship, 144–45
social integration, 163; community organizing and, 22, 67; for LA Voice and CRS, 50–51; prophetic redemption and, 45–46; social reception and, 45
social movements, 168; CBOs and, 16; criminal justice reform as, 42; CRS and, 95; elite civic organizations and, 30; prisoner reentry as, 34; prison reform as, 29; probation privatization and, 29–30; racism and, 169; therapeutic techniques and, 106–7
structural barrier narratives, 146, 152, 156; cultural racism and, 154; records discrimination in, 153–54, 158; social problems in, 153
substance abuse, 21
superpredators, 35
surveillance, 11
Swarts, Heidi, 95

testimonies: Boyle and, 139; collective action and FORCE, 107–11; of Homeboy Industries, 135–39; of Homeboys LOC,

142, 168; of Osuna, 138–39; on personal reform, 136–37
therapeutic techniques and discourse: collective and political action and, 70, 114; redemption scripts as, 70; social movements and, 106–7
Thrasher, Frederic, 11
threat, political, 29–30, 41
three-strikes law, 87
Toll, Henry Wolcott, 11
top-down policy reform, 165; of Chicago School of sociology, 169; CSG and, 29; grassroots activism and, 166
top-down reentry initiatives: federal, 41; My Brother's Keeper as, 28; Prisoner Reentry Initiative as, 28; Serious and Violent Offender Reentry Initiative as, 28, 41
Travis, Jeremy, 34, 37

University of Chicago. *See* Chicago School of sociology
Urban Institute, 29, 34, 35, 37

vocabularies of motive, 71, 90
volunteerism, 54
voting rights, 5

Walgreens campaign: corporate campaign against, 46–47, 74, 93–94, 95, 164; insurgent prophetic redemption and, 95
Washington, Booker T., 9, 10
Welfare Reform Act (1996), 29, 41; Charitable Choice clause of, 32
White House Office of Faith-Based and Community Initiatives (OFBCI), 35–36
Wiesendanger, Alex, 92, 93–94, 96, 101–2, 105, 111–13
Williams, Quintin, 99

ABOUT THE AUTHOR

Edward Orozco Flores is Associate Professor of Sociology at the University of California, Merced. He is the author of *God's Gangs: Barrio Ministry, Masculinity and Gang Recovery*.